W9-DAG-235

Critical Essays On Joel Chandler Harris

Critical Essays On
Joel Chandler Harris

R. Bruce Bickley, Jr.

G. K. Hall & Co. • Boston, Massachusetts

UPSALA COLLEGE LIBRARY
WIRTHS CAMPUS

Ps
1814
.C7

Copyright © 1981 by R. Bruce Bickley

Library of Congress Cataloging in Publication Data
Main entry under title:
Critical essays on Joel Chandler Harris.
   (Critical essays on American literature)
   Includes index.
   1. Harris, Joel Chandler, 1848-1908—Criticism and
interpretation. I. Bickley, R. Bruce, 1942-
II. Series.
PS1814.C7   818'.409   81-6816
ISBN 0-8161-8381-3   AACR2

This publication is printed on permanent/durable acid-free paper
MANUFACTURED IN THE UNITED STATES OF AMERICA

CRITICAL ESSAYS ON AMERICAN LITERATURE

This series seeks to collect the most important previously published criticism on writers and topics in American literature along with, in various volumes, original essays, interviews, bibliographies, letters, manuscript sections, and other materials brought to public attention for the first time. R. Bruce Bickley, Jr., has assembled the first collection of criticism ever published on Joel Chandler Harris. It contains 46 reviews and 18 critical essays, including three written especially for this volume. In these Florence Baer has written perceptively on Harris and folklore, Louis Budd on Harris's local color humor and the genteel tradition, and Joseph Griska on what the unpublished letters reveal about Harris's personality and career. We are confident that this collection will make a permanent and significant contribution to American literary study.

JAMES NAGEL, GENERAL EDITOR

Northeastern University

10581

Especially for Karen,
since I did not ask her to help write this one

CONTENTS

INTRODUCTION

Critical Essays on Joel Chandler Harris is the first volume of Harris criticism that has ever been compiled. It brings together a century of commentary—from the earliest reviews of *Uncle Remus: His Songs and His Sayings*, in 1880, to essays commissioned especially for this book in 1980. In many respects *Critical Essays* naturally evolved from, and serves as the companion volume to, *Joel Chandler Harris: A Reference Guide* (G. K. Hall, 1978). In preparing that book I read and annotated over 1400 English-language reviews, articles, dissertations, books, and discussions in books on Harris, from 1862 through 1976; and the further I read in Harris scholarship the more apparent it became that a generous selection from contemporaneous reviews and a culling of the very best essays and articles on Harris across the years were overdue. For Joel Chandler Harris left a richer legacy than has generally been realized—a legacy that his reviewers and astutest critics themselves have become part of, even as they have helped others interpret it.

The author of over thirty books, and thousands of column-inches in the prestigious Atlanta *Constitution* and other Georgia newspapers, Harris in effect earned five reputations. He was a popular humorist who bridged the traditions of the Old Southwest literary comedians and the more socially significant humorists and satirists of the post-Civil-War South; he was one of the three or four most influential journalists of the Reconstruction and post-Reconstruction periods; he was the first compiler of authentic American Negro folklore; he was a widely admired writer of children's stories; and as the most talented Southern local colorist prior to Twain, Harris was the first author to create fully realized black and poor white characters in fiction and to portray sensitively their social and economic milieux. Harris would deserve a permanent place in literary histories of America if he had left only the Uncle Remus tales as his cultural contribution; but in fact the pathologically shy Georgian left a great deal more. *Critical Essays on Joel Chandler Harris* displays the full range of Harris's legacy, as his most thoughtful reviewers and authoritative critics have appraised it, in its strengths and weaknesses. Harris was a prolific writer, but he was an uneven one. He wrote too facilely at times and too often let his well-advertized themes of North-South reconciliation and "neighborliness" resolve plots that might otherwise have ended more tragically—or at least more realistically. And as more than one reviewer of *Sister Jane* and *Gabriel Tolliver* complained, the otherwise-talented creator of Uncle Remus should never have tried to write *novels*.

The first section of *Critical Essays* reprints in chronological order forty-six carefully chosen, representative reviews of Harris's works: two reviews each on eighteen of his more important books, characteristic single reviews of nine of his other volumes, and a thoughtful obituary essay published by the *American Review of Reviews*. The second half of this volume collects eighteen major essays on Harris, again in chronological arrangement, from Mark Twain's lightly humorous but sensitive portrait of Harris in *Life on the Mississippi* (1883) and Thomas Nelson Page's unabashedly admiring review-essay on the 1895 edition of *Uncle Remus*, to discerning and provocative analyses in our own century by Allen Tate, Thomas English, Darwin Turner, Robert Bone, Louis Rubin, and other authoritative critics. The last three articles in the book—Florence Baer's essay on Harris's futile efforts to gain the full respect of professional folklorists, Louis Budd's frank appraisal of his humor and flawed performance as a local colorist, and Joseph Griska's reassessment of his personality and career in the light of unpublished letters—were written expressly for this collection and help to redirect or refocus earlier views of Harris's achievement and character traits.

It will be valuable at the outset to survey the broad parameters of scholarship and criticism on Harris over the past century in order to establish the larger context for the reviews and articles gathered in this volume. The following summary of scholarship is in part a synthesis of my previously published reviews of Harris criticism, in the prefatory essay to *Joel Chandler Harris: A Reference Guide*[1] and in the surveys of scholarship that introduce three of the chapters in my 1978 Twayne biography of Harris.[2] *Critical Essays on Joel Chandler Harris* now makes it possible, however, to study the critical response to Harris at close range (and from the vantage point of recent revisionist perspectives) and at a longer range simultaneously.

I. Biographies, Critical Studies, and Bibliographies

The first significant biographical and critical study of Harris is William Baskervill's monograph published in 1896,[3] an appreciative essay but one that offered an essentially balanced overview of Harris's reputation in the 1890s as a Middle Georgia humorist and folklorist and as a local colorist. For Harris's creation of characters like Mingo, Free Joe, Balaam, and other figures was in many ways as important as his giving the world that "Ethiopian Aesop," Uncle Remus. Yet Harris's reputation was still growing in 1896, and simultaneously anecdotes about his impregnable shyness and self-consciousness were regularly making the rounds of the reviewers' columns. The *American Review of Reviews* obituary, reprinted in this collection, typifies the response of Harris's devoted readers at the end of his varied career: he was loved all the more because of his personality quirks, and although his local-color stories themselves could have earned

him a lasting reputation, the Uncle Remus tales had made him truly immortal. Ten years after his death the first full-length biographies would
appear. Julia Collier Harris writes too fondly at times of her father-in-law
in *The Life and Letters of Joel Chandler Harris* (1918),[4] but her
biography is still regarded as the standard one; it includes valuable letters
and personal reminiscences of Harris's immediate family and friends.
Published in the same year as *The Life and Letters*, Robert L. Wiggins's
*The Life of Joel Chandler Harris: From Obscurity in Boyhood to Fame in
Early Manhood*[5] belies its sentimentalized title and provides important
perspectives and documents on Harris's apprenticeship years at Turnwold
Plantation and as a newspaperman, through 1879.

The two most important general assessments of Harris's life and
works to appear during the half-century between Julia's biography and
Paul Cousins's *Joel Chandler Harris: A Biography* (1968)[6] are Thomas H.
English's "In Memory of Uncle Remus," reprinted below, and Jay B.
Hubbell's essay on the local colorist in his monumental *The South in
American Literature.*[7] Both authorities review Harris's career, discuss his
diffident personality, and fairly appraise his contributions as a journalist
and Southern regionalist. Cousins's biography, the final chapter of which
is also included in this volume, stresses Harris's formative years in Middle
Georgia, especially those spent on Joseph Addison Turner's plantation,
and draws on interviews with some of Harris's surviving personal acquaintances to add details about his public and private life and beliefs.
Cousins's study helped to revive interest in Harris and the social scene he
sought to portray during Reconstruction and immediately afterwards.
Arlin Turner's review-essay on Cousins's biography, also reprinted in
this volume, offers a compact but authoritative summary of the social
changes and uncertainties that Harris was caught up in and responded to
in his local-color writings and journalism. The first two chapters of my
Twayne biography synthesize the research of Harris's major biographers
and provide an economical overview of his life and career.

Julia Collier Harris's *Life and Letters* remains the largest gathering
to date of Harris letters. Meanwhile, Joseph Griska of Shaw University is
compiling a full edition of letters. Bradley Strickland's "A Check List of
the Periodical Contributions of Joel Chandler Harris (1848–1908)," with
its supplement,[8] is the most inclusive bibliography in print of Harris's
magazine publications; Julia Collier, Paul Cousins, and I have listed Harris's books in our biographies. The standard secondary bibliography is my
Reference Guide, cited earlier.

II. Harris's Journalistic Career

Harris's importance as a New South journalist, literary critic, and
humorist still has not been adequately studied. Julia assembled representative essays from Harris's political and social journalism and his literary

criticism in *Joel Chandler Harris: Editor and Essayist* (1931),[9] and her running commentary in this volume is helpful in tracing his various themes and concerns. Harris composed thousands of unsigned editorials and essays for the Atlanta *Constitution* that can never be authoritatively ascribed to him, since Henry Grady and other writers on the staff were striking up many of the same themes in their own unsigned articles. But the student of the New South will certainly want to peruse Julia's book and read Allen Tate's hitherto unreprinted (and apparently unnoticed) review-essay on her volume in the *New Republic*, printed in these pages. Tate shares with the reader his surprise at discovering in Harris's "fugitive writings" (if this was not an intentional pun, it should have been) a whole second career of major consequence, and in Harris's literary criticism "a complete and matured attitude toward the writer and his materials." Tate argues that Harris's work is a more important contribution than Whitman's to a "native" American literature and that Harris's corrective of Henry James's limited notion of what constitutes the "provincial" in literature leads Harris to a beautifully universal definition of what literature itself is. Provocatively, Tate also finds affinities between Trotsky's essay "Literature and Revolution" and Harris's criticism, parallels that are more striking than those between Trotsky and Dos Passos, or Trotsky and Max Eastman. Tate's review-essay is a discerning response both to the literary climate of the 1930s and to Harris's significance as a critic and newspaper and periodical journalist during and immediately after Reconstruction.

The two contemporaneous reviews of Harris's more ephemeral and facile journalism—his hastily assembled *Life of Grady* (1890) and his grade-school reader, *Stories of Georgia* (1896), which are reprinted in the first section of this book—sufficiently represent the content and quality, or lack of it, in this phase of his journalism. But three full-length articles gathered in this volume—Thomas English's "In Memory of Uncle Remus" (1940), Jay Martin's "Joel Chandler Harris and the Cornfield Journalist," reprinted from his astute literary and sociological history, *Harvests of Change* (1967), and Louis Budd's "Joel Chandler Harris and the Genteeling of American Humor," one of the commissioned essays—are broad-ranging, insightful analyses of Harris's surprisingly full career as a journalist. English is surely fair to the image of Harris in his own time and to his reputation in our day in concluding that Harris "interpreted the Negro to a generation to whom the Negro had almost ceased to be a person and had become a problem." Martin's approach is more overtly psychological. Professionally, Harris was a jovial and optimistic journalist who supported the New South cause, but privately Harris the creative writer identified with the Edenic world of the Old South plantation and satirized the socio-economic push of the post-war era. Harris's stuttering and fear of novel situations, suggests Martin, were visible signs of his split personality and of his contradictory values.

Budd's article is so richly conceived and executed as to defy easy summary. Budd ranges across Harris's career as a humorist and local colorist, pointing out the tempering effects of his editors on a style of humor that might otherwise have embodied more of the earthiness of the Old Southwest comedy in which Harris's roots were planted; he also identifies the Bergsonian repetitiveness and formulaic patterning of too many of his local-color stories and his less-than-realistic realism, even though Harris himself, in his literary criticism, faulted his contemporaries for failing to grapple with the more tragic aspects of human experience. And in his discussion of the white biases in some of Harris's most celebrated black characters and of his superficial presentation of human love and sexuality, Budd questions whether Harris succeeded in enlivening clichés—if this was his intention. Yet Budd's essay also affirms Harris's value as a serious political and social critic and as a regional writer who contributed significantly to the legacy of the black and the poor white as viable characters in fiction, a legacy that Faulkner and others of our century would inherit and make richer. Many of Budd's observations, especially those on the comic devices and dialect humor that Harris's editors and readers enjoyed, are confirmed in the contemporaneous reviews I have included in this volume; one should note, for example, the witty 1881 *Spectator* review of *Uncle Remus* or the 1899 *Saturday Evening Post* essay on the *Chronicles of Aunt Minervy Ann* for their savoring of Harris's Middle Georgian recipe for humor.

III. Harris as a Folklorist and Dialect Writer

Harris published eight collections of Uncle Remus tales during his lifetime, and three more volumes would appear posthumously. But so far as the folklorists and dialecticians are concerned, Harris made his reputation with his first book, *Uncle Remus: His Songs and His Sayings* (1880). Since I have reviewed the critical and popular response to Harris's dialect tales elsewhere,[10] let me simply highlight major studies here, drawing special attention to the reviews and essays that are compiled in this volume. There are now two book-length studies of Harris's folklore: Stella Brewer Brookes's *Joel Chandler Harris—Folklorist* (1950),[11] which primarily classifies and describes his use of trickster tales, myths, supernatural tales, proverbs, and other folk materials, and Florence Baer's monograph, *Sources and Analogues of the Uncle Remus Tales* (1980—Baer's study is being published as this collection goes to press),[12] the title of which is self-explanatory. As Professor Baer explains in the article she wrote for this volume, even though the professional folklorists would not officially accept Harris as a fellow scientist, they praised him for compiling the first important collection of American Negro folklore and for over a century have been vigorously arguing about possible lines of transmission and analogues for the tar-baby tale and other stories. (Aurelio M. Espinosa, to cite the most indefatigable researcher, seems to have made a career of chasing down tar-baby parallels: in one of his last articles, Espinosa reports on his analysis of 267 variations of the tale.[13])

Most of Harris's reviewers could not resist the temptation to play amateur comparative folklorists when they discussed his plantation fables. Of the reviews gathered in this text the *New York Times* piece on the first Uncle Remus book, the *Nation*'s review of *Nights with Uncle Remus* (1883), and the *Times* essay on the 1895 edition of *Uncle Remus*, illustrated so capably by A. B. Frost, represent both the enthusiasm and the knowledgeableness that many of Harris's critics brought to their columns. A great deal could be learned about the popular folklore of the various regions of America at the end of the last century by a systematic study of the newspaper reviews of Harris's Uncle Remus books. Of course, the more scientific essays on Harris's folklore, from T. F. Crane's article in 1881[14] forward, constitute another eminently researchable set of responses to the black folklore that Harris preserved. Of the more recent studies of Harris's folklore, I have found especially intriguing Kathleen Light's article on Harris's problem in reconciling his assumptions about cultural evolution with the complexities of supposedly "primitive" folk stories; Light's 1975 essay is reprinted here, as is Florence Baer's commissioned study that counters Light's view with a different explanation for Harris's losing his early enthusiasm for folkloristic research and collecting.

That Harris was America's first accomplished writer of Southern dialect, black and white, was affirmed by his earliest reviewers; that opinion still stands today. In *Huckleberry Finn* (1885) Mark Twain may surpass Harris in dialect differentiation among Southern whites, although David Carkeet has recently suggested that Twain probably used Harris as a model in the Arkansas gossips' tour-de-force of dialect in Chapter XLI.[15] But Twain's praise of Harris two years earlier (see the reprinted commentary from *Life on the Mississippi* on page TK), which is echoed in extant personal letters through 1885, is not the hyperbolic flourish of a friend: so far as Twain was concerned—and we can be sure he was genuinely concerned—Harris was the *only* master of American Negro dialect. Another celebrated contemporary of Harris who had also earned a reputation for his handling of Southern black dialect, Thomas Nelson Page, in his review-essay on the 1895 Frost edition of *Uncle Remus*, declared unequivocally that "No man who has ever written has known one-tenth part about the negro that Mr. Harris knows," and that Harris's works were the "best thesaurus" for the "real language" of the old-time Negro. Page, whose most famous volume of plantation tales appeared seven years after the 1880 *Uncle Remus*, must have felt a little self-irony when he referred in his review to the "host of imitators" that Harris had raised and to the "shudder" that the public had come to feel whenever a new dialect-story was published; Page's essay is reprinted here in its entirety.

Harris's dialect has been studied most carefully by Sumner Ives, although various commentaries have appeared on the subject for the past century. Because of the technical nature of Ives's work, I have not chosen to reprint any of it here, but students of Harris should be aware of his three major studies: "A Theory of Literary Dialect" (1950)[16], which uses the Uncle Remus stories as the sample for analysis; the monograph, *The Phonology of The Uncle Remus Tales* (1954)[17]; and "Dialect Differentiation in the Stories of Joel Chandler Harris" (1955).[18]

IV. Harris and Local Color

Reviews and published commentaries on the Uncle Remus materials are, of course, at the same time studies of one important phase of Harris's work as a local colorist, but with the publication of *Mingo and Other Sketches in Black and White* in 1884 critics were quick to recognize Harris's talent as a writer of regional short fiction worthy of comparison with the works of George Washington Cable, Mary Noailles Murfree, Bret Harte, and Twain. I have gathered in the first part of this volume typical contemporaneous reviews of the *Mingo* volume, *Free Joe and Other Georgian Sketches* (1887), *Balaam and His Master and Other Sketches and Stories* (1891), *Tales of the Home Folks in Peace and War* (1898), *On the Wing of Occasions* (1900), and *The Making of a Statesman and Other Stories* (1902), which are the major collections of local color short fiction. But the reader will also want to see the reviews of the *Daddy Jake* volume (1889) as well as those that treat the Uncle Remus books for a wider sampling of how favorably, for the most part, Harris's local-color writings were received. I have discussed the short stories in Chapter 5 of the Twayne critical biography, and Louis Budd, Darwin Turner, Michael Flusche, and others whose essays are reprinted here treat the local-color fiction to varying degrees. The current consensus about Harris's achievement as an author of short fiction is that he wrote two or three fine stories ("Free Joe" and "Mingo" are usually cited first) and several others that certainly portray the sense of their region and its people and are therefore worth knowing about; but many of Harris's short stories are formulaic and overly sentimental.

Harris was never a reputable novelist. His first attempt at the genre, which also happened to be his first try at any kind of fiction-writing—*The Romance of Rockville*, serialized in the Atlanta *Constitution* in 1878—should have persuaded him to abandon extended narrative for shorter modes of composition more suited to his talents as a newspaper columnist and prose sketcher. Harris's most ambitious novels, *Sister Jane* (1896) and *Gabriel Tolliver* (1902), suffer from the same structural problems that afflict *The Romance of Rockville:* meandering and uncertain plotting, too many family skeletons in too many closets, and insufficient dramatic conflict. Reviewers, so long enamored of Harris, often went out of their way to find things to praise in his novels: his predictably authentic use of regional dialect, his sense of humor, his eye for details of setting. And modern commentators have said that *Gabriel Tolliver*, despite its flaws in execution, is the most perceptive and balanced Reconstruction novel that we have. Harris's late novels, *A Little Union Scout* (1904) and *The Shadow Between His Shoulder-Blades* and *The Bishop and the Boogerman* (both published posthumously in 1909), are slight productions; I have included only one review of each of these books. But Harris's ambitious attempt at ironic first-person narration and the obvious autobiographical elements of *Sister Jane* make that novel a complex and intriguing psychological study, and Harris's sensitive portrait of the uncertain ebb and flow of social change and racial tensions during Reconstruction redeems *Gabriel Tolliver* from the case for obscurity that many of the reviewers made for that work.

More favorably received in Harris's day, and more readable in our own, are his autobiographical novel, *On the Plantation: A Story of a Georgia Boy's Adventures During the War* (1892), and the interlocked collection of humorous tales, *The Chronicles of Aunt Minervy Ann* (1899). The somewhat simplistic narrative structure and tone of *On the Plantation* confirm what is implied by Harris's handling of social themes in the book: it was written for younger audiences. Yet the narrative does afford valuable insights into Harris's personal history and makeup and into the disruptive effects of the Civil War on rural Georgia and, by extension, on the South generally.[19] Aunt Minervy Ann is a "white-folks' nigger" who is always quick to put the fear of God into the hearts and nervous systems of her more backsliding kinsmen, and as I have observed elsewhere her "chronicles" might more aptly be termed escapades—the book is primarily an entertaining period-piece featuring a vigorous and unflappable black heroine.

V. Mythological, Sociological, and Psychological Studies

The most thoughtful and provocative essays on Harris have been informed by a kind of enlightened eclecticism—they are partly mythological and folkloristic, partly psychological, and partly sociological. Moreover, the complexities and contradictions in Harris's own personality have made the process of evaluating his artistry especially challenging. From his youth onward he was extremely self-conscious about his short stature and carrot-red hair and embarrassed about his illegitimate birth, the latter anxiety apparently heightening the former to produce, or at least to reinforce, a severe stammering disorder in his speech. Harris could never read his stories in public or even to his own children, one learns. And he was a compulsive practical joker all his days—as well as an accomplished newspaper humorist and, in time, an important literary comedian. Although one may well want to heed Louis Budd's advice and be cautious about playing the amateur Freudian, one cannot help wondering whether Harris's sense of humor helped him displace tensions while it helped him earn a living. And as Joseph Griska in his commissioned essay, and others (including this writer) have suggested, might Joseph Addison Turner, Harris's plantation mentor, have served as a temporary substitute for the father that Harris never had, and could Uncle Remus—of whom Harris was at least as fond as his readers were—have functioned in a similar way in Harris's imagination? But Harris himself should have the last word on the subject. After summarizing the various and contradictory theories that the professional folklorists had posited to explain the evolution and transmission of folktales, Harris observed with characteristic humor—and universality of application: "at the end of investigation and discussion Speculation stands grinning."[20]

Two essays that I did not have space for in this volume but which are well worth reading for their combination of mythological and folkloristic analysis with literary interpretation are John Stafford's "Patterns of Meaning in *Nights with Uncle Remus*" (1946)[21] and Louise Dauner's "Myth and Humor in the Uncle Remus Fables" (1948).[22] Stafford draws upon Kenneth Burke and William Empson in showing how the *Nights* volume (1883) is a more complex one than *Uncle Remus* (1880) because of Harris's use of overlapping rhetorical strategies: he speaks to his readers from the point of view of the Southern white man, from that of the long-repressed Negro, and from a magical-religious perspective. Dauner looks behind the surface simplicity of the animal stories to probe psychological, symbolical, and metaphysical dimensions that even Harris himself was not aware of; as have many folklorists and critics, Dauner emphasizes the Trickster as the primary demiurgic figure in the tales. Among the essays included in this collection that treat some of the more traditional folkloristic or mythological motifs in the Uncle Remus fables, I mention again Kathleen Light's essay on Harris and theories of cultural evolution and Florence Baer's profile of his career as an "accidental" folklorist who tried to become a more serious professional scholar. In reprinting the pages on Harris from Ellen Leyburn's definitive study, *Satiric Allegory: Mirror of Man* (1956), I also want to underscore Harris's contribution to the larger tradition of allegorical animal fables; Leyburn succinctly demonstrates why Harris's fables work so well on the identifiably human level and on the level of social satire and moral allegory.

One of the most astute analyses ever to have been published on Harris is the 1881 *Spectator* review of *Uncle Remus*, reprinted here, which comes directly to the richest question posed by the allegory of the fables: Harris in his preface and his loyal retainer Uncle Remus in the framed stories both seem to defend the old plantation system, and yet "in reality" the tales illustrate "the habits of cunning, deceit, and dishonesty, and the delight in them" in which Uncle Remus and other blacks were steeped, and the "infinite gullibility" of the so-called stronger race. The *Spectator* review is the first contribution to an entire tradition in Harris criticism—a school of criticism that explores the ways in which the black slave subverts, or seems to subvert, his white master and the social system he represents (when it is contrasted with the racist assumptions of the 1880 and 1895 *New York Times* essays on *Uncle Remus*, the English review is even more remarkable).

I have reprinted the most authoritative and challenging articles to appear on this complex subject over the years. Bernard Wolfe's "Uncle Remus and the Malevolent Rabbit" (1949) is a masterfully constructed analysis of the several rhetorical effects and layers of meaning in the tales. Also compelling is Jesse Bier's commentary, from *The Rise and Fall of American Humor* (1968), on Harris's duplicity and his subversion of Southern values in the Uncle Remus stories. Provocative, too, is Robert Bone's study of Harris as a maverick member of the "Plantation School" of Southern letters; complexly, the Uncle Remus tales on one level seemed to reinforce Southern prejudices about the Negro and to reflect nostalgically upon the Lost Cause, while on another level they challenged the values represented by the Old South. Both Professor Bone and Darwin Turner, in his celebrated "Daddy Joel Harris and His Old-Time Darkies," reprinted from the *Southern Literary Journal* (1968), praise Harris for preserving in a relatively authentic frame a major body of Afro-American material that might otherwise have been lost forever; but Turner faults Harris for dealing too often in black stereotypes and for portraying sexless male Negroes who can only express their repressed drives and social and psychological emasculation through animal fantasies in which the servant finally displaces the master.

As I have suggested above, it is almost inevitable that the sociology and psychology of Harris's art reflect his own insecurities and life history, and some of the most fruitful commentaries on Harris have openly examined both levels of implication. Julia Collier Harris could not have anticipated the psychobiographical fallout that would be precipitated by her reprinting her father-in-law's letter about his "other fellow"—his second self that turned its back scornfully on newspaper hackwork and wrote folklore and fiction.[23] Jay Hubbell in *The South in American Literature* reflected briefly upon the two different legacies left by Harris the reform-minded New South journalist and Harris the nostalgic creative writer longing for an earlier era.[24] But Jay Martin's "Joel Chandler Harris and the Cornfield Journalist" (1967) is a critical gem on the subject of Harris's double-vision as the manifestation of a complex split in his own personality. Harris's stuttering, his avoidance of new or threatening situations and public appearances, and his refusal to change his style of clothing in his later years were signs of his split psyche. Although he publicly espoused Henry Grady's call for a new, industrialized, and socially reformed South, Harris's personae Uncle Remus and Billy Sanders questioned New

South values and, especially in the animal tales, celebrated the Edenic world of the old plantation. Louis Rubin's "Uncle Remus and the Ubiquitous Rabbit," first published in 1974, offers a balanced and articulate overview of Harris's career and his diffident personality and of the larger critical issues raised by the Uncle Remus tales. Harris was a segregationist who saw blacks as biologically and socially inferior, but an underdog himself he sympathized with the downtrodden Negro and his diabolically clever hero, Brer Rabbit. Although he was probably not aware of all of the implications of the folktales he retold, the stories evince Harris's humane and imaginative attempt to understand the oppressed condition of the black man in a white society.

Michael Flusche sees signs of Harris's insecurity and pessimism about his own times not only in the Uncle Remus tales but in his short stories and novels as well. As the title of his reprinted *Mississippi Quarterly* essay implies, "underlying despair" darkened Harris's literary vision: Harris compensated for his inadequacies by his practical joking and his humorous writing, but below the surface of both his personality and his fiction lay hostility and loneliness. In his commissioned article based on research among unpublished Harris letters, Joseph Griska documents Harris's pathological shyness and insecurity and his very real need to be "braced" by close friends and by his family. Griska's neo-Freudian analysis stresses Harris's imagined rejection by his father and the profound depression and sense of inferiority that this and other causes produced. Contrary to the popular image of Harris—one that he helped to promote—that he was only an "accidental" author, Griska shows how tenaciously Harris sought literary recognition and financial rewards for his writing.

VI. Perspectives for Criticism

Some of the largest questions about Harris's contributions to folklore and American literature deserve a great deal more study. For example, to what extent were the Uncle Remus tales American Negro versions of West African folk stories, and to what extent were they modified by American slaves to symbolize or allegorize black experience and role-playing during slavery?[25] A related question, probably no longer answerable since Harris did not have the means to transcribe scientifically what he heard from his original sources, should still be asked: how much did Harris embellish his sources? And there is the thornier problem (to borrow a metaphor from Uncle Remus) of the extent of Harris's own intellectual awareness of the complex social and psychological themes that the folktales appear to embody, at least for a modern audience. Two more strictly literary issues also need further exploring: Harris's position in the stream of American humor, as it flowed from the up-river literary comedians of the Old Southwest and through him into the richer delta of Twain and later satirists; and the analogues between Harris's full portraits of the black and poor white in his local-color fiction and Twain's as well as Faulkner's portraits of the same classes of people. Although all three writers were drawing their material from comparable milieux, it may be that Twain and Faulkner are more in Harris's debt than is realized.

In closing it is well to remember how popular Harris has been with so many different audiences over the decades and why he has had such appeal. Harris has been praised by professional folklorists (even though they kept him out of their club), by authors and critics (both white and black, although sometimes reluctantly by the latter), by social historians (of diverse biases), by industrial, labor, and political leaders (he was admired by Andrew Carnegie and Samuel Gompers, by Teddy Roosevelt, Henry Grady, and Booker T. Washington), and by common readers and the children of common readers. And it is wise to recall, perhaps as an antidote to overdoses of psychobiography, that the reason Harris has been so universally popular is that he entertained his readers with seemingly effortless and artless tales that more often than not invested the common man—or as in the case of Brer Rabbit, a symbol for the common man—with canniness, insight, humor, and strength. He has thus been an author for all times and all peoples.

R. BRUCE BICKLEY, JR.

Florida State University

Notes

1. See the Preface, pp. ix–xiv in R. Bruce Bickley, Jr., *Joel Chandler Harris: A Reference Guide* (Boston: G. K. Hall, 1978).

2. For a review of criticism on Harris's most important Uncle Remus collections see pp. 63–70 of "The Major Uncle Remus Books," Ch. 3 of R. Bruce Bickley, Jr., *Joel Chandler Harris* (Boston: Twayne, 1978). Pp. 104–05 of "The Short Fiction," Ch. 5 of the critical biography, briefly review the scholarship on Harris's local color stories, and pp. 130–31 of Ch. 6, "Chronicles and Novels," highlight representative responses to his major novels. Important books and articles on Harris are individually reviewed in the secondary bibliography of the Twayne study, pp. 163–68.

3. William Malone Baskervill, *Southern Writers. Biographical and Critical Studies. Joel Chandler Harris* (Nashville: Barbee & Smith, 1896).

4. Julia Collier Harris, *The Life and Letters of Joel Chandler Harris* (Boston and New York: Houghton Mifflin, 1918).

5. Robert Lemuel Wiggins, *The Life of Joel Chandler Harris: From Obscurity in Boyhood to Fame in Early Manhood* (Nashville, Dallas, Richmond: Publishing House Methodist Episcopal Church, South, 1918).

6. Paul M. Cousins, *Joel Chandler Harris: A Biography* (Baton Rouge: Louisiana State University Press, 1968).

7. Jay B. Hubbell, *The South in American Literature 1607–1900* (Durham: Duke University Press, 1954).

8. William Bradley Strickland, "A Check List of the Periodical Contributions of Joel Chandler Harris (1848–1908)," *American Literary Realism*, 9 (Summer 1976), [205]–229. For

the supplement, see R. Bruce Bickley, Jr., and William Bradley Strickland, "A Checklist of the Periodical Contributions of Joel Chandler Harris: Part 2," *American Literary Realism*, 11 (Spring 1978), 139–40.

9. Julia Collier Harris, ed., *Joel Chandler Harris: Editor and Essayist* (Chapel Hill: University of North Carolina Press, 1931).

10. Bickley, *Joel Chandler Harris*, pp. 63–70.

11. Stella Brewer Brookes, *Joel Chandler Harris—Folklorist* (Athens: University of Georgia Press, 1950).

12. Florence E. Baer, *Sources and Analogues of the Uncle Remus Tales* (Helsinki: Academia Scientiarum Fennica, 1980).

13. Aurelio M. Espinosa, "A New Classification of the Fundamental Elements of the Tar-Baby Story on the Basis of Two Hundred and Sixty-Seven Versions," *Journal of American Folklore*, 56 (January-March 1943), 31–37.

14. T. F. Crane, "Plantation Folk-Lore," *Popular Science Monthly*, 18 (April 1881), 824–33.

15. David Carkeet, "The Dialects in *Huckleberry Finn*," *American Literature*, 51 (November 1979), 323–24.

16. Sumner Ives, "A Theory of Literary Dialect," *Tulane Studies in English*, 2 (1950), 137–82.

17. Ives, *The Phonology of the Uncle Remus Tales*, Publication of the American Dialect Society, No. 22 (Gainesville: American Dialect Society, 1954).

18. Ives, "Dialect Differentiation in the Stories of Joel Chandler Harris," *American Literature*, 27 (March 1955), 88–96.

19. *On the Plantation* was reprinted in 1980 by the University of Georgia Press, in a handsome edition with a brief foreword by Erskine Caldwell.

20. Harris, "Introduction," *Uncle Remus and His Friends: Old Plantation Stories, Songs, and Ballads with Sketches of Negro Character* (Boston and New York: Houghton, Mifflin, 1892), p. vii.

21. John Stafford, "Patterns of Meaning in *Nights with Uncle Remus*," *American Literature*, 18 (May 1946), 89–108.

22. Louise Dauner, "Myth and Humor in the Uncle Remus Fables," *American Literature*, 20 (May 1948), 129–43.

23. Harris, *The Life and Letters*, p. 386.

24. Hubbell, *The South in American Literature*, pp. 793–94.

25. Recently, George Fenwick Jones has argued that at least two of the tales in the first Uncle Remus volume were "literary transmissions" that came to America via William Caxton's edition of *Reynard the Fox*, rather than folktales from African or Afro-American oral tradition; Jones believes that Harris may have understandably confused the plantation stories he heard as a boy at Turnwold with tales he read later. Jones's speculations are suggestive, but the preponderance of evidence, especially Harris's careful methods for "verifying" his tales and the extensive source and analogue studies of modern folklorists, reconfirms an oral line of transmission for the great majority of the Uncle Remus tales. Of course, it is possible that some of Harris's informants who sent him outlines of folktales on occasion confused oral with literary stories heard in their own childhoods. See Jones, "Reineke Fuchs and Brer Rabbit: Oral or Written Tradition?" in *Vistas and Vectors: Essays Honoring the Memory of Helmut Rehder*, ed. Lee B. Jennings and George Schulz-Behrend (Austin: University of Texas Press, 1979), pp. 44–53.

Editorial Note

In the reviews and essays that follow, non-standard punctuation has been silently emended, a few inaccurate publication dates and titles for Harris's works corrected, characters' misspelled names restored, and footnotes renumbered and revised where necessary to conform to the recommendations of the 1977 *MLA Handbook*. In the few instances where economy required that I omit material, I have so indicated by explanatory notes or bracketed ellipses. All other ellipses are those of the original authors. Where two reviews of a Harris book are reprinted, the full publication reference for the volume accompanies the first review, only.

REVIEWS

"Negro Folk-Lore"

Anonymous*

We are just discovering what admirable literary material there is at home, what a great mine there is to explore, and how quaint and peculiar is the material which can be dug up. Mr. Harris's book may be looked on in a double light—either as a pleasant volume recounting the stories told by a typical old colored man to a child, or as a valuable contribution to our somewhat meagre folk-lore. Descanting but slightly on such *mise en scene* as the author has very wisely chosen, still admiring the happy little bits of by-play, with which the numerous stories are introduced for the delectation of "Miss Sally's" 7-year old child, we would rather confine ourselves to the strange myths which are still kept alive by the negroes in Southern plantations, and the dialects, which curious subjects Mr. Harris has cleverly arranged and presented to us with a great deal of skill and judgment.

To Northern readers the story of Brer (Brother–Brudder) Rabbit may be novel. To those familiar with plantation life, who have listened to these quaint old stories, who have still tender reminiscences of some good old Mauma who told these wondrous adventures to them when they were children, Brer Rabbit, the Tar Baby, and Brer Fox come back again with all the past pleasures of younger days. It is indeed curious to notice how the negro in all his stories places the rabbit first in the scale of animal intelligence, and the fox second, reversing the white man's ideas of their comparative standing. The rabbit myth, as is stated in the preface, exists to a certain extent among numerous African and Eastern races. If in Japan the badger is among the most cunning of creatures the rabbit is fully his equal. Undoubtedly the supremacy of the rabbit, as believed by the American negro, comes from legends which his African forefather brought with him when the first slavers landed their black merchandise. Sometimes in speculating over the story of the rabbit and his conspicuous position, questions of the survival of animals may be suggested as a reason for the persistence of this creature in folk-lore. Rabbits have been introduced of late years into New Zealand and New South Wales. They have increased and multiplied there to such an enormous extent that to-

*Review of *Uncle Remus: His Songs and His Sayings* (New York: D. Appleton, 1881 [1880]). Reprinted from *New York Times*, 1 December 1880, p. 3, cols 1–2.

3

day in some sections of the antipodes they absolutely threaten destruction to every green thing that grows. It might have been that in early times such enormous numbers of rabbits existed that the memory of them has come down to us as a permanent type, while other animals of greater importance have been forgotten.

Innumerable are the stories the negro tells of the "cuteness" of cotton tail. He is the Solomon of beasts, and joins to his wisdom a faculty of trickery, of getting the better of all the other animals, which is peculiar to him alone. He is mischievous for mischief's sake. One of the most curious and incomprehensible of all the adjuncts to the negro story is the presence of a certain human, womanly character, a Miss Meadows, with whom the rabbit and fox, bear and terrapin are on the most familiar terms. She never loses her higher characteristics of being a woman. She comes in over and over again something like a Greek chorus. The *vraisemblable* never, somehow, is upset by her introduction. Miss Meadows must be present as a matter of course, and a little one in middle Georgia, sitting on the knee of an old colored friend, always asks Uncle Primus or Maum Amorette, "and what did Miss Meadows say then?"

Of late there have been many variations of one particular story, "The Rabbit and the Tar Baby," presented to an admiring public, but Mr. Harris, through Uncle Remus, presents the pure unalloyed version. There is a delightful nonsensicality about some of these stories, as "How Mr. Rabbit Saved His Meat," which cannot but please even the most prosaic reader.

As a fair specimen of that fineness of ear which Mr. Harris possesses, and the knack he has of giving phonographs of negro dialect, we take the following:

> "Soon's Brer Wolf hear talk er der patterrollers [patrol] he scramble off inter de underbresh like he bin shot out'n a gun. En he want mo'n gone to Brer Rabbit, he whirl in en skunt [skinned] de cow and salt de hide down, 'en den he tuck'n cut up de kyarkiss en stow it 'way in de smoke-'ouse, en den he tuck'n stick de een' er de cow-tail in de groun'. Atter he gone en done all dis, den Brer Rabbit he quall out fer Brer Wolf: 'Run yer, Brer Wolf! Run yer! Yo cow gwine in de groun'! Run yer!'
>
> "W'en ole Brer Wolf got dar, w'ich he come er scootin', dar wuz Brer Rabbit hol'in' on ter de cow-tail, fer ter keep it fum gwine in de groun'. Brer Wolf, he kotch holt, en dey 'gin a pull er two en up come de tail. Den Brer Rabbit, he wink his off eye en say—sezee,
>
> " 'Dar! de tail done pull out en den cow gone!' Sezee."

Old Remus brings to light numbers of those queer turns of phrases which are only in use by the negro south of Maryland. "Gwineter" is composite, and mosaics "is-going-to-be" in one agglomeration. A negro never says "this minute is going to be my last," but turns it this way: "He dunner

(don't know) w'at minnit gwineter be de nex'." The prefix a, as in old style
a-going, is always er, as "he come er-scooting." The conjunction "and" is
shorn of its affix and prefix, and left as an n, as he "took and," which
becomes "tuck'n." The combination of b and l, with or without a vowel,
or p and l under similar circumstances, are always shibboleths, and
"obliged" becomes bleedzd. Bs at the beginning of a word with a final d
are also troublesome, and bird becomes "bud." A Savannah or Charleston
cook who has to pick rice-birds will say, "I shell de bud." Shell serves the
purpose of pick, as she uses the same verb for pluming birds or opening
oysters. The verb "to do," introduced inappropriately, is constant, as "de
tail done pull out," or "I han't done done it," or "he gone done done it,"
or "he gone done dead." Of course there is no very great persistence as to
characteristic words, for the civil war introduced military phraseology
among the negroes, which war talk they have kept, with the last of those
old blue overcoats. "Raid" came in 1861, and will last through our time;
so will skedaddle, ranch, corral. Your negro has a quick ear, and though
he may not understand a word, so it has an expressive sound, he will
adopt it. Hence, slang terms are in time taken up by him, though they appear when white men have forgotten them. A negro loves to say, "Here I
come 'a-biling,' " or " 'a-bulging,' " and, suiting actions to words, he will
start all his limbs in motion. A word a negro uses in conjunction with
bees, to express their humming, might belong to the history of the Snark.
"De bees is a 'zoonin." No word could be more expressive than this. Can it
be old English? It is so pretty that it is worthy of poetic adoption. Very
often negro pronunciation is unintelligible to English ears. The writer of
this was once with a highly educated Englishman who prided himself on
his philological acumen, as a proficient in Grimm's laws. An old negro
woman was crooning over her basket of sea-cotton:

"Romanoff in hebben for me."

and repeated the refrain of her song over and over again.
"Bless me!" said the Englishman. "Is this a Russian hymn glorifying
the reigning family!"
The old Mauma was singing,

"Room enough in heaven for me."

Mr. Harris shows cleverly the distinction between Middle Georgia
and Southern Georgia negro dialects. It is a language apart. When Gen.
Sherman's soldiers went to Savannah and discovered the rice-field
negroes, their language was incomprehensible, and the rank and file
called them "Dutch niggers." A colored man from the Chatahoochee
would never understand his brother who worked on the banks of the
Ogochee. The rice plantation hand is a small, coal-black negro, not very
high in the stage of civilization, who has an English of his own. Here is a
specimen of rice-field dialect: " 'Taint mi chile sek tarra one—sek tarra

time bin mine—dis my dart'r chile—'o awful scar—he tink de chile gwine die," tarra meaning "other," and sek, sick, and he and she being of all genders.

Mr. Harris gives a number of negro proverbs, some of which are excellent, as: "Meller mushmillion hollers at you from over de fence." "Nigger wid a pocket-hand'kcher better be looked arter." "One-eyed mule can't be handle on de blinde side." "Moon may shine but a lightered knot's mightily handy." "Hit's a mighty deaf nigger dat don't year de dinner ho'n." "Hit take a bee fer ter git de sweetness out'n de hoar-houn blossom." "Watch out w'en you'er gitting all you want. Fattenin' hogs ain't in luck."

Mr. Harris's book is altogether excellent of its kind, and in preserving certain quaint legends, and giving us exactly the sounds of the negro dialect, he has established on a firm basis the first real book of American folk lore.

"Uncle Remus"

Anonymous*

This charming little book appears to be written by a partisan of "the peculiar institution," and so very thorough a partisan, that he speaks of Mrs. Stowe's "wonderful defence of slavery as it existed in the South." "Mrs. Stowe," he goes on, "let me hasten to say, attacked the possibilities of slavery with all the eloquence of genius; but the same genius painted the portrait of the Southern slave-owner, and defended him." In the same sense, and no other, Mr. Harris obviously regards this book as a defence of the slave-system. Because it depicts the slave of the old plantations as often warmly attached to the family in which he was domesticated, as full of sympathetic qualities, full of humour and fancy, and full, too, of a certain kind of social independence, Mr. Harris appears to suppose that it is an apology for the system. In reality, this book illustrates the habits of cunning, deceit, and dishonesty, and the delight in them, in which even these highly favourable specimens of the slave were steeped, quite as much as it illustrates their attachment to the house to which they belonged, and their fascinating qualities of head and heart.

However, the interest of the book is not in its illustrations of slavery, but in its picture of the kind of imaginations in which the negro slave most delighted. In his preface, Mr. Harris says:

> The story of the Rabbit and the Fox, as told by the Southern
> negroes, is artistically dramatic in this; it progresses in an

*Review of English edition of *Uncle Remus: His Songs and His Sayings*, published as *Uncle Remus and His Legends of the Old Plantation* (London: David Bogue, 1881). Reprinted from *Spectator*, 2 April 1881, p. 445, cols. 1–2; p. 446, cols. 1–2.

orderly way from a beginning to a well-defined conclusion, and is full of striking episodes that suggest the culmination. It seems to me to be to a certain extent allegorical, albeit, such an interpretation may be unreasonable. At least it is a fable thoroughly characteristic of the Negro; and it needs no scientific investigation to show why he selects as his hero the weakest and most harmless of all animals, and brings him out victorious in contests with the bear, the wolf, and the fox. It is not virtue that triumphs, but helplessness; it is not malice, but mischievousness.

And, perhaps, that admission is quite sufficient—if anything were needful for that purpose—to cancel the effect of all the author's admiring insinuations as to the value of the institution which has produced these charming legends. Mr. Harris should have said, "It is not virtue that triumphs, but cunning," for mere "helplessness" can never triumph; and the object of all these legends is to show that races of inferior physical strength are *not* helpless, but more able to help themselves by cunning than their adversaries by tooth and claw. However, whatever be the drift of the author, the idea of preserving and publishing these legends in the form in which the old-plantation negroes actually tell them, is altogether one of the happiest literary conceptions of the day. And very admirably is the work done.

What strikes us most, perhaps, is the curious simplicity of the trickery which is supposed to win the victory over superior force. The rabbit, who is always, or almost always, the negro's hero amongst animals—sometimes the terrapin, a kind of fresh-water tortoise, we believe, takes his place—gets out of his scrapes by the sort of inventiveness which, if it were conceivable at all, would be not so much an evidence of his superior cunning, as of the infinite and immeasurable gullibility of the fox, or wolf, or bear with whom he has to contend. And evidently the imagination of the negro delighted itself more in grotesquely exaggerating in every way this gullibility of the stronger races, than even in dwelling upon the cunning of the weaker races. These legends embody better the contempt of the weak for the humorously exaggerated stupidity of the strong, than their delight in the astuteness of the weak. One of the earlier stories, however, tells how the rabbit is, at first, taken in by the fox, who makes a sort of lay figure of a baby all smeared over with tar, which is called a "tar-baby." The curiosity of the rabbit entangles him with this sticky lay-figure, so as to put him in the fox's power, though he afterwards outwits the fox; and it is to this story that the question refers with which the following extract begins:

[Reprints Legend VI of *Uncle Remus*, "Mr. Rabbit Grossly Deceives Mr. Fox," the third paragraph through the end. This tale recounts Brer Rabbit's celebrated use of reverse psychology—"please, Brer Fox, don't fling me in dat brier-patch"—to effect his escape.]

Nothing could show better how the negro imagination ran riot in imputing stupidity to those who were known to be stronger than themselves, than the charming legend where the Rabbit actually boasts that his family have always made a riding-horse of the Fox, with the express intention *not* of putting him on his guard, but of making him into a riding-horse, and succeeds none the less. The touches of humor in the story are exquisite. The refusal to account for Miss Meadows in any way beyond stating that she was "in the tale"; the demeanour of Brother Rabbit when Miss Meadows and her daughters are laughing at him, sitting there "sorter lam' like," and then crossing his legs and winking his eye "slow"; making his false boast, and paying his " 'specks," and "tipping his beaver," and walking off as stuck-up as a "fire-stick"; and the description of the fox looking as "peart as a circus pony" in the saddle and bridle and blinkers in which he tamely came on purpose to prove that he had never been the Rabbit's riding-horse; the account of the putting-on of the spurs; the fault the fastidious horseman finds with his horse for losing his pace; and the old negro's final objection to giving out more cloth at one time than is needful for one pair of trousers—are all telling features in a most humorous tale. But, for ourselves, we think we even prefer the story of the contest of the Fox with the Terrapin, in which, again, a degree of stupidity is attributed to the fox far more charmingly grotesque than the cunning attributed to the tortoise:

[Reprints Legend XII of *Uncle Remus*, "Mr. Fox Tackles Old Man Tarrypin."]

Brother Terrapin, allowing to himself that when the fox comes up "he'd sorter keep one eye open," his pococurante way of saying he'd been "lounjun 'roun'," and "suffer'n'," and his gentle patronage of the fox for not knowing what trouble is; his ill-advised indignation at the idea that his tail had been burnt off, and the unfortunate demonstration of the existence of that member into which it surprises him; and finally, the extraordinarily simple trap into which the fox falls by being led to suppose that he had got hold of a stump-root, and not of the terrapin's tail, are all of them charming touches of humour, and of humour obviously enjoying the consciousness of its own extravagance. So, too, when the rabbit gets the wolf into the chest, and before beginning operations against him, deliberately goes to the looking-glass to wink at himself; and again, when the political indignation of the crayfishes breaks out because the elephant "puts his foot down" on one of them, and they "sorter swawmed tergedder, en draw'd up a kind o' peramble wid some wharfoes in it, en read her out in de 'sembly"; and once more, when we listen to the delightful bravado with which the old negro parades the fine, bushy tail of the rabbit of old times, in the hope of exciting his little auditor's wonder, we appreciate the popular humour of these legends as we have hardly ever appreciated any humour so gay and childlike. We must give the last in full:

"One time," said Uncle Remus, sighing heavily and settling himself back in his seat with an air of melancholy resignation, "one time Brer Rabbit wuz gwine 'long down de road shakin' his big bushy tail, en feelin' des ez scrumpshus ez a bee-martin wid a fresh bug." Here the old man paused and glanced at the little boy, but it was evident that the youngster had become so accustomed to the marvellous developments of Uncle Remus's stories, that the extraordinary statement made no unusual impression on him. Therefore the old man began again, and this time in a louder and more insinuating tone: "One time ole man Rabbit, he wuz gwine 'long down de road shakin' his long, bushy tail, en feelin' mighty biggity." This was effective. "Great goodness, Uncle Remus!" exclaimed the little boy, in open-eyed wonder, "everybody knows that rabbits haven't got long, bushy tails." The old man shifted his position in his chair and allowed his venerable head to drop forward until his whole appearance was suggestive of the deepest dejection; and this was intensified by a groan that seemed to be the result of great mental agony. Finally he spoke, but not as addressing himself to the little boy. "I notices dat dem folks w'at makes a great 'miration 'bout w'at dey knows, is des de folks w'ich you can't put no 'pennunce in w'en de 'cashun come up. Yer one un um no, en he done come en excuse me er 'lowin' dat rabbits is got long, bushy tails, w'ich goodness knows ef I'd a dremp' it, I'd a whirl in en ondremp' it."—"Well, but Uncle Remus, you said rabbits had long, bushy tails," replied the little boy. "Now you know you did."—"Ef I ain't fergit it off'n my mine, I say date ole Brer Rabbit wuz gwine down de big road shakin' his long, bushy tail. D'at w'at I say, en dat I stan's by." The little boy looked puzzled, but he didn't say anything. After a while the old man continued: "Now, den, ef dat's 'greed ter, I'm gwine on, en ef tain't 'greed ter, den I'm gwineter pick up my cane en look atter my own intrust. I got wuk lyin' roun' yer dat's des natally gittin' moldy."

What could be more admirable than the dignity with which Uncle Remus confronts what the boy has inferred from what he said, with what he actually said, and accuses him of false witness, and reduces him to abject submission, before he will consent to go on a single syllable with his story? In such touches lies the charm of this fascinating little volume of legends, which deserves to be placed on a level with *Reineke Fuchs* [*Reynard the Fox*] for its quaint humour, without reference to the ethnological interest possessed by these stories, as indicating, perhaps, a common origin for very widely severed races.

[*Nights with Uncle Remus:* An "Extraordinary *Tour de Force*"]

Anonymous*

Mr. Harris's reputation was made at a single stroke by his *Uncle Remus: His Songs and His Sayings*, which appeared just three years ago in book form. It was then seen that, in spite of his disclaimer that he was simply a chronicler of negro folk-lore, he was an exquisite humorist, whose mastery of the negro dialect and skill as a story-teller placed him in the front rank of American writers. He now comes forward with a second volume, no longer a medley, but wholly given up to the "creetur" tales which made the first so enjoyable and so valuable, and thus proves the sincerity of his protest that he was a man with a mission. The mine of which he first fairly revealed the richness has, meantime, been still further opened up by his own explorations and the help of friends, until in addition to the thirty-four of the former series we have seventy-one new tales placed before us. It cannot be supposed that the vein is worked out, even if it should seem that the best ore lay on the surface. Opinions will differ as to whether there is anything in the present collection to be preferred, say, to the "Tar Baby," the explanation of Brer Possum's love of peace, or the trial of strength in which Brer Tarrypin surpasses Brer B'ar. But in all other respects, unquestionably, this work more than holds its own, and indeed, regard being had to the literary skill displayed in setting so large a number of stories, must be thought an extraordinary *tour de force*.

The ease and confidence with which Mr. Harris handles his materials are shown in various ways. There is a certain development in the two leading characters. "The little boy" is felt to be getting older and more mature; Uncle Remus grows more mellow, and his finer traits are brought out by contrast with an aged "Affiky" man, Daddy Jack, from the rice plantations, and with two of the women house servants. These three newcomers all relieve Uncle Remus in telling stories, and Mr. Harris's crowning art lies in maintaining the peculiar speech and psychic quality of each. In other words, he drives a dialectic four-in-hand with unrivalled dexterity. Nothing could be better here than the way in which Daddy Jack takes a tale away from Uncle Remus and proceeds to tell it himself, but the former will not father it, and quietly resumes (p. 207): "Now, den, we er got ter go 'way back behine dish yer yallergater doin's w'at Brer Jack bin mixin' us up wid. Ef I makes no mistakes wid my 'membrence, de place wharbouts I lef' off wuz whar Brer Rabbit had so many 'p'intments fer ter keep out der way er de t'er creeturs dat he 'gun ter feel

*Review of *Nights with Uncle Remus: Myths and Legends of the Old Plantation* (Boston: James R. Osgood, 1883). Reprinted from *Nation*, 15 November 1883, p. 422, cols. 2–3.

monst'ous humbly-fied." Another striking example is a succession of three variants of one theme, told by Uncle Remus, Daddy Jack, and Aunt Tempy respectively. Space fails us, however, to quote freely from these laughable pages. How many delicate touches there are like this (p. 99): "Brer Wolf he keep on, he did, twel he done stop up de hole good, *en den he bresh de trash off'n his cloze,* en put out fer home." Or take this consummate piece of deception and anti-climax (p. 71): "Brer Rabbit say he a good frien' to Brer Fox, en he aint got no room ter talk 'bout 'im, but yit w'en he see 'im 'stroyin' King Deer goats, en chunkin' at his chickens, *en rattlin' on de palin's fer ter make de dog bark,* he bleedz ter come lay de case 'fo' de fambly."

Our author has had compassion on his Northern readers, and adds many helpful foot-notes in explanation of the obscurer terms, besides furnishing a special Daddy Jack vocabulary. His introduction gives an interesting account of the difficulties of gathering his later stories, which are still current, and he makes the acute criticism on Theal's *Kaffir Folk-Lore* that the fact of these tales having all "undergone a thorough revision by a circle of natives" raises a fair presumption that they were more or less cooked, and that the body of Kaffir folk-lore corresponding to that of the Southern States has still to be extracted from reluctant informants. However, Theal supplies some curious parallels with the stories related by Mr. Harris; and so does Bleek, but the Kaffir hare *(hlakanyana)* has already given way to the Hottentot fox. It is also made nearly certain that the Amazonian tortoise-myths recorded by the late Professor Hartt were derived by the Indians from contact with the blacks. The same thing has happened to our American Indians. The introduction concludes with a rhymed Creole animal story lately published by Prof. James A. Harrison, of Washington and Lee University.

We cannot dismiss this work without noticing its confirmation of Mr. Harris's capacity for higher and more sustained efforts, as already evidenced in "At Teague Poteet's." His accurate and sympathetic observation, his poetic imagination, his strength and tenderness in character drawing, a certain dramatic instinct, moreover, show that he may yet make a name in fiction as in folk-lore. His publishers, we are glad to see, announce as in preparation *Mingo, and Other Sketches.*

[*Nights with Uncle Remus:* Another Skillful Collection]

Anonymous*

Everybody will welcome another collection of stories by Uncle Remus [. . .] for whether we regard them as contributions to the science of folk-lore, illustrations of dialect, or simply as good stories, few recent publications have met with equal favor. It is a good thick volume too, containing seventy-one stories, a few of which have already seen the light in the pages of magazines, and on the average the stories will, we think, be found fully as good as those in the first collection. We learn from the preface that "the thirty-five legends in the first volume were merely selections from the large body of plantation folk-lore familiar to the author from his childhood, and these selections were made less with an eye to their ethnological importance than with a view to presenting certain quaint and curious race characteristics, of which the world at large had either vague or greatly exaggerated notions." The present volume undertakes to be as complete as it could be made, although no doubt other legends exist which somebody will by and by pick up. The skill with which the tales are introduced, the descriptions of the old man's demeanor, and his by-talk with the little boy, all show a high degree of dramatic power on the part of the author. A good illustration of this is found where Aunt Tempy and Daddy Jack are introduced, in order to give an opportunity for tales in a different dialect. Uncle Remus is an "up country" negro, and when Daddy Jack, from the sea-islands, tells his story, the contrast is very striking. This sea-island dialect, Mr. Harris says, as compared with that of Uncle Remus, is "simpler and more direct; it is the negro dialect in its most primitive state."

[*Mingo and Other Sketches:* Enjoyable and Picturesque Tales of Contrasts]

Anonymous†

Those who remember the striking story, "At Teague Poteet's," which appeared first in one of the magazines and proved that Mr. Joel Chandler Harris could write a fine and picturesque tale quite independent of the dialect stories that made him famous as "Uncle Remus," will be glad to have it in book form, bound with a few other "sketches in black and

*Reprinted from *Dial,* 4 (December 1883), 195.
†Review of *Mingo and Other Sketches in Black and White* (Boston: James R. Osgood, 1884). Reprinted from *Critic,* 2 August 1884, p. 51, col. 2.

white," which it is only necessary to recommend by saying that they are his. Those who have enjoyed "Uncle Remus" will find in these "sketches" the same qualities that originally endeared the author to them, while those who felt that the troublesome dialect of "B'rer Rabbit" was the only barrier that separated them from a deep and longed-for enjoyment, will rejoice to find in "Mingo" just enough of the dialect to give a unique piquancy, added to a delineation of the "white" element in the story as vivid and entertaining as that of the "black" has been before. To our own mind, Mr. Harris's work gains greatly by this association of contrasts. In the story of "Mingo," for instance, which opens the book and gives to it its name, the amusing "poor white" element adds greatly to the effectiveness of the faithful old negro, Mingo himself—one of those slaves of whom undoubtedly there were many, who looked along the road that led to freedom, but said with a doubtful, and faithful, shake of the head, "Mebbe you leads to freedom, but bress de Lord, I'm gwine back!" The original of "Aunt Jane" in the story of "Malbone" once said to a friend who offered to show her the baby, "My dear, have you forgotten that I hate babies?" "No, indeed," was the reply. "Of course you hate babies, but I knew you didn't hate *me*, and I thought perhaps you might like to see me with a baby. It was the combination, Aunt Jane." We are tempted to assure those who have fretted a little at the dialect that has made it hard for them to enjoy what they knew was enjoyable in "B'rer Rabbit," that in "Mingo" they have a combination of "Uncle Remus" with Joel Chandler Harris which will leave them in these "sketches in black and white" nothing to be desired and everything to be enjoyed.

[*Mingo and Other Sketches:* Harris Is "Very Close to the Untutored Spirit of Humanity"]

Anonymous*

Mingo and Other Sketches does not discredit the fame of "Uncle Remus." It is not hard to account for Mr. Harris's success as a story-teller in negro and poor-white lingo. He is very close to the untutored spirit of humanity. He discriminates nicely between natural emotions in the widest sense and those which are a class inheritance. He uses rude or corrupt language to express only primitive passion and thought—fierce hate, unreasoning love, a dog's gratitude for kindness, a savage's impulse toward revenge; he never offends or wearies by palpable incongruity between idea and form. In this respect his perception is subtler and more truthful than Bret Harte's, with whom he may be legitimately compared.

*Reprinted from *Nation*, 7 August 1884, p. 115, col. 1.

Both authors have keen instincts and insights, but Harris's are finer and deeper. Harte's characters are by far the more picturesque, his incidents are more thrilling, but Harris's people wind themselves about our hearts and owe little to circumstance. Mrs. Feratia Bivins in "Mingo" is a perfect illustration of fitness between sense and sound. In acquiring a purer form of speech, her animosities, at once terrible and trivial, must have suffered modification; and no other tongue than Mingo's could have conveyed all the pathos and unconscious humor in his story, beginning: "Bimeby soon one mornin' I make a break. I wrop up my little han'ful er duds in a hankcher, en I tie de hankcher on my walkin' cane, en I put out arter de army." "Teague Poteet" and his comrades embody the Declaration of Independence and something more, for they convince us that the right to distil [sic] whiskey on Hog Mountain, without reference to revenue, is among the rights inalienable to man. The ladies of the Mountain, Mrs. Sue Parmalee, Mrs. Puritha Hightower, and Mrs. Puss Poteet are as delightful as are their names, and the only weak figure in this story is the conventional lover of Sis Poteet. In "Blue Dave," too, the conventional characters are lifeless, but there is compensation in the solemn importance of Brother Brannum and Brother Roach, and in the hunted, desolate negro, Dave. In "A Piece of Land" we are so sure of Miss Jane Inchly's soft heart that we can laugh at her sharp tongue; but the other characters are somewhat beneath the author's usual taste in selection, and they have not that air of spontaneous creation which is one of his shining merits.

" 'Uncle Remus's' Sketches"

Anonymous*

In this volume may be found "Free Joe," "Little Compton," "Aunt Fountain's Prisoner," "Trouble on Lost Mountain," and "Azalia." We know of no story which for simple pathos equals "Free Joe," Joe being that poor old colored man, freed by an accident, and to whom freedom had been a curse. How with a few words Mr. Harris gives us the character of Spite Calderwood, who just for "cussedness" separates Joe from Lucinda, until there is no one he has to love but his black cur dog, Little Dan. What is particularly to be admired in Mr. Harris is that he never truckles to the opinions of the past nor is subservient to those of today. There were Spite Calderwoods both in the North and South, men to be despised.

It is around and about Hillsborough and Rockville that most of Mr. Harris's stories occur, and the author is happy in the descriptions of his

*Review of *Free Joe and Other Georgian Sketches* (New York: Charles Scribner's Sons, 1887). Reprinted from *New York Times*, 15 January 1888, p. 14, cols. 6–7.

own State, Georgia. If it be a special tenderness Mr. Harris gives his Aunt
Fountain or Uncle Prince, though we may smile at their queer methods of
expression, one never can laugh at them. Uncle Remus, though he was
black as the ace of spades, has more admirers than Miss Sally's little boy.
"Azalia" is the longest of the stories, and the adventures of Miss
Tewksbury, an angular New-England spinster, and her pretty niece Miss
Eustis, in the piney woods of Georgia are pleasantly told. Here is a little
lesson, which the author gives in a neat way. General Garwood, an ex-
Confederate officer, leaves a railroad station, and his old colored mammy
comes to see her master off. "Tell um all howdy for me, Marse Peyton, all
un um. No diffunce ef I ain't know um all, 'tain't gwine ter do no harm fer
ter tell um dat ole Jincy say howdy. . . . I wish ter de Lord I uz gwine
'long wid you, Marse Peyton! Yit I speck time I got dar I'd whirl in en
wish myse'f back home." When the train was ready to start the gentleman
shook hands with the negro woman. The woman seemed to be very much
affected. "God A'mighty bless you, Marse Peyton, honey!" she exclaimed.
As Miss Tewksbury and her niece are in the cars the somewhat sour Aunt
berates the South, but Miss Eustis recalls the scene they have just witnessed. "Poor thing," said Miss Tewksbury, with a sigh, "she sadly needs
instruction." "Ah, yes! that's a theory we should stand to, but how shall
we instruct her to run and cry after us?" inquires Miss Eustis. In this story
there is a little dapper, gentlemanly clergyman, who, delivering a sermon
in his florid manner, says: "All things become homogeneous through the
medium of sympathy and the knowledge of mutual suffering." In some
unknown skirmish in Virginia Miss Eustis's brother and General
Garwood's brother fell. As they lay dying side by side they had clasped
one another's hands, and so young Garwood's faithful servant Uncle
Prince had found them, and the two dead heroes were carried to Georgia
and there buried side by side, and for that Helen Eustis loved General
Garwood, and the vinegarish maiden aunt was pacified, and when there
was a marriage "the notice in the *Reporter* was from the pen of Henry P.
Bassett, the novelist."

[*Free Joe and Other Georgian Sketches:* "Unaffectedness and Spontaneity"]

Anonymous*

One of the most charming young women in modern fiction is Helen
Eustis in "Azalia," one of Joel Chandler Harris's short stories collected in
his last book, *Free Joe and Other Georgian Sketches* [. . . .] The title

*Reprinted from *Catholic World*, 46 (March 1888), 836–37.

"Azalia" would, judging by the ordinary short story, lead one to suppose it was a girl's name, and that the girl was perhaps an untutored Cracker maiden who, meeting a "city chap," fell in love with him and died in the most pathetic way. It is an agreeable disappointment to find that Azalia is the name of a place in Georgia. Helen is a witty and unaffected Bostonian. Mr. Harris does not tell us this; he lets us make Helen's acquaintance. Miss Tewksbury, Helen's aunt, is afraid of the Ku-klux[sic], and when the young lady is ordered to Azalia for her health Miss Tewksbury's fear of danger becomes almost a certainty.

> "Dr. Buxton," Helen says, "is a life-long Democrat, consequently he must know all about it. Father used to tell him he liked his medicine better than his politics, bitter as some of it was; but in a case of this kind Dr. Buxton's politics have a distinct value. He will give us the grips, the signs, and the passwords, dear aunt, and I dare say we shall get along comfortably."

And they do. Their experiences in the South are pleasant. Goolsby, the book-agent, is delightful. He says to the ex-Confederate General Garwood, speaking of a book he is selling:

> "It's a history of our own great conflict, *The Rise and Fall of the Rebellion,* by Schuyler Paddleford. I don't know what the blamed publishers wanted to put it 'rebellion' for. I told 'em, says I, 'Gentlemen, it'll be uphill work with this in the Sunny South. Call it "The Conflict," ' says I. But they wouldn't listen, and now I have to work like a blind nigger splittin' rails. If sech a book is got to be circulated around here, it better be circulated by some good Southron—a man that's a kind of antidote to the poison, as it were."

The discussions between General Garwood and Miss Tewksbury on slavery are amusing. Miss Tewksbury insists that there was no good in slavery:

> "You must admit that but for slavery the negroes who are here would be savages in Africa. As it is, they have had the benefit of more than two hundred years' contact with the white race. If they are at all fitted for citizenship, the result is due to the civilizing influence of slavery. It seems to me that they are vastly better off as American citizens, even though they have endured the discipline of slavery, than they would be as savages in Africa."

"Azalia," with its pleasant atmosphere, in which good-humor plays the part of oxygen, is an excellent story. The other tales in the book possess that unaffectedness and spontaneity characteristic of Mr. Harris' method [. . . .]

"Daddy Jake the Runaway"

Anonymous*

Putnam County, Georgia, bids fair to become the classic soil of the South as Athens is dubbed by Milton the "eye of Greece"; for in this famous country the immortal "Uncle Remus" is at home; here Col. R. M. Johnston "locates" (in the expressive Americanism) his picturesque comedy of the Georgia "Crackers"; and here again Joel Chandler Harris sets a-going the wonderful wheels of Negro myth-lore and prehistoric story-telling in the ups and downs, the miseries and mirth of "Daddy Jake," Lucien and Lillian. Putnam County thus becomes like the Central Plateau of the Hindu-Kush Mountains—"east of the moon and west of the sun"—so dear to the myth-mongers and philologists of the Müller school: the centre of diffusion of a marvellous ring of myths that encircles the Negro memory of that quarter like the nebulous ring of Saturn, and expands outward through that State and contiguous States in ever-enlarging circles. The periphery of this circle touches the islands of the Carolina coast, where the "long-tailed" cotton grows; but its centre and sensitive nerve is ever the all-famous "Putnam."

This new collection of Mr. Harris's Negro stories rotates about the year 1863, and has the War of the Confederacy for its dramatic background. The core of the tales, however, is the inexhaustible curiosity of the "little boy"—here "bisected," as it were, into a boy and a girl. These charming infants—Lucien and Lillian—ply the "old man" of the former collection—now rechristened "Daddy Jake"—with the usual childish multitude of questions; they are as eager for a "story" as ever; and Brer Coon and Brer Rabbit are nearly as fertile in these as the living ones are in skipping and scampering offspring. It is Aesop come to life again after his reincarnation in an Ethiopian mould. Aesop, too, was a slave, like Uncle Remus and Daddy Jake and Epictetus and many and many another of the great philosophers and saints; and the fables of Greece and Rome and India are hardly more striking than the Negro "marooners" in their simple *naïveté* and imaginative humor. It will probably never be practicable to separate the myths of Putnam County from the myths of the broader "Africa" from which they spring; yet one must always be thankful that an artist has arisen fearless enough to seize and publish them with all their accompaniment of quaint dialect and Southern plantation life. They have value for the philologist as well as for the lover of comparative mythology.

"Uncle Remus" is here, too, in *propriâ personâ;* for after the introductory story is concluded (57 pages), we have a new cycle of Remus-legends and animal fables, such as "How Black Snake Caught the Wolf," "The Creature with no Claws," "The Foolish Woman," "The Rattlesnake

*Review of *Daddy Jake the Runaway and Short Stories Told After Dark* (New York: Century, 1889). Reprinted from *Critic*, 2 November 1889, p. 212, cols. 1–2.

and the Polecat," and "Why the Guineas Stay Awake." One at least of these new stories has a remarkable variant or parallelism in a Kafir legend of South Africa, and all thirteen show the undiminished vivacity of Uncle Remus's recollection. The book is delightfully printed, and forms a most auspicious prelude to the burst of "juvenile" books soon to come.

[Harris's *Life of Grady:* A "Hasty Compilation"]

Anonymous*

The title-page of the memorial Grady volume grossly misstates the character of its contents. It should read, *Speeches of Henry W. Grady, with a sketch of his life by Joel Chandler Harris, and Various Tributes to his Memory.* The volume is a hasty compilation—so hasty that the proofs have not had any critical revision; and though Mr. Harris appears upon the title-page not only as biographer, but also as editor, his editorial work must have been nominal. Thus, while he gives April 24, 1850, as the date of Mr. Grady's birth, the next contributor gives May 17, 1851, and the reader who pays his money is obliged to take his choice without any editorial or other help. In a felicitous quotation from George Eliot in Mr. Grady's Elberon speech, "A sweet habit of the blood" appears as "a sweet habit of the blest," and there are many typographical slips which no theological bias can excuse [. . . .]

Mr. Harris is evidently but ill pleased with his part of the book. He describes it as "a hurriedly written sketch, which is thrown together to meet the modern exigencies of publishing"; and, further along in the same paragraph, he says: "These reminiscences have taken on a disjointed shape sadly at variance with the demands of literary art." These judgments of the author the candid reader will approve [. . . .]

Mr. Grady was preëminently a man of sentiment. We do not feel so sure as Mr. Harris that his sentiment never degenerated into sentimentality. We think it sometimes did, and that sometimes it obscured for him the lines of truth and justice in political and social matters. But for the most part it was sound and sweet. It was the source, in part, of his wide popularity. It furnished his speeches and orations with their Celtic warmth. It made him hosts of friends. In all private and personal relations it is evident that he was most loving and most lovable. For children and young people he had a very great affection. The same tenderness and passion that went to his private relations went to his feeling for Atlanta, for Georgia, for the South, and for the Union [. . . .]

*Review of *Joel Chandler Harris' Life of Henry W. Grady* (New York: Cassell, 1890). Reprinted from *Nation,* 15 May 1890, p. 398, cols. 2–3; p. 399, cols. 1–3.

[*Balaam and His Master:* Excellent "General Art" and "Minute Shadings"]

Anonymous*

Ever since Uncle Remus and Uncle Remus's little white boy were created, followers in the same line of story-telling have been common. There are many who are clever in catching the dialect, the form of phrasing of the negro, but these imitative qualities do not alone suffice. There was Thackeray's Irishman. Phonetically, his spelling was marvelous, but the Thackerayan Celt was not alone perfect in speech but in action, and it is exactly Mr. Joel Chandler Harris's general art which makes him so excellent. It is not the negro alone, how he talks and acts, but it is his entire surroundings which this writer holds within his grasp. Mr. Chandler Harris does not tell of the negro in Mississippi or Alabama, but rather of the colored man in Georgia, and the minute shadings which he gives are understood by those who have lived in Georgia. Take, for instance, "Ananias," the shambling and apparently "good-for-nothing nigger"— the dog with a bad name—who stole sweet potatoes so that his old broken-down master and his young "Miss" might not starve. Take Lawyer Terrell who defends the slouchy Ananias. Terrell brings back the memories of those remarkable men the Milledgeses, the Cummingses of other times, who, through thick and thin, stood out for human justice. In "Where's Duncan?" Mr. Chandler Harris shows a terrible Southern drama. This story is of Augusta before the thirties, and this city of Georgia had been settled by Celts, of the kind favored by Oliver Cromwell. Mom Bi is purely South Carolinian. Such an old woman, African born, gained the love and, strangely enough, the dread of her white family. The natural savagery in her had never been quite tamed. Had she lived a hundred years, the wild streak in her would come out. This dialect, as shown in "Daddy Jake," many attempt and few succeed in representing. It is an English reduced to its most limited scope. If a Russian serf had but 200 words for his entire vocabulary, the transplanted African of a former period had less. It is a type entirely gone out of existence. "The Old Bascom Place" is a charming little romance, abounding with humor. Mrs. Bass, the termagant, who won't let the mild Mr. Bass "collogue with niggers," is the foil for Mildred, Judge Bascom's daughter. The Judge's insanity, his belief that he still is master of the Old Place, is touchingly told. Mr. Joel Chandler Harris's stories will live, for they help to preserve the best idea of white and colored existence just prior to and after the civil war, and in 100 years from now such a story as "Balaam and his Master" will be read for the exact facts presented, maybe for the pathos in it.

* Review of *Balaam and His Master and Other Sketches and Stories* (Boston and New York: Houghton, Mifflin, 1891). Reprinted from *New York Times*, 7 June 1891, p. 19, col. 4.

[*Balaam and His Master:*
No Writer Approaches Harris's
Knowledge of the Negro]

Anonymous*

Still keeping in the South, we come along the same parallel to Mr. Joel Chandler Harris, the inventor and introducer of Uncle Remus. The names of Mr. Harris and Mr. Page, for reasons not too clearly ascertained, are often spoken in the same breath. They both treat of the South, before the war and since the war, and they both have to do with master and slave, as any man must who chooses such a subject. In both, also, is the strong tendency to drama which is one of the unifying signs of the writers of the new South. But here resemblance ceases and difference begins. Mr. Page is the more brilliant, the more versatile, of the two. He has perhaps a stronger hold upon character—with a very important exception, presently to be noted—and he is certainly more often master of that logic of events by which a sketch is graduated into a story. "Balaam and His Master" and "Ananias," impressive as they are from more than one point of view, are no match in construction for "Elsket," or even for the too much "arranged" " 'George Washington's' Last Duel." But Mr. Harris has a great and distinguishing gift. This gift is his knowledge of the negro—a knowledge in which no other writer has approached him. "Balaam and His Master," "Ananias," "Where's Duncan?" and "Mom Bi," being four of the six pieces in Mr. Harris's new volume, are all studies, and remarkable studies, of the race. The public, highly entertained with the queerness and quaintness of the folk lore embodied for the first time in Uncle Remus, were to be excused for not seeing that here was a new and subtle student of a people who have been as much conventionalized in art as the Irishman or the lily. The two end men of that conventionality are Uncle Tom and Zip Coon, or, if one would rather, Jim Crow. That is, there has been the pious darky and the merry darky, and the negro of literature and the stage has usually kept close to one accepted type or the other.

To say that Mr. Harris's favorite exemplars are more like Uncle Tom than like Zip Coon would be a gross generality, and useful only to imply that the grave in the sons of Ham, rather than the gay, attracts Mr. Harris; for the methods of attacking slavery in *Uncle Tom's Cabin* and in Turgénef's *Annals of a Sportsman* are not farther apart than Mrs. Stowe's eloquent symbol and the real negro as he appears in Mingo, in Free Joe, and in Balaam. It is not meant for a moment that Mr. Page and other Southern writers have not depicted sad negroes—Marse Chan would be in itself an answer to such a statement—or that Mr. Harris has not depicted glad ones. But the keenness of this writer's observation is shown in the

*Reprinted from *Atlantic Monthly*, 69 (February 1892), 263–64.

unusual variety of individual characters with which he illustrates his favorite type; and if, in this latest volume, patience, long-suffering, fidelity, and the melancholy that underlies the African humor predominate, to the utter exclusion of the banjo and the breakdown, it cannot be said that monotony has been allowed to creep into the view. Balaam following the fortunes of his young master to prison and death, and Ananias risking both for the fortunes of the old master of whom the war had made him free, are alike only in their faithfulness, and have personalities of their own as definite as those of the more out-of-the-way and more sharply drawn Duncan and Mom Bi. Ananias—"the name seemed to fit him exactly. A meaner-looking negro Lawyer Terrell had never seen"—the story of Ananias is probably immoral, as it makes stealing (for another) seem half divine. Its immorality, too, will be progressive, for, among all the darkies of fiction, few will possess the memory more securely than this faithful soul in a mean body, whose mother had named him Ananias, not after the liar, but after the prophet. The charge of theatricality may, not wholly without reason, be brought against the tale of Duncan, the mysterious and ill-fated son of a white man and a mulatto woman, and also that of the terrible old slave-woman who held the divided function of prophetess and friend of the family. But the theatricality is, we feel, in the choice of subject rather than in the treatment of it; and the illustration of character is so bold, so free, so unmistakably true to race, that the rest does not much matter. Mr. Harris is not always so fortunate in his white people; in them his exaggerations take the direction of Dickens, and Colonel Watson, "The virile paralytic" of "A Conscript's Christmas," is a kind of Georgia Smallweed.

One attribute of these stories by the author of Uncle Remus is curious indeed, and it has passed, so far as we can discover, altogether unnoted in print. This is the apparently unconscious production from time to time of some effect of fairy or folk lore. Mom Bi has of course an avowed element of the grotesque, but we like to believe that Mr. Harris did not set out to produce the elfin impression of Danny Lemmons the hunchback, who went singing ahead of the soldiers, in "A Conscript's Christmas." The man with the bag over his shoulder, who comes suddenly out of the wood in "Where's Duncan?" brings with him a whiff of the Germany fairy story. His clever dealing with the mules, also, and his music, of the kind which is understood to wile the bird from the tree, although they do not offend probability, have yet a little of the atmosphere of legend. It must be left to the learned in folk lore to explain this action of negro superstition upon the Anglo-Saxon mind, or, if one prefers, this cropping out of Teuton myth in middle Georgia. We are content with pointing out a curious, attractive, and not unnatural presence in the talent of one whose pen occupied itself first with the legends of Uncle Remus.

[A *Plantation Printer:* Uncle Remus's Influence Is Present]

Anonymous*

In *A Plantation Printer* [. . .] Mr. Joel Chandler Harris relates the adventures of "a Georgia boy" during the War of Secession, and those who never tire of Uncle Remus and his stories—with whom we would be accounted—will delight in Joe Maxwell and his exploits. Uncle Remus, to be sure, does not appear in person in these boyish adventures among the Georgian forests and swamps; but his influence is present, and is active enough to put a spirit of youth in the reader who loves to hear once more of Brer Rabbit and Mr. Beaver, talking birds, strange stories of negro and Indian superstitions, and spirited descriptions of 'coon-hunting in the dismal swamp, and fox-hunting that is not after the mode of the Shires. Then, too, there is a witch story, as wild and moving as any in the repertory of Uncle Remus.

"On the Plantation"

Anonymous†

Mr. Thomas Nelson Page has delightfully chronicled the adventures of *Two Little Confederates;* the same epic period now affords "Uncle Remus" the opportunity of telling the story of *one* little Confederate, this time a Georgian, as contrasted with Mr. Page's Virginians. Verisimilitude runs all through the pages. The Southern war plantation is henceforth to be the background of its "Tale of Troy," the picturesque *mise-en-scène* of many a drama for many a rhapsode yet to come. Mr. Harris "knows it like a book," in its Georgian aspects at least, plain yet powerful in the simple forms of its tragedy and humor, in the exhibition of rural human nature, in the quaintness of its ways and manners, and in its threads and skeins of folk-lore. *On the Plantation* is essentially a boy's book—written by an "Old Boy"—one familiar with slave life in its gentler associations and acquainted with the plantation as distinguished from the "farm," of more northern latitudes. The plantation life is—and was—as different from the life of the farm as a river, broad, generous, brimming, is from a stream or streamlet—as different as the wildwood from the placid garden. The

---

*Review of the English edition of *On the Plantation: A Story of a Georgia Boy's Adventures During the War* (New York: D. Appleton, 1892), published as *A Plantation Printer: The Adventures of a Georgia Boy During the War* (London: Osgood, McIlvaine, 1892). Reprinted from *Saturday Review,* 2 April 1892, p. 403, col. 1.

†Reprinted from *Critic,* 6 August 1892, p. 65, cols. 1–2.

enormous estates of the Southern planters generated an atmosphere, a local color, a rich, rounded experience often like those of the smaller principalities of Greece or Germany, and quite unlike the contracted prosaic doings on a farmpatch of a few hundred acres. The owner of a thousand slaves—we speak from knowledge—would associate with himself a chaplain and a physician; a beautiful chapel would be built and dedicated for the use of the family; miles of roads would be hewn out of the virgin forest for his teams to traverse; gin-houses on the various "places" would seed the fleecy cotton; and hamlets of pretty cots surrounded by gardens would dot the slopes of the undulating country and house the Africans after their toil in the sun.

It is of plantation life like this that Mr. Harris talks (autobiographically, it would seem) in this new Georgia book, which reproduces the sentiment of the plantation very perfectly, and recalls it from the dead in a way that makes it live again. For it is of the "old plantation" that he speaks, and of his experiences there during the war as printer's devil in editing a country paper, and of the fox and 'possum huts, and Christmas and its quaint revelries. The chapter called "Tracking a Runaway" is a marvellous piece of word-painting, rivalled only by "A Georgia Fox-Hunt" in the same book. In these and in the poetical stories of the "Owl and the Acorn" and such like Mr. Harris excells and is at his best—an epic story-teller who has stolen fire from the Arabians and is worthy to sit cross-legged beside them in a *khan* of Damascus.

[*Uncle Remus and His Friends:* Uncle Remus Is "Just the Same as Ever"]

John Habberton*

It is high time for a new book from Unc' Remus, for the older ones have been thumbed to pieces in thousands of families. The old man is just the same as ever, and his home audience consists principally of the little boy, but the stories and songs are new, and quite as funny as the old ones. Thousands of bedtime hours will be made merry for the little ones by this new collection of tales, and hundreds of thousands of boys and girls at the North will wish, in spite of their comfortable homes and good parents, they could have been born down South and slipped down to the old darkey's cabin with that other "little boy" who seems as important to Remus as Boswell was to Johnson. As to Mr. Harris, scores of writers envy

*Review of *Uncle Remus and His Friends: Old Plantation Stories, Songs, and Ballads with Sketches of Negro Character* (Boston and New York: Houghton, Mifflin, 1892). Reprinted from *Godey's*, 126 (February 1893), 234.

him the honor which will be done him in the future—long distant may it be—when some tourist will scrawl on his tombstone "Author of Uncle Remus."

[*Uncle Remus and His Friends:* Sadly, a "Good-Bye" Volume]

Anonymous*

Uncle Remus and His Friends, [. . .] by Mr. Joel Chandler Harris, gives us a new collection of stories and songs transcribed from the lips of the plantation negro. Our delight in the collection is only tempered by the author's announcement that the book contains "Uncle Remus's good-by" to the public. We cannot have too much matter of this sort, particularly matter collected and edited with so happy a mixture of sympathy with intelligence, and we trust that Mr. Harris may yet be led to reconsider his resolution. Many of the stories now published were gathered from Mr. Harris's household servants. He tells us that "there has been a general understanding in my household for a dozen years or more that preference was to be given in the kitchen to a cook of the plantation type." After this statement we are not surprised when told that "it has sometimes happened that digestion was sacrificed to sentiment." The author's children, also, were enlisted as detectives in the work of ferreting out bits of half-forgotten folk-lore, and proved themselves most efficient aids in the work.

[*Little Mr. Thimblefinger:* "Odds and Ends of the Old Storyteller"]

Anonymous†

Mr. Joel Chandler Harris is a man of his word, and hence "Uncle Remus" is no more. But there were odds and ends of the old story-teller not worth associating with his fame if they were certainly his; and these, with sundry fairyland inventions of Mr. Harris's own, make up a plump volume entitled *Little Mr. Thimblefinger and His Queer Country: What the Children Saw and Heard There* [. . . .] "The little boy" who drew out Uncle Remus is replaced by Sweetest Susan and Buster John and their

---

*Reprinted from *Dial,* 16 March 1893, p. 186, col. 2.

†**Review** of *Little Mr. Thimblefinger and His Queer Country: What the Children Saw and Heard There* (Boston and New York: Houghton, Mifflin, 1894). Reprinted from *Nation,* 13 December 1894, p. 448, col. 3.

dusky child nurse Drusilla. The queer country lies under the spring, and the children find Brother Rabbit *emeritus* passing his tranquil old age with Mrs. Meadows—"de gals" presumably having got married off. Brother Rabbit now takes up the parable in his own behalf, and consequently has no use for negro English, which is relegated to Drusilla. Some of his tales are very droll, in spite of this loss of the dialect flavor. Mr. Harris challenges comparison with the author of *Alice* in his fantasy of the "Looking-Glass Children," and does not suffer, within the limits imposed. Mr. Oliver Herford's outline illustrations are among the best that Mr. Harris has yet inspired.

"Mr. Frost's Edition of
Uncle Remus"

Anonymous*

"Uncle Remus," after its fifteen years of popularity, is found in this new edition more valuable than ever, because we are further removed by just so many years from opportunities of studying the type that has been so accurately represented by the author's extraordinary skill. The dialect— that very dangerous medium for the maker of literature—is clear enough to those who are fortunate enough to have had some acquaintance with the Southern negro, but we can readily imagine that fifty years from now it will be an undecipherable jargon to the general reader. It is, however, not merely cleverly rendered; it is profoundly studied, following in every inflection and suggestion the personality it represents.

It is amusing to all readers, of course, as only the dialect of the most pathetic of races can be amusing, but it is intensely serious as well. It fixes for us the subtle characteristics of a people who, in the nature of things, must soon pass, and who, but for writers like the historian of Uncle Remus, would be practically unknown to the rising generation: for the educated negro of the coming years is quite another person from his ancestor, who lived "befo' de wah." This educated twig of the rough parent stalk meets with the strongest disapprobation from Uncle Remus himself—he had better "be home pickin' up chips. W'at a nigger gwineter l'arn outen books? I kin take a bar'l stave," Remus mildly asserts, "an' fling mo' sense inter a nigger in one minnit dan all de schoolhouses betwixt dis an' de State er Midgigin. Don't talk, honey! Wid one bar'l stave I kin fa'rly lif' de veil er ignunce."

If Uncle Remus scorns education, he is not above solving the ethnological problem of the white and black races. It is his modest theory

*Review of the 1895 edition of *Uncle Remus: His Songs and His Sayings* (New York: D. Appleton). Reprinted from *New York Times*, 16 October 1895, p. 16, col. 1.

that, although "niggers is niggers now," there was a time "way back yander" when we "uz all niggers tergedder," and he hasn't heard, he tells the little boy who hangs upon his words, but what folks were getting along in those days as well as they do now. The way the transformation was effected was a peculiar one. The news came that a pond of water existed in the neighborhood (the neighborhood of the world, we wonder?) which would wash whomsoever should get into it "nice an' w'ite." One black person made the plunge and came out "w'ite ez a town gal," and then "bless grashus!" when the folks saw it they all made a break for the pond. The "soopless" got in first and came out all white; next came the "nex' soopless," and they came out mulattos. By this time the water was almost used up, and the late comers could only dabble their hands and paddle with their feet, so the true negro remains black, with the exception of the palms of his hands and the soles of his feet.

This new and perfectly simple account of the origin of the races interested the little boy very much, Mr. Harris tells us, but it probably did not convey to him, as to older hearers, the reminder of that fundamental element in the negro character which crops out in so many of its manifestations—the element, that is, of vanity. The true negro, he who succeeded only in "paddlin' wid his foots an dabblin' wid his han's" in the wonderful pond, is probably the most consistently vain creature upon this planet. What other race could have found itself the toy as well as the target of nations and have preserved so vast a self-complacency? What other race could consent to amuse its master race with the wildest buffoonery and take pride and pleasure in its success?

It is essentially a child nature that belongs to the slaves and children of slaves who, happily, will have played only a brief part in the completed drama of American history, and it has many surprises for the student of human nature. Compounded of aboriginal African elements and the strain of culture that has crept in through association with a superior people, it retains its credulity, its active fancy, its imitative instinct, and adds to these, by a strange contradiction that speaks of the gentle African spirit, pride of family, loyalty, and a cunning humor inimitable and indescribable, but not, as Mr. Harris has proved, impossible to transcribe. Uncle Remus has a very full but not an exaggerated share of the traits of his kind. How effectually he disciplines the eager little boy, hardly more a child than himself, when he finds him playing with "dem Favers," who "wa'n't no 'count 'fo' de wah, en dey wa'n't no 'count endurin' er de wah, en dey ain't no 'count atterwards"; how gleefully he accepts the little boy's bribes of mince pie and cream cake, and how altogether dignified and reproachful he is when the little boy catches him in error. He proves, too, that this race is born to animism as the sparks fly upward. Even the toothache is invested by him with a soul, and a very evil one at that. The little pain that "crep' up" the lower jaw and went back "an' tol' Mary" and then the "two crope up together," is a personality that will appeal to any reader who has suffered.

It is a matter of fact that Uncle Remus's stories are of positive interest to folk-lore students, and that the familiar histories of Brer Fox and his neighbors are found as much at home in South Africa as in the plantation States.

Mr. Frost's pictures of animals would be an additional charm to almost any book, and in the present instance they breathe the very spirit of the text.

"Mr. Harris's Masterpiece"

Anonymous*

Of the new *Uncle Remus* the author says in his introductory letter to the illustrator, Mr. Frost: "The book was mine, but now you have made it yours, both sap and pith." The implied praise is not too great, for Mr. Frost's drawings are among the cleverest things ever done in their line. At some points they fall below Mr. Church's drawings for the original edition. They are not as imaginative, nor do they decorate the page so well, but Brer Frost has a more intimate knowledge of Negro and animal life and can combine the two natures in the one individual in a more convincing manner. He humanizes his Fox and Bear and Rabbit, as Uncle Remus himself does; the humanity with which he endows them is always of the African sort, the clothing also, and he knows nearly as much about the beauty of rags and patches as Mr. Whistler, or even Rembrandt. What a dissipated, worthless "nigger" he makes Brer Fox, stretched upon the ground, watching Jack Sparrer. How the Negro mechanic comes out in Brer Rabbit boring a gimlet hole in the cover of the chest in which he has imprisoned Brer Wolf. The illustrations to Uncle Remus's "Songs" and "Sayings," which follow the "Legends of the Old Plantation," are quite as good. No two faces or figures are alike, yet every one is unmistakably a black man. The half-tone pictures are not nearly so good as the pen-and-ink illustrations, which gain nothing by having been printed upon clay-laden paper. Mr. Frost's original drawings were noticed in last week's *Critic* [. . . .] In *Mr. Rabbit At Home* we renew our acquaintance with little Mr. Thimblefinger and his queer country under the well, where Mr. Rabbit and Miss Meadows now live and entertain their occasional visitors, Buster John, Sweetest Susan and Drusilla, with fantastic tales of the "Jumping-off Place" and "The Rabbit and the Moon." These have a totally distinct flavor from the Uncle Remus stories, and in them the interest centres, not in the storyteller, nor in his characters, but in the listeners. The text is, of course, by Mr. Harris; the delightful illustrations are by Mr. Oliver Herford [. . . .]

*Review of the 1895 edition of *Uncle Remus: His Songs and His Sayings* and of *Mr. Rabbit at Home: A Sequel to Little Mr. Thimblefinger and His Queer Country* (Boston and New York: Houghton, Mifflin, 1895). Reprinted from *Critic*, 23 November 1895, p. 343, col. 1.

[*Stories of Georgia:*
"Vivified and Realized"
Georgia History]

Anonymous*

The pen of Mr. Joel Chandler Harris has been making excursions into the field of history. It has traveled over much-worn roads, but the eyes of the author singled out fresh beauties and vivified and realized old ones.

Mr. Harris has written, not a history of Georgia, but some stories of Georgia. The title of the volume tells the full story of its contents—*Stories of Georgia.* Strung together in connected form, giving a coherent and absorbing story of our state's history, are a cluster of well-told narratives dealing with the foremost events and personages of Georgian history.

Mr. Harris has not written a conventional history. Mr. Harris is not conventional; he is Mr. Harris. He does things in his own unique way and when he put his pen to his latest task he invested the dry, dull story with the color and vitality of life and made a thrilling story which the youth of the state will read with the relish of a novel. He has, as he himself puts it, clothed the dry bones of fact with the flesh and blood of narrative, and he has given us strong, vivid pictures of some of the people who figured first in our history. His strong characterization of the Indian woman, Mary Musgrove, and his sympathetic story of her adventures and misadventures, holds the mind and fascinates the imagination as a strongly written piece of fiction or an absorbing play.

He gives us a fresh insight into the character and motives of that first gentleman to establish government over this territory, Mr. James Oglethorpe. He has woven into his story of Mr. Oglethorpe's coming to America all the incidents of that gentleman's career which the histories furnish, and he has put them in interesting form.

Mr. Harris covers in the fifteen or more divisions of his book each separate important phase of Georgia's history. He has not departed one whit from the facts, but he has related our history just as he would relate a story when the data was before him.

Mr. Harris has told us familiar and unfamiliar facts in that captivating way which characterizes all his work. He touches a subject but to give it life and color and beauty and he has performed for Georgia history a feat which no other man has done. It is a task which other states would do well to emulate, but it would be wise in doing so to get a Harris to work the miracle.

Mr. Harris's book is just out. It is a handsome volume, neatly and attractively printed. It will attract a great deal of attention throughout the state. It should be in every home and every Georgia youth should read it.

*Review of *Stories of Georgia* (New York, Cincinnati, Chicago: American Book Co., 1896). Reprinted from *Atlanta Constitution*, 1 November 1896, p. 5, cols. 1–2.

[*Daddy Jake the Runaway* and *The Story of Aaron:* Snatches of "Life among the Lowly"]

Anonymous*

A pure coincidence, surely, brings out together a new edition of *Daddy Jake* and a first edition (may there be many) of *The Story of Aaron*. They are both snatches of that "Life among the Lowly" which Mrs. Stowe was not the first to depict under the veil of romance, and Mr. Harris will not be the last. In other words, they take their place on the shelf beside *Archy Moore* and *Uncle Tom's Cabin*, but with the capital moral and historic distinction that they are the product of a Southern pen.

The art of "Daddy Jake" was admirable, but the mechanism was all terrestrial and human. It opened directly and in the most matter-of-fact way with "an uproar on the Gaston plantation, in Putnam County, in the State of Georgia," "one fine day in September, in the year 1863." This plantation "lay along the Oconee River" "not far from Roach's Ferry." Uncle Jake, the carriage-driver, strikes and thinks he has killed the overseer, who presumes to give him orders and to assault him, and, fearful of the consequences, takes to the woods. Dr. Gaston's young children, Lucien and Lillian, go in quest of him in a bateau let drift down the Oconee. In "The Story of Aaron" we are still "on a large plantation in middle Georgia," but Lucien and Lillian are transformed into our classic friends Buster John and Sweetest Susan, with their back-door relations with "Mr. Thimblefinger's queer country," while Daddy Jake gives place to Aaron, the offspring of an Arab slave hunter who was properly punished by being confounded with the Africans he was marketing, and an Arab girl who shared the same fate and was transported with him to this country. Aaron shows his pedigree in his carriage and in his spirit, was early regarded and treated as a "dangerous nigger," and later passed for a conjurer among his fellow slaves. In fact, Brer Rabbit had directed Buster John and Sweetest Susan to him to learn the language of animals, and, this acquired, the story of Aaron is most cleverly pieced out in turn by the subject of it himself, by the gray pony, the track dog, the white pig, the black stallion, and by Free Polly.

We do not mean to spoil the pleasure of younger or older readers by revealing the plot. Aaron, too, becomes a runaway, and seeks refuge in the swamp, the lair of the white pig. The aspects of slavery which Mr. Harris incidentally displays are the slave coffle, the slave auction, the op-

*Review of the 1896 edition of *Daddy Jake the Runaway* (New York: Century) and of *The Story of Aaron (So Named) The Son of Ben Ali: Told by His Friends and Acquaintances* (Boston and New York: Houghton, Mifflin, 1896). Reprinted from *Nation*, 5 November 1896, p. 353, cols. 2–3.

pression of small proprietors by large slave-owners, and lynch law in operation upon an abolitionist, along with the passion of the Southern temperament and its instinctive resort to the shot gun whether for good or for evil purposes. In the end, the rescue of the abolitionist, before the war, redounds to the security of the Abercrombie plantation when Sherman passes that way on his march to the sea, and the great General figures in the narrative like any other personage, but in the unwonted light (in Southern eyes) of a benefactor. The story is neither as dramatic nor as pathetic as "Daddy Jake," but the skill of it is consummate, and its fidelity to the life not inferior, while its supernatural element will perhaps render it more attractive to that imaginative age which can make a happy family of "Ole Brer Tarrypin," Tecumseh Sherman, and "Miss Meadows and de gals."

[*Sister Jane:* "A Dull Book"]

Anonymous*

Sister Jane is a dull book, and it is a pity that Mr. Harris should have published it. The supposititious author of the narrative is a bashful, good-natured person in whom Mr. Harris would doubtless like us to see a type of manly sweetness. But Mr. William Wornum is not sweet; he hovers on the brink of the maudlin through chapters long drawn out, and if there is anything strenuous in the episodes which are imported into the book at long intervals it is certainly not communicated to him to make him interesting in spite of himself. To be sure, "Sister Jane" is supposed to be the central figure in the book, but her aphorisms have a manufactured air, and the strength of character for which she is assumed to be remarkable does not impress one by any effective manifestations. Mr. Harris gives us to understand that he is writing about some intensely human creatures, but they never prove this for him. It would seem, in short, that the author of some of the most excellent pages of discursive narrative in recent American fiction is not necessarily qualified to write a novel. *Sister Jane*, which obviously tries to be a novel, is really an amorphous production through which pale, soulless, bodiless personages ramble with scarcely a glimmer of vitality among them all. Mr. Harris puts his knowledge of a Southern village into his work, and his scenes are well drawn, but they need to be populated by reasonable beings before they can have any value to the public.

*Review of *Sister Jane: Her Friends and Acquaintances* (Boston and New York: Houghton, Mifflin, 1896). Reprinted from *New York Daily Tribune*, 20 December 1896, Part III, p. 2, col. 4.

[*Sister Jane:* A "Quiet Picture," but a Flawed One]

Anonymous*

The incidents narrated by Mr. Joel Chandler Harris in *Sister Jane* are old fashioned, romantic, improbable, quite in the atmosphere of middle Georgia before the war. The manner is grave, repressed, a little stilted— qualities natural to a middle-aged bachelor, observant and reflective, and very much under the thumb of a bustling sister made up of a sharp tongue, a soft heart, and pronounced taste for management. Mr. Harris's quiet picture of an old-time Southern community is vivid and interesting, and seems to be true to fact. There is no violent contrast between the condition of the master and that of the slave, but an easy, harmonious assimilation, based on recognition of common humanity, without much reference to difference of color. Of course his representation does not cover the whole South, but only a section where the spirit of true democracy had not been contaminated; where, as he says, "the aristocracy of caste could hardly find a spot of ground on which to plant its dainty feet," and where integrity went farther than wealth. All his people own slaves, but are not therefore proud, splendid, and barbaric. The finest person socially, and the villain of the plot, is a colonel by courtesy, but his family is intimate with "Sister Jane," the tailoress, and exchanges "howdy" familiarly with all the village. The dialect used is similar to that which is pushed to incomprehensibility by Mr. [Richard] Malcolm Johnston. Mr. Harris employs it with discretion as a medium for heightening color in funny old men (Grandsir Johnny Roach and Uncle Jimmy Cosby), for adding individuality to the irony of Mrs. Beshears and pathos to the distress of Mandy Satterlee.

The last chapters of *Sister Jane* are somewhat tiresome and bewildering. There is too much strain on capacity for joy by the return of a long-lost uncle and long-lost son, together with so much repenting and forgiving that the mind fails to distinguish between the sinner and the sinned against. We moderns resent such complications in life, and skip them in stories; but Mr. Harris, writing about simple Georgians of the forties, probably shared the primitive enthusiasm for strange coincidence and sentimental adjustments, and so fell into what would have pleased his characters, taking no thought for the duty of pleasing his readers.

*Reprinted from *Nation*, 28 January 1897, p. 71, col. 3; p. 72, col. 1.

[*The Story of Aaron:*
Harris Sympathizes with
Children, Darkies,
and Animals]

Anonymous*

Mr. Joel Chandler Harris has a familiar. How else can we explain his ability to read the mind of horses and smaller cattle? The charm of *The Story of Aaron* [. . .] lies much in the crossing and recrossing of the belt which stretches between the natural and the supernatural, but always he is human, sympathetic, at home with unsophisticated children, darkies, and the animals which stupid people call dumb.

[*Aaron in the Wildwoods:*
Reviving an Old Plea
for Slavery?]

Anonymous**

Mr. Joel Chandler Harris's *Aaron in the Wildwoods* [. . .] is not a sequel to *The Story of Aaron*, but a picking-up of dropped threads. Both the full understanding and the full enjoyment of it depend upon that and other recent volumes in the same cycle, in which the author has attempted an adumbration of slavery as it was, for youthful minds. As a whole, the new volume is at once less artistic and pathetic than its predecessors, yet adds something to the picture. A passage (p. 196) which explains amateur slave-catching by the "vigor of youth seeking an outlet" and regarding it "merely in the nature of a frolic for them to ride half the night patrolling, and sit out the other half watching for Aaron [the swamp fugitive]," sheds light on one of the causes of the perpetuity of lynching. On the other hand, children will be perplexed by the revivial of the old plea in extenuation for slavery that God was using its tender mercies for the civilization of the victims of the African slave trade. And, again per contra, we see here the beginning of a Southern Lincoln legend, which boldly proclaims the liberator "the greatest American of our time." Mr. Harris's art is conspicuous in his personification of the Swamp. In this he invites comparison with Kipling and the Jungle, and if his style must be pronounced inferior, his poetic feeling will stand the test, while a certain tenderness finds no parallel in the more renowned and prolific story-teller.

*Reprinted from *Atlantic Monthly*, 79 (March 1897), 424.

**Review of *Aaron in the Wildwoods* (Boston and New York: Houghton, Mifflin, 1897). Reprinted from *Nation*, 28 October 1897, p. 340, col. 2.

[*Tales of the Home Folks in Peace and War:* Kindness, Geniality, and Humor]

Anonymous*

Mr. Joel Chandler Harris has written many tales of Georgia, the civil war, and the colored brother, but has had the discretion not to overwrite. We are already familiar with the kind of people who move through his latest volume, *Tales of the Home Folks,* and meet them without expectation of novelty, but with hope of being well entertained. The author's kind, genial, and humorous personality lives in every episode, and unfailingly excites the desirable sensations of pleasure and satisfaction. In one sketch, "The Late Mr. Watkins of Georgia," Mr. Harris recounts with excellent humor the troubles brought upon him by the "Uncle Remus" tales. The learned to the earth's remotest ends appear to have taken him with embarrassing solemnity, and call upon him in many tongues to engage in the most acrimonious controversies about folk-lore and myth.

[*Tales of the Home Folks in Peace and War:* "A Belle of St. Valerien" Is a Delight]

Anonymous*

Mr. Harris's place in literature has long been so distinctly defined that it ceased years ago to be necessary to do more than announce a new book by him. Yet there is always more or less eagerness to know whether the work comes from Uncle Remus or the White Folks, and there is usually a shade of disappointment in the latter case. For, while the White Folks' tales are fine, they are not classic, as Uncle Remus's fables are. So that it is with satisfaction rather than with enthusiasm that the new volume is received. Most of the stories are of the sort that the author is fond of telling—simple happenings in Southern country life, mingling sadness and mirth. As usual, some of the characters are white and some are black as regards the colour of their skin. In other respects they are all pure white, for the author's skill has never been bent toward the delineation of the evil in mankind, whatever the race. The nearest approach to it

*Review of *Tales of the Home Folks in Peace and War* (Boston and New York: Houghton, Mifflin, 1898). Reprinted from *Nation,* 26 May 1898, p. 407, col. 3.

*Reprinted from *Bookman,* 7 (June 1898), 353.

in the present collection of tales is the description of the unfortunate hunchback father of "A Baby in the Siege," and he seems afflicted rather than wicked. The only notable departure from the author's well-known manner and familiar line will be found in the fifth story, "A Belle of St. Valerien," which is a complete surprise. There is no reason, certainly, why anything admirable should be a surprise from Mr. Harris's pen; but this little study of New France is so entirely unlike the rest of his work, so absolutely Gallic in the exquisite frivolity of its beginning and in the invocation of the Church's influence at its close, that it appears absolutely foreign to the author's ideals, models, and methods. It would fit more readily into the writings of the old French masters. But surely the last thing to complain of is that an author's work is not all of a piece, and this perfect bit in the new book may be enjoyed without other comment than an exclamation of delight.

"Chronicles of
Aunt Minervy Ann"

Agnes Repplier*

With infinite humor and a touch of pathos, with ample knowledge and unfailing sympathy, Mr. Joel Chandler Harris has related to us the *Chronicles of Aunt Minervy Ann*. All that is best and worst in the negro character, all that the South knows so well and that the North does not know at all, may be studied to advantage in this vivacious narrative. Minervy Ann, big, masterful, devoted, with a warm heart, a bad temper, and a genius for cooking, is well matched by her husband, Hamp, a "no account nigger," worthless enough to be promptly elected to the Georgia Legislature as the first-fruits of franchise. But the "Honorable Hampton Tumlin" awakens only the old affectionate contempt in his spouse's ample bosom, and she is as careless with her hands as if she were not boxing the ears of a Representative.

Nevertheless, Minervy Ann stoutly protects the "Honnerbul Hampton" from all ill usage save her own; and she is disposed, moreover, to take an optimistic view of her race and its future. "It looks like dat de niggers what been growin' up sense freedom is des tryin' der han' fer ter see how no 'count dey kin be. Dey'll git better; dey er bleege ter git better, kase dey caan't git no wuss." An argument as sound as any we have heard on a subject endlessly argued. If Mr. Harris knows more than he has yet told us about Aunt Minervy Ann we hope he'll tell it soon.

*Review of *The Chronicles of Aunt Minervy Ann* (New York: Charles Scribner's Sons, 1899). Reprinted from *Saturday Evening Post*, 30 September 1899, p. 236, col. 1.

[*Plantation Pageants* and *The Chronicles of Aunt Minervy Ann:* In Harris's Familiar Vein]

Anonymous*

Mr. Joel Chandler Harris's *Plantation Pageants* [. . .] and *The Chronicles of Aunt Minervy Ann* [. . .] are in the familiar vein of his most recent publications, continuing, as they do, the eventful lives of those interesting personages, Aaron and the children of the Abercrombie plantation, with Aunt Minervy Ann and Major Tumlin Perdue. "Glancing back over its pages, it seems to be but a patchwork of memories and fancies, a confused dream of old times," is the author's characterization of *Plantation Pageants*, and it will, perhaps, answer as well as any for this rambling collection of scenes and events, insufficiently linked together for a coherent tale, and with rather too much of the mythical thrown in. Yet it is not wholly devoid of that charm which has made the creator of Brer Rabbit so dear to the hearts of young and old, and it carries on the picture of reconstruction or pulling together at the South after the civil war. It is in the stirring narrative, told in the rich dialect of Aunt Minervy Ann, that Mr. Harris appears at his best. This typical "Aunty," strong in physique and in executive ability, and still devoted, in spite of newly acquired liberty, to her quondam owner, describes in vigorous language and with delicious humor the return of the moneyless proprietor to his despoiled plantation, the makeshifts to keep the pot a-boiling, and the general social demoralization attendant upon the reversed relations of white and black. Excellent illustrations by A. B. Frost add not a little to the attractiveness of these tales, and are in strong contrast to the poor efforts of E. Boyd Smith in the *Plantation Pageants*.

"Uncle Remus's War Stories"

Anonymous†

These stories deal with some more or less imaginary episodes in the unwritten history of the civil war, and they cause the reader to realize how much more interesting certain unwritten records are than some that

---

*Review of *Plantation Pageants* (Boston and New York: Houghton, Mifflin, 1899) and of *The Chronicles of Aunt Minervy Ann*. Reprinted from *Nation*, 14 December 1899, p. 451, cols. 1–2.

†Review of *On the Wing of Occasions: Being the Authorised Version of Certain Curious Episodes of the Late Civil War* (New York: Doubleday, Page, 1900). Reprinted from *Chicago Daily Tribune*, 20 October 1900, Part 2, [p. 10], col. 2.

have been accepted as history. The stories are full of action and of skill-fully managed plot, and though we have no actual battle scenes they are yet tales of warfare, with battle fields within doors, where the weapons are human wits. A certain New York hotel, where the head waiter is a famous Captain McCarthy, where all the employés are members of a Secret Service committee, and where to ask for a plate of fried onions or a glass of water is to give a signal to a confederate, plays an important part in these stories, particularly in the first one, "Why the Confederacy Failed."

But the flower of the collection is a lengthy short story entitled "The Kidnapping of President Lincoln." It tells of how young Francis Bethune and his wise old friend, Billy Sanders, having been granted permission to cross the Yankee lines in order to escort home a troublesome feminine spy, decided to improve the opportunity to kidnap the President. Billy Sanders is one of Mr. Harris' most delightfully successful creations. He is illiterate, as far as book knowledge goes, but he has an immense fund of horse sense and shrewd native wit which makes him an invaluable companion for such a mission. The spy proves to be a young aunt of Bethune's, Mrs. Elsie Clopton, a wrong-headed, heart-in-the-right-place sort of woman, who is determined to save the Southern cause. The two conspirators find this lady comfortably nested in the bosom of the Lincoln family and glorying in the way she has suffered for her country. Mr. Sanders thus expressed his doubts as to the intensity of these hardships.

> "You don't look like you've been sufferin' for your country much. Appearances is mighty deceivin' if you ain't been havin' three square meals a day, fried meat an' biscuit, an' hot coffee for breakfast, collards, an' dumplin's, an' buttermilk for din-ner, an' ashcake an' molasses for supper."
>
> "You see how the men mistake us," protested Elsie, turning to Mrs. Lincoln. "Our keenest anguish is mental, but the men never think they are suffering unless they are in physical pain. And the men think the women are too timid to take any risks. Look at me, Mr. Sanders."
>
> "I see you, Leese," said Mr. Sanders, so dryly that Mrs. Lin-coln burst out laughing.
>
> "Don't mind him, dear friend; he always was comical. And then there was your grandmother, Mr. Sanders, Nancy Hart. Didn't she suffer for her country?"
>
> "She staid at home an' hit the Tories a lick when they pestered her, two for one, maybe; but she didn't complain of no sufferin', so far as I know. The sufferin' was all wi' them that pestered her. Anyhow, we've come to take you home, an' when we git there I'm goin' to build a pen to keep you in. Goodness knows. I don't want to be runnin' my head in no more hornets' nests."
>
> "Why, you don't call this a hornets' nest, I hope," said Mrs. Lincoln, smiling.

"By no means, mum," replied Mr. Sanders, with a bow. "This is the only homelike place I've struck sence I left Shady Dale. But I hear you're a Southerner, an' Mr. Lincoln is Georgy all over, an' that accounts for it. If we wa'n't here, where'd we be?"

Thus did Mr. Sanders regale the Lincoln family, and the President was always glad to listen to his amusing yarns. On the other hand the two kidnapers were equally delighted with the President, and the way in which they let their opportunity slip by is told with captivating humor. The whole story, in its swift yet natural action, its clever situations, and its witty dialogue is a model of what a story should be. It represents the high water mark of the author's art.

[*On the Wing of Occasions:*
An Uneven Collection]

Anonymous*

Lest the glory of fresh conquest should obliterate the memory of battles long ago, Mr. Harris has, perhaps, deemed the moment opportune to print "Certain Curious Episodes of the Late Civil War." The episodes are not very curious, and not at all incredible. The narration drags over unimportant matters and then leaps, leaving gaps as if Mr. Harris had forgotten the really critical moves in the games of political conspiracy. Capt. McCarthy, the soul of Confederate intrigue, and, during several agitating years, the imposing head waiter of the New York Hotel, appears to have been an interesting and resourceful person, yet, by his gloomy confidence that Providence had decided against the South, rather disqualified for work requiring for success a hearty belief that God was with him. Apart from intrinsic improbability and a stumbling start, "The Kidnapping of President Lincoln" is an excellent tale. The President's remarkable personality is vividly presented, and all the detail adds to the accepted portrait of that "patient, kindly man, with the bright smile and sad eyes, with melancholy at one elbow and mirth at the other."

*Reprinted from *Nation*, 29 November 1900, p. 430, col. 3.

"Joel Chandler Harris's New Stories"

Anonymous*

To take up a volume by Mr. Harris is to be instantly pervaded by a pleasurable anticipatory glow. As one reads the four stories contained in *The Making of a Statesman* this glow suffers a little chill. They are agreeably told, the book will not be amiss as a transient hammock companion, but the tales are, by no means, up to the level of Mr. Harris's best work, and will not add to his reputation.

The sacrifice made by the hero of the first story is happily impossible to such a man as he is described, and is so far from commendable that it suggests George Eliot's warning: "Don't melt yourself down for the benefit of the tallow trade."

There is a pleasant glimpse of Mr. Billy Sanders; but Aunt Minervy Ann, for once in her life, is disappointing in her methods and her humor. It is feared—let it be said with bated breath—that she is even a little tiresome. "Flingin' Jim and His Fool-Killer" is the most characteristic tale, but not in its author's delightfully spontaneous vein.

If authors only knew how to harden their hearts against publishers, and to refuse to write unless the spirit moves!

[*The Making of a Statesman and Other Stories:* Southern Politics and Negro Character]

Anonymous†

The Making of a Statesman tells of an era preceding that of definite recognition of politics as a business. It represents those presumably good old times when a political career, in the South especially, was the privilege of a gentleman, and intimately connected with oratory embellished by quotations from the classics. Yet Mr. Featherstone, who rose to be a leader in the State of Georgia, and whose public record was most honorable, was, from the beginning, tainted with dishonor. He was more culpable than Mr. Gallegher,[1] because he rose to power by the theft of

---

*Review of *The Making of a Statesman and Other Stories* (New York: McClure, Phillips, 1902). Reprinted from *New York Times Saturday Review of Books*, 19 April 1902, p. 266, col. 4.

†Reprinted from *Nation*, 12 June 1902, p. 471, cols. 1–2.

[1]Ed. note: Gallegher is a self-seeking businessman in W. L. Alden's *Drewitt's Dream* (1902), cited in the preceding review.

another man's brains. The voluntary self-sacrifice of Billy Spence is not probable, but, that being granted, all that follows is natural and pathetic. The remaining tales in the volume sustain Mr. Harris's reputation for revealing negro character in negro dialect. Aunt Minervy Ann, telling about Miss Puss's parasol, is a perfect specimen of the immortal "Mammy."

[*Gabriel Tolliver:* Should We Congratulate Harris for Disclaiming Art?]

Anonymous*

Mr. Harris's *Gabriel Tolliver* is a volume of the reminiscent sort. Regarded as a novel, it is very poor work, rambling, shuffling; indeed, without characterization, form, or style. From a passage in the "prelude" we gather that the prelude was an afterthought, meant to declare that the author knows the book to be careless and tedious and unimpressive, and that he is proud of all that. We do not understand such pride, but we feel that it is distinctly not creditable. As a confession of incapacity for a task undertaken, the task of writing a novel, the following passage is incomparable:

> Let those who can do so continue to import harmony and unity into their fabrications and call it art. Whether it be art or artificiality, the trick is beyond my power. I can only deal with things as they were; on many occasions they were far from what I would have had them to be; but as I was powerless to change them, so am I powerless to twist individuals and events to suit the demands or necessities of what is called art.

Perhaps with such original notions of what art is, it would be quite impossible to do anything even remotely artistic; therefore we should perhaps congratulate Mr. Harris on not having tried for art. Besides this pearl of reflection, the "prelude" includes an African legend, the legend of Dilly Bal, a gentleman who sweeps the cobwebs out of the skies. This legend is beautifully told—we would say "most artistically rendered," if it were not for the fear of hurting Mr. Harris's feelings.

---

*Review of *Gabriel Tolliver: A Story of Reconstruction* (New York: McClure, Phillips, 1902). Reprinted from *Nation*, 11 December 1902, p. 467, col. 3.

[*Gabriel Tolliver:*
Characterization Is
Its Strength]

Anonymous*

We have had several good novels of the reconstruction period of late years, among which Mr. Page's *Red Rock* is probably the best. By the side of that masterpiece we must now place *Gabriel Tolliver*, the most extended work of fiction that has been attempted by Mr. Joel Chandler Harris. The strength of this work is in its delineation of the types of character, black and white, that were to be found in rural Alabama [sic] in the sixties. Here Mr. Harris has for his only serious rival the late Colonel Richard Malcolm Johnston, and the two men have in common the same eye for individual idiosyncrasies and the same sense of genial humor. The plot of *Gabriel Tolliver* is of the simplest kind. There is the love story of Gabriel and Nan, the arrest of Gabriel on a false charge supported by an unfortunate array of circumstantial evidence, his rescue by an ingenious device, and the eventual union with his sweetheart. There are numerous minor complications, involving the other personalities concerned, and the total effect of the story is to give us an intimate picture of life in the country town where the action takes place. The problem of reconstruction is represented by a carpet-bagger whose death we hardly regret, and the measures taken by the Knights of the White Camellia to persuade his deluded negro followers that they had better leave politics alone. The charm of this book is very evident, but it is the charm of a series of episodes and character sketches rather than of a narrative of continuous interest.

"Harris—*Wally Wanderoon*"

Anonymous*

American folk-lore owes a debt of gratitude to the author of *Uncle Remus*. There is a finish to his story-telling, and the tales in *Wally Wanderoon* are told in the spirit of the "good old times," and begin and end in the "good old way." This is a book that suggests afternoons curled up in an armchair, unconscious of the flight of time.

*Reprinted in *Dial*, 1 April 1903, p. 243, col. 1.

*Review of *Wally Wanderoon and His Story-Telling Machine* (New York: McClure, Phillips, 1903). Reprinted from *Critic*, NS 43 (December 1903), 573.

[A *Little Union Scout:*
A Tale of Both
Sides of the War]

Anonymous*

Scouting during the civil war appears to have been easier work than it was in South Africa, or is now in Mantchuria [sic]. According to writers of fiction, much of the scouting for North and South was done by girls, dressed up as boys, to be sure, but, from all reliable accounts, more obviously girls than if they had stuck to petticoats. "The Little Union Scout" of Mr. Harris's tale had already made fame as Capt. Frank Leroy before the adventures here narrated befell. Her proper name was Jane Ryder—such a sensible-sounding name that one can hardly think of its owner so foolishly masquerading. Undoubtedly the combatants knew Capt. Leroy for a girl and permitted her to prance between them, for the sake of distraction from the grimmer affairs of war. Her tale is told with Mr. Harris's accustomed ease, and shows, as do so many of his tales, his familiarity with details of the war and with the feeling on both sides.

[A *Little Union Scout:*
"Rather Confused and
Inconsequential"]

Anonymous*

This is a rather pretty little love-story laid between the lines during the Civil War. The scout is a young girl who masquerades as a boy; the chief man character is a Southerner, who, of course, falls in love with the scout, and there is much capturing and escaping, many love scenes, and a little blood now and then for variety. The war part is only a setting, and the whole thing is a rather confused and inconsequential short story, expanded into a short novel. It adds nothing to the literature of the war, and nothing to Mr. Harris's reputation, but it serves to pass an hour pleasantly enough, if one is not feeling strenuous.

*Review of *A Little Union Scout* (New York: McClure, Phillips, 1904). Reprinted from *Nation*, 23 June 1904, p. 500, col. 3; p. 501, col. 1.
*Reprinted from *Literary World*, 35 (August 1904), 231.

[*The Tar-Baby and Other Rhymes of Uncle Remus:* Harris's Saga-Man Is a Poet of "Style and Distinction"]

Anonymous*

Some one has called the rhymes of Uncle Remus indispensable, and the adjective is hardly too strong for the fact. Certainly we do well to cherish to the uttermost a strain that is never to be replaced or imitated. Beside these songs of the ancient negro our own popular songs are thin and acrid. Uncle Remus is a poet with style and distinction and humor and pathos and joy of heart. He opens to us a simple world full of both wisdom and folly, in which tropical temperaments take their ease and find ready expression for a luxuriant imagination. Mr. Harris in all his collections has maintained the characteristic indigenous quality of the negro chants and ditties, and the present collection is particularly rich in archaeological value. His note to "Baylor's Mail," for example, explains that the title had its origin in the method of intercommunication by which before and during the war the negroes transmitted intelligence from point to point. "When Sherman swung loose from Atlanta for his march across Georgia," he says, "the fact became known to all the negroes on a plantation in Middle Georgia—and to one white person—within the course of twelve hours." This system prevails in both India and Africa, and after an investigation covering forty years Mr. Harris has gained the information—which he calls "as scanty as it is unimportant"—that it was introduced on the Southern plantations by a negro named Qua, who died at an extreme old age in the thirties. His grandson, whose name was M'Bulu (corrupted into Baylor), gave it its designation. "The system of intercommunication was known among the older negroes," Mr. Harris says, "as M'Bulu Irruwanda—literally Baylor's waist cloth or breechclout—the means by which a signal or series of signals is given in Africa. But it may be made to mean the song, the holla, or any other method by means of which intelligence is transmitted." Here are three verses of the song in which the memory of this primitive and efficient mail service is perpetuated:

> Run, little Brothers, run!
> Yo' journey's des begun.
> An' many a long mile stretches
> Fum settin' ter risin' sun;
> An' it's whack! ef de patroller ketches,
> An' it's whoop when yo' journey's done!
> It's fun fer de one dat fetches,
> Fer de one dat carries, none!

*Review of *The Tar-Baby and Other Rhymes of Uncle Remus* (New York: D. Appleton, 1904). Reprinted from *New York Times Saturday Review of Books*, 12 November 1904, p. 766. col. 1.

Oh, run in de bushes, Brothers!
    Down de long corn-furrers run!
Run in de heat what smothers,
    In de frost what grips you, mon!
It's Way-o! fer de hills what beckon,
    Wy-o! fer de low-groun's wide!
You're movin' now, I reckon,
    When you rock fum side ter side!

Run, little Brothers, run!
    'Twix' settin' an' risin' Sun;
Watch out fer dem what foller
    Wid track-dogs an' wid gun;
Break thoo de swampy holler—
    Yo' journey will soon be done!
Pas' de place whar de wil'-hogs waller—
    De race is mighty nigh won!

In the camp meeting songs we have the fervor and intensity lacking in the songs of the plantation, and in the dancing songs we have the pure essence of irresponsibility, the ecstasy of pagan joy, the racial harmony, with exuberant forms of sentiment. Uncle Remus is more than a delightful story-teller—he is a saga-man of a race that has been almost entirely obliterated and that no possible combination of circumstances can restore. In his preface Mr. Harris explains that Remus has paid small attention to "the misleading rules of the professors of prosody, who seem to have not the slightest notion of the science of English verse," but, with instinctive love of melody and appreciation of the simplest rhythmical movement, has ignored syllables and accents and depends wholly on "the time movement that is inseparable from English verse."

"Uncle Remus Again"

Anonymous*

Joel Chandler Harris's new Remus stories are as full of the humor and charm of negro lore as ever. Uncle Remus is, of course, older, but he still loves "tater custards" and little boys. It is a new little boy in this book, a son of the old little boy who has, since the first Uncle Remus stories, "growed up" and got married. In the new volume Uncle Remus explains in storied fashion why, among other things, Mr. Cricket has elbows in his legs; why Mr. Dog is tame, and how Old Craney-Crow lost his head.

To one who is slightly acquainted with negro lore in other parts of the world some of Uncle Remus's stories come in the nature of a momentary and agreeable shock. Many of them are nearly identical with stories

*Review of *Told by Uncle Remus: New Stories of the Old Plantation* (New York: McClure, Phillips, 1905). Reprinted from *New York Times Holiday Book Number*, 1 December 1905, p. 836, col. 3.

told by negro raconteurs in the West Indies and Africa. That the old Gagool of the West Coast or the Mammie of the West Indian bush did not borrow from Mr. Harris should be clear when it is stated that stories of the Uncle Remus type and of great similarity in narration have been told in the jaboo of the gold coast, the French patois of Martinique, and the mixed Dutch of Curacao for hundreds of years.

In the West Indies the Joel Chandler Harris or the Uncle Remus has not yet been born or created to give the negro stories of that part of the world to the world. To have read Uncle Remus, however, is to have gained a full education on the story lore which the Africans, as many an argument was concluded, brought with them from the jungle. Time and again efforts have been made to trace the origin of the stories, but always the trail has led to the west coast and there been lost in the Dark Continent.

In the West Indies there are no rabbits, foxes, or wolves, but there is Brer Spider, Brer Hawk, Sis Ground Dove, and a host of other animal characters. The play is always the same, but there are, perforce, the actors. The cunning spider called Annancy seems to be Brer Rabbit, and to hear his adventures told in any language one understands is to be convulsed with the same droll mirth that has endeared Uncle Remus.

Annancy, the West Indian Brer Rabbit (and this is a further south Remus story), never liked Brer John Crow, because he and all the John Crow family were always poking their noses into other people's affairs. Brer Annancy thought hard and one day invited all the John Crows to a feast. When the guests arrived Brer Annancy had a big barrel in the clearing and himself was boiling a kettle of water over a big fire.

"Now," said Brer Annancy (in Dutch, French, or Spanish patois—he speaks them all), "you John Crows put your heads in that barrel, and shut your eyes until I say open them, for I've got a big surprise for you."

The inherent curiosity of the John Crows was aroused. They solemnly stood around the barrel and put their heads into it. Then Brer Annancy took the kettle off the fire, tiptoed behind the John Crows, and poured the boiling water into the barrel full of heads.

"That's why John Crows have bald pates," concludes the West Indian Remus, "and that's what folks get for poking their noses into things."

Just think of how Uncle Remus would have told that. Perhaps, however, Uncle Remus will take a trip to the West Indies in his old age, although from his latest book it does not seem that his fund of story and humor is anyway near being run out.

[*Told by Uncle Remus:* His Story-Telling Is Unimpaired by Age]

Anonymous*

In response to an urgent demand for more Uncle Remus stories, Mr. Joel Chandler Harris has written *Told by Uncle Remus* [. . .] a collection of new stories of negro folklore, which are permeated by the same sly humor that has given Uncle Remus his unique position among lovers of good stories. Brer Rabbit, Brer Fox, Brer Wolf, and all the rest of the gay brotherhood reappear in the new book, and Messrs. Frost, Condé, and Verbeck have contributed pictures, in full-page size and also in little vignettes that are quite as characteristic. "The Reason Why" is the name of the introductory story, which tells how Uncle Remus, after years of silence, happened to begin story-telling again. The reason is as ingenious and convincing as if an excuse for such a proceeding was really needed. The stories explain such interesting matters as "Why Mr. Cricket Has Elbows on His Legs," "How Wiley Wolf Rode in the Bag," "When Brother Rabbit Was King," "Why Mr. Dog is Tame," and many others. Uncle Remus has presumably aged somewhat since his first appearance, but his story-telling faculty is unimpaired by time and disuse.

"The Author of *Uncle Remus*"

Anonymous†

Joel Chandler Harris did not look like a literary man, did not talk or act like one, and, for that matter, always refused to consider himself as one. But *Uncle Remus* has been translated into twenty-seven languages, and it would not be easy to name any American author who will be surer of his readers' hearts a hundred years hence.

Mr. Harris was a Georgia newspaper man, a very quiet, shy person of homely tastes in everything save reading, an author who was obscured by immediate panic when a strange admirer worshipped before him. He was, however, the truest and most unaffected friend in his own little circle—a man who could enjoy taking the reins of the street-car horse that plodded toward his office while the driver ate his dinner inside, as much as he could suffer when a strange interviewer invaded his sanctum, bent on exploiting him.

*Reprinted from *Dial*, 16 December 1905, p. 444, col. 2; p. 445, col. 1.

†An obituary essay reprinted from *American Review of Reviews*, 38 (August 1908), [214–15].

He always felt that the "Uncle Remus" stories were a sort of accident in which he bore a comparatively unimportant part. The stories appeared first in the Atlanta *Constitution* in the '70's. Harris had at the age of twelve entered a count[r]y newspaper office as printer's devil. He had gone through the multifarious "grind" of a provincial newspaper man in Savannah, Macon, and elsewhere, when in 1876 Colonel Howell brought him to the Atlanta *Constitution* as editorial writer and capable journalistic man-of-all-work. Soon after this "Si" Small, who had been doing dialect sketching for the *Constitution*, resigned, and Colonel Howell, with some difficulty, persuaded Harris to step into the breach and keep the readers amused.

The only thing the young editor could think of was to write down the old plantation stories he had heard in the negro cabins while, after the fashion of Southern boys, he had loafed with the darkies in front of the big open fireplace, with hoecake browning and bacon sizzling. So he ransacked his memory for the most characteristic of these darky stories, printed them in the *Constitution,* and became famous.

This last result surprised him not a little. When he began to get letters from all over the world from "fellows of this and professors of that, to say nothing of doctors of the other," he became aware for the first time that he had invaded the preserves of learned philologists and students of folklore, who were mightily interested in finding that the same stories were being told on the plantations of Georgia that amused the small coolies in the rice fields of India. While the learned people were so profoundly impressed by "Uncle Remus," it does not appear that he was much impressed by them, save for the appeal to his shrewd sense of humor. His was the most charming disposition to take fright when asked to take himself seriously.

But though Mr. Harris considered "Uncle Remus" an accident and himself a fifth-rate literary man, one does not need to read further than the immortal adventure of the Tar Baby to feel that there is more in the matter than chance and the ordinary abilities of country journalism. The best key to the accident is to be found in the habits and recreation of young Joel in those years during the great war, when most of his day was taken up with setting type, carrying "forms," collecting bills, soliciting advertising, and otherwise making himself useful on Colonel Turner's little newspaper, *The Countryman.* The youngster had a way of going straight to the best reading for youngsters in Colonel Turner's very reasonably well appointed library, where he devoured Scott, Dickens, Hugo, Goethe, and Goldsmith. This enables us better to understand the kindly philosophy, that shrewd humor, with something of the universality of appeal of an Aesop or a La Fontaine, that make Uncle Remus, Bre'r Fox, and Bre'r Rabbit irresistible and inimitable. The cotton plantation, the negroes, the folklore stories common in their essentials to those of Europe, Asia, and Africa, these made the opportunity for Harris. In the meantime he had by companionship with the great hearts and minds of men of letters and by diligent application to his craft made himself ready to take the opportunity so naturally and easily that he literally knew not what was being done when he gave a new character to the story-tellers of the ages.

Joel Chandler Harris produced many works besides the "Uncle Remus" series sufficient in quality to have given him a respectable reputation if the masterpiece had not given him a great reputation. Most of them were volumes of short stories of Georgia life, in the same family with Thompson's "Courtship of Colonel Jones" and Richard Malcolm Johnston's charming Georgia sketches; one was a novel, *Gabriel Tolliver*, and two were historical—a life of Henry W. Grady, founder[sic] of the Atlanta *Constitution*, and a history of Georgia.

After a quarter-century of quiet, steady editorial work on the *Constitution*, Mr. Harris retired from his desk in 1900, and for the next few years applied himself to his literary labors. He had married in 1873 and had six children. The enormous success of "Uncle Remus" in Europe as well as America brought him material comfort for his large family. During the past two years he had thrown all his energies into a new Southern monthly, the *Uncle Remus Magazine*, conducted by himself and his son Julian.

As a modest, large-hearted man who pursued his quiet way with whole-souled devotion to the work before him, Mr. Harris will be affectionately remembered by every one who was fortunate enough to be his friend. As the author of *Uncle Remus* he will undoubtedly hold an affection not less deep and true from many generations who come after those who knew him in this life.

"Mysterious Cally-Lou"

Anonymous*

The debt of gratitude which so many thousands of readers already owed to Joel Chandler Harris is increased by *The Bishop and the Boogerman*, one of the last books that came from his pen. It is a charmingly quaint, delightful bit of whimsicality, and, like his *Uncle Remus* books, so simple and childlike that it is an ideal story for children, and at the same time so true in its pictures of people and of life, so wise, and so full of wholesome humor, that "grown-ups" will enjoy it even more than the children do. It goes back forty years for its beginning, into the Georgia of just after the war, and tells the story of how a little girl, suddenly left an

*Review of *The Bishop and the Boogerman* (New York: Doubleday, Page, 1909). Reprinted from *New York Times Saturday Review of Books*, 20 February 1909, p. 103, cols. 1–2. Copyright © 1909 by The New York Times Company. Reprinted by permission.

orphan, went to live with her crabbed old Uncle Jonas, she and the mysterious Cally-Lou.

This Cally-Lou came to be a most important personage in Uncle Jonas's household. She was just little Adelaide's imaginary playmate, to whom and about whom the children talked as if she were a real person. All the others gradually accepted her as a reality, except practical old Uncle Jonas, who could never be made to admit that he had almost seen her, and after a while Cally-Lou came to be the name for—a sort of intangible embodiment of—all sorts of evasive, immaterial influence and motives that the people of the household might feel. It is the sort of thing that on the printed page requires the most delicate of handling.

Mr. Harris, however, has made Cally-Lou quite as real a creature as "Miss Meadows and de Gals," or the Tar Baby, and at the same time he has made it all look as simple and as artless as does one of the adventures of Bre'r Rabbit. The Bishop is just a humor-loving neighbor of Uncle Jonas, upon whom Adelaide bestows the title, because he has as kindly a face as a Bishop who had once been kind to her, and the Boogerman is a young negro whom Adelaide shot with her cornstalk gun when she and the Bishop patrolled the garden on the watch for that awesome character.

A faint thread of a story runs through the book, which is hardly more than a series of sketches carrying the same characters through various happenings. It is very charming, with its unexpected turns of thought and quaint forms of expression, its understanding of the child heart and the workings of the child brain, its kindliness, and its sweet, bubbling humor.

"An Unmitigated Villain"

Anonymous*

"Mr. Billy Sander's" latest story—alas, it is also his last—narrates a stirring adventure of the war between the States.

The Shadow Between His Shoulder Blades [. . .] treats of an unmitigated villain, and ends with his well-merited but gruesome taking off.

It is relieved, however, by many touches of humor and racy forms of speech. It has the inimitable flavor of all Mr. Harris has written, and will be received with the welcome due the posthumous child of the author, known and loved throughout the English-speaking world as "Uncle Remus."

*Review of *The Shadow Between His Shoulder-Blades* (Boston: Small, Maynard, 1909). Reprinted from *New York Times Saturday Review of Books*, 6 November 1909, p. 689, col. 2. Copyright © 1909 by The New York Times Company. Reprinted by permission.

[*Uncle Remus and the Little Boy:* Remus Is "His Perfect Self"]

Stephenson Browne*

Six tales and seven songs make the last volume of the lo[r]e of Uncle Remus, and the fathers who read the first stories thirty years ago will be as little inclined as their sons to neglect this group. It bears the title *Uncle Remus and the Little Boy*, and has over fifty illustrations, eight in color, representing Uncle Remus himself as unaltered by the lapse of years, the little boy as looking much like his father. One of the child's achievements is to write a letter, which, according to Uncle Remus, "wipes out de whole war." The boy accounts for its length by quoting his [m]other's statement that "when you travel it improves the mind." Uncle Remus is his perfect self.

[*Uncle Remus Returns:* More Adventures and More Philosophy]

Anonymous†

Uncle Remus is an old man now, and he tells these stories to the son of the "little boy" of the early stories. Brother Rabbit, Brother Fox and Brother Bear have some more adventures, and Uncle Remus muses philosophically on the mumps, politics, the "true inwardness of the mule," and hard times. Appeared during 1905–'06 in the *Metropolitan Magazine*. Drawings by A. B. Frost and J. M. Condé.

---

*Review of *Uncle Remus and the Little Boy* (Boston: Small, Maynard, 1910). Reprinted from *New York Times Saturday Review of Books*, 10 September 1910, p. 498, col. 1. Copyright © 1910 by The New York Times Company. Reprinted by permission.
†Review of *Uncle Remus Returns* (Boston and New York: Houghton Mifflin, 1918). Reprinted by permission of the American Library Association from *ALA Booklist*, 15 (November 1918). [73].

ARTICLES
AND ESSAYS

[America's Immortally Shy Master of Negro Dialect]

Mark Twain*

Mr. Joel Chandler Harris ("Uncle Remus") was to arrive from Atlanta at seven o'clock Sunday morning; so we[1] got up and received him. We were able to detect him among the crowd of arrivals at the hotel-counter by his correspondence with a description of him which had been furnished us from a trustworthy source.[2] He was said to be undersized, red-haired, and somewhat freckled. He was the only man in the party whose outside tallied with this bill of particulars. He was said to be very shy. He is a shy man. Of this there is no doubt. It may not show on the surface, but the shyness is there. After days of intimacy one wonders to see that it is still in about as strong force as ever. There is a fine and beautiful nature hidden behind it, as all know who have read the Uncle Remus book; and a fine genius, too, as all know by the same sign. I seem to be talking quite freely about this neighbor; but in talking to the public I am but talking to his personal friends, and these things are permissible among friends.

He deeply disappointed a number of children who had flocked eagerly to Mr. Cable's house to get a glimpse of the illustrious sage and oracle of the nation's nurseries. They said:

"Why, he's white!"

They were grieved about it. So, to console them, the book was brought, that they might hear Uncle Remus's Tar-Baby story from the lips of Uncle Remus himself—or what, in their outraged eyes, was left of him. But it turned out that he had never read aloud to people, and was too shy to venture the attempt now. Mr. Cable and I read from books of ours, to show him what an easy trick it was; but his immortal shyness was proof against even this sagacious strategy, so we had to read about Brer Rabbit ourselves.

*Reprinted from Mark Twain, "Uncle Remus and Mr. Cable," Ch. XLVIII in *Life on the Mississippi* (Boston: James R. Osgood, 1883), pp. [471]–72. Harris visited Clemens and George Washington Cable in New Orleans on 30 April and 1 May 1882, primarily to discuss Clemens' proposal for a joint lecture tour. Yet it was almost inevitable that the habitually shy Harris, who refused to read his stories even to his own children, would decline the lecture proposal.

Mr. Harris ought to be able to read the negro dialect better than anybody else, for in the matter of writing it he is the only master the country has produced.

Notes

1. Ed. Note: Clemens and, presumedly, James R. Osgood, his literary advisor and publisher who had accompanied him to New Orleans.

2. Ed. Note: Jo Twichell, Clemens's good friend from Hartford, had called on Harris in Atlanta earlier in the spring of 1882 and is probably the "trustworthy source" Clemens refers to.

"Immortal Uncle Remus"

Thomas Nelson Page*

Fifteen years ago, out of a region known rather for its acting men and talking men than for its writing men (though several volumes of sketches wonderfully racy of the soil had come from it, even in the old times), there appeared a book so humorous and unlike all that had gone before it that, though at first sight it seemed to be in an almost unknown tongue, the public at once seized on it, first with curiosity and then with delight. It purported to be a record of the stories, songs and sayings told or sung by an old negro—a former slave—to the little grandson of his old master and mistress, and on the outside the stories were a series of fables of animals and birds, relating in the main to the strife between Brer Fox and Brer Rabbit, and these stories were recognized by those who had been brought up in the South as at core the same which they had heard in their childhood from the old "uncles" and "aunties" of the plantation. But there was more. Instead of the old darkies, there was the best story-teller of the time to make his characters as real as the wolf in Little Red Riding Hood, or the Beast who kept Beauty captive. Some found in the book animal-myths valuable as links in the chain with which they hope[d] to penetrate the mysterious and always vanishing recesses of the ethnological labyrinth. Others welcomed it as a contribution to the history of the negro race, in which they were philanthropically interested. But the great majority found in it more. Under the apparently unknown tongue when they had mastered it sufficiently to appreciate its soft elisions and musical inflections, were found to lie humor, wit, philosophy, "unadulterated human nature" and a charming picture of the relation between the old family servant and the family of his master.

It possessed, besides, that fidelity to life, that simplicity of recital and that subtle, indefinable essence which is the unmistakable birthmark of genius. It brought back to them their youth, and changed them to children again, yet with a quickened apprehension which only age and

---

*A review-essay of the 1895 edition of *Uncle Remus: His Songs and His Sayings*. Reprinted from *Book Buyer*, 12 (December 1895), [642]–45. Page (1853–1922) is best remembered for his romanticized portraits of Virginia antebellum plantation life, a vision well represented in his first collection of local color tales, *In Ole Virginia* (1887). Page's short stories and his Reconstruction novel, *Red Rock* (1898), have been frequently compared to Harris's local color tales and to his *Gabriel Tolliver: A Story of Reconstruction* (1902).

experience can give. With Miss Sally's little boy they sat and heard not mere stories of animal life, but discerned under them wit, wisdom and the philosophy of life. The narrator became no longer only Miss Sally's Little Boy's Uncle Remus, but their Uncle Remus, as well, and Brer Fox and Brer Rabbit took their places among the small but distinguished company who, touched by the light of genius, have become immortal in the realm of literature.

Mr. Harris has achieved the distinction of creating three characters who have already taken their place in this high company. Brer Fox and Brer Rabbit are familiar characters in our speech and have oftener than once been cited as illustrations in the House of Commons and in our own highest deliberative assembly. As might have been foreseen, this success has raised a host of imitators and followers, who have as a rule caught only the outside and followed after a long interval. The result has been a deluge of what are called "dialect-stories," until the public, surfeited by them, has begun almost to shudder at the very name. These writers have supposed that they were writing dialect when they were only writing distorted words and illiterate grammar, not knowing that the master here has used the vehicle only to carry the thought, and that the secret of his craft lies not in the manner so much as in the matter. Herbert Spencer says that, "Astonished at the performances of the English plough, the Hindoos paint it, set it up, and worship it, thus turning a tool into an idol: linguists do the same with language." Uncle Remus, with all his lingo, might be as dull as any of the other stories which, based on the mere counterfeit of mutilated words, have followed in his shining track, but for the stuff which is in it. It is not the abbreviated words nor the elision; but the habit of thought as of speech, the quaint turn of phrase overflowing with humorous suggestion, where sometimes a word carries a whole train of thought, which make up the dialect of Uncle Remus, nor yet is it only these; but it is far more the knowledge of animals, particularly of the animal, Man—"the unadulterated human nature"—which constitutes the stuff in all his stories, and makes them what they are when taken together, perhaps almost the best contribution to our literature which has been given since the war. No wonder that it opened the way for others.

No man who has ever written has known one-tenth part about the negro that Mr. Harris knows, and for those who hereafter shall wish to find not merely the words, but the real language of the negro of that section, and the habits of mind of all American negroes of the old time, his works will prove the best thesaurus. The old-time negro is passing away, and his speech with him, as a certain type of old-time gentleman is passing. The new issue, that succeeds him, may be more gifted in grammatical speech, more able to fulfil the intricate demands of a truly independent Pullman-Portership; more able to hoe the new row of free and insolent citizenship, or to represent the government at home or abroad; and perhaps he will find in time his proper historiographer. But to some who knew the other, the true gentility of the Uncle Remuses, in however homely a garb, calls forth from the past memories which we would never wish to forget; and to us Mr. Harris has done an inestimable service.

The new edition now brought forth by Messrs. Appleton is worthy of the matter. It is in beautiful new type, in a warm, dignified and fitting binding, and is copiously illustrated by Mr. A. B. Frost, with illustrations so apt and admirable—that is, so truly illustrative of the spirit of the work—that Mr. Harris graciously says in his preface that Mr. Frost has made the book his. Whether he has done this or not, he has undoubtedly added to it the additional lustre of his genius, which has this exceptional merit that it is as distinctly American and original as Mr. Harris's own. One could not say more.

"The Cornfield Journalist"

Allen Tate*

This valuable collection of the fugitive writings of Joel Chandler Harris will not immediately increase his reputation, but in the long run it will alter the public notion of his career. Before that can happen, however, the profession of letters—if such a profession survive the upheavals of this decade—will have to study Harris's philosophy of literature, and disentangle its permanent features from the casual and frequently merely whimsical forms that he wrote in: it was with great surprise that the present reviewer discovered, in these fragmentary essays, a complete and matured attitude toward the writer and his materials. This attitude is of great importance. Our conception of Harris has been, of course, a very limited one—a provincial Georgian, with a genius for Negro dialect, who created a character called Uncle Remus. It is an enviable reputation, but it leaves out of consideration an entire phase of his career and, I think, the most valuable phase.

If one whole side of his work has been neglected, it must be confessed that the explanation lies in his own conception of his career. He never saw himself as a man of letters. He had an invincible modesty, a steady and perfectly sincere belief that he had never written anything of value. It is easy, I think, to overestimate the effect of this belief on the inadequate form of his social and critical writings. Most probably he could not see himself as a man of letters chiefly because there was no profession of letters in the South at that time; there was no model for him to go by, no solidarity of writers for him to join. His voluminous correspondence with the New York editors, his trips to the East, even the efforts of G. W. Cable to get him on the lecture platform, failed to bring him out of his isolation; and in the end the price he paid for independence and integrity was the oblivion of half of his writings, in the files of *The Atlanta Constitution*.

*A review-essay on Julia Collier Harris, ed., *Joel Chandler Harris: Editor and Essayist* (Chapel Hill: Univ. of North Carolina Press, 1931). Reprinted from *New Republic*, 3 August 1932, p. 320, cols. 1–2; p. 321, col. 1. Tate (1899–1979), the distinguished Southern poet and critic and member of the Fugitives and the Agrarians, served as an editor of *The Fugitive*, *Hound and Horn*, and *Sewanee Review*. Among other honors, Tate was named to the American Academy of Arts and Letters and the American Academy of Arts and Sciences, and won the Bollingen Prize for Poetry (1956) and the Academy of American Poets Award (1963).

The editor of this volume, Mrs. Julia Collier Harris, his daughter-in-law and the author of his life, has done her work with admirable tact and skill. The book is a model of editing. It is arranged roughly in chronological order in four divisions. The first section, called "The Cornfield Journalist," contains specimens of his early writings; here one finds, at the outset, the greatest variety of subject and the most casual treatment. The second division is a selection from his opinions on the problem of the Negro. The third and fourth sections show the concentration of a mature mind, although the form is still diffuse: his interests in later life are politics, society and literature, and the early vein of genteel magazine sentiment—"The Glory of Summer," "At the Sign of the Wren's Nest"—has disappeared.

The agitation in the last fifteen years for a "native" American literature has been based almost exclusively on Whitman, but a far sounder text could have been found in a few passages from the writings of Joel Chandler Harris. Whitman's gospel for the American writer is too deeply involved in a sentimental politics to be of permanent value, and is likely to be forgotten more and more as the "frontier psychology" vanishes. Harris's view, however, is applicable to any state of society at any time, and it contains no special plea whatever; in fact, Harris explicitly disavows the political impulse as esthetically unsound:

> Literature that is Georgian or Southern is necessarily American, and in the broadest sense. The sectionalism that is the most marked feature of our modern politics can never intrude into literature. Its intrusion is fatal, and it is this fatality that has pursued and overtaken and destroyed literary effort in the South. The truth might as well be told. We have no Southern literature worthy of the name, because an attempt has been made to give it the peculiarities of sectionalism rather than to impart to it the flavor of localism.

That last phrase, of course, is Harris's journalese, but the intended distinction is fundamental, and Harris meant to convey its full implications. In an article written two months later than the passage I have quoted, he said: "An interesting phase of the continual call for what is technically known as 'Southern Literature' is the accompanying demand for controversial fiction." The tyranny of politics over the Southern writer he fiercely resented. The sentimental, romantic school of Southern fiction, the school headed by Thomas Nelson Page, was dominated by politics: the writer could not lose himself in his material because he was goaded by public opinion into presenting it aggressively. He was a "sectionalist," not a "localist"; if we use the latter term to mean the writer who approaches his subject purely and naturally, I believe we come near to Harris's meaning.

This idea was first expressed in 1879. Eleven years later Harris wrote an article on the reception that Henry James's essay on Hawthorne had received in Boston. James, in his characteristic attitude, had denounced American literature as "provincial" and had taken New England to task for the provincial limitations of Hawthorne. Harris was amused at the replies to James; the Bostonians hastened to assure the world that they were not provincial at all. Harris was astute enough to see that the denial of "vice" betrayed its presence in its least respectable form; and he went on to say:

> Under the circumstances, there is nothing left for Boston to do but to borrow a theory from Atlanta, the cracker city of Georgia, and defend it. That theory is, that no enduring work of the imagination has ever been produced save by a mind in which the provincial instinct was the controlling influence.

Not only did Boston fail to borrow the theory; critical opinion since it was expounded has ignored it.

It should be observed that Harris does not overstate his case; he says that the provincial instinct must be the controlling influence, not the sole influence. The imaginative writer must be preoccupied with a scene that has become so familiar to him that it is inseparable from the character; for art is sensuous and it must have a sensuous groundwork for any superstructure of ideas that the author, from whatever source, may have acquired. In 1882 he wrote to a young woman who had asked for his literary advice:

> It will be no trouble for you to attract attention in *The Constitution* provided that what you write deserves attention. Permit me to suggest a series of "Street Car Studies," or something in that line—something about people and things with which you are perfectly familiar. It is a great step towards success when a young writer gains his or her consent to treat of things with which he or she is familiar.

American writers from the beginning have not been comfortable in a local scene, and it has been due undoubtedly to the domination of politics in a democratic society. There are other causes—chiefly colonialism and the sense of insufficiency that it fostered. The political domination—and this is what Harris meant by the evil of sectionalism—it has been hard to distinguish from the pioneer imperialism which is still the leading motive of the American mind. No man can contemplate and love the grove that he intends to cut down. The political tyranny of the older America of agriculture and commerce has been replaced by the tyranny of Big Business. The elder form of the vice, with all its faults, was doubtless better than the younger; for politics at its height in this country understood ideas, but business seems to understand nothing, not even itself.

The fate of Harris's reputation in the next thirty years cannot be predicted: I have said that his conception of literature is applicable to any state of society. That is not strictly true; it is applicable to any relatively stable society, whatever the social organization may be. The mere study of a sound theory is not sufficient to make it available to writers; yet a writer like Harris, at this time, has a distinct critical value. His point of view is the central and permanent point of view to which literature, after periods of heresy, always returns. Although our time is concerned about the ascendancy of industrialism, or Big Business, over the arts, this criticism, even when it seems to be literary, is a political counter-attack. Much of the Communist criticism of capitalistic art sounds less like the best pages of Trotsky's "Literature and Revolution" than like the standard denunciation of art by the Humanists, whose economics is conservative capitalism. The tyranny of politics gave way before the more powerful tyranny of Big Business; now we have a new tyranny, that of Revolution. Trotsky and Harris, on the fundamentals of literature, are closer together than Trotsky and Dos Passos, or Trotsky and Max Eastman. This new heresy is just developing. It will probably be a generation before fine letters can regain its bearings—for a little while; and then some new heresy will have its day.

"In Memory of Uncle Remus"

Thomas H. English*

In the long run it is the homely virtues of honesty, industry, and neighborliness, which are only more familiar aspects of the cardinal virtues—faith, hope, and charity—that make it possible for humankind to bear the shocks of the disastrous epochs of progress in the modern world, and of those more disastrous times which threaten to destroy the very principle of progress. Joel Chandler Harris's boyhood embraced the years of the Civil War; his youth and young manhood were passed in the "tragic era" of the Reconstruction. His mature years were those of the industrial reorganization of the South, which have seemed to some observers even more disastrous than those which had gone before, for the New South had joined forces with the conqueror to obliterate the last vestiges of the Old South. Peace was completing what war had only too well begun. Joel Chandler Harris was to be known far and wide for the stand which he took with Henry Grady of the Atlanta *Constitution* in welcoming the new era of urban and industrial progress. But the philosophy which he had made his own and was to preach all his life in the columns of his newspaper and the pages of his books was one of rural simplicity. The integrity of the individual and of the section might be summed up in the trinity of homely virtues—honesty, industry, neighborliness.

Joel Chandler Harris was born at Eatonton, in Middle Georgia, on December 9, 1848. Supported by a hard-working mother, to whose support he must contribute as soon as possible, he had few of what are called advantages of rearing and education, yet his boyhood was normally happy. His faith in democracy was early established by the experience of growing up in a democratic stronghold of back-country America, where the extremes of poverty and affluence, of social position and influence were lost in the sense that all folk were neighbors. Of course there were Negro slaves in the village and on the plantations of Putnam County, but

*Reprinted with the permission of the author from *Southern Literary Messenger*, 2 (February 1940), 77–83. Mr. English, Professor Emeritus of English, Emory University, since 1970 has been Executive Secretary of the Friends of the Emory University Library; from 1945–64 he was editor of the *Emory University Quarterly*. The author of several articles on Harris and editor of various uncollected writings by him, Professor English has also written *Emory University 1915–1965: A Semicentennial History* (1966), published a volume of poetry, and co-authored, with Willard B. Pope, *What to Read* (1929).

all evidence points to the conclusion that human kindness did not stop short of this humble society. In the cotton fields and in the quarters was developed a character of good will and loyalty which was to be immortalized in Uncle Remus.

A few terms in the schools of Eatonton comprised Joe Harris's formal education. On the lookout for congenial employment, he obtained a position in which his education was to be informally completed and directed into the channel of the profession which was to be his for life. Not far from the village was the large plantation of Turnwold, whose proprietor, Mr. Joseph Addison Turner, prided himself on uniting in himself the divergent characters of planter and man of letters. He had written and published widely before 1862, in which year he proposed to found a weekly newspaper to be printed on and issued from his plantation. When he advertised for an apprentice in the first issue of *The Countryman*, Joe Harris saw his opportunity. The next five years of the boy's life were passed in Mr. Turner's plantation printing office, where he first made himself master of the craft of printing and then went on to learn the rudiments of the art of journalism. *The Countryman* was much more than a news sheet, although political and war news were not lacking in its pages. But the editor had proposed, in the leading article of the first issue, principally to emulate the examples of his namesake's *Spectator* and of Goldsmith's *Bee*, and throughout its brief existence bellettristic aims were dominant.

Mr. Turner was a wisely indulgent employer. Finding that his apprentice had a keen though unschooled appetite for books, he allowed him to borrow volumes from his large library and recommended titles which might develop a sound literary taste. Later when he was convinced that the boy seriously wished to learn to write, he took pains in criticizing his first offerings for *The Countryman*, and when Joe rose to meet the standards he set, freely opened its columns to the contributions of the "*Countryman's* Devil." The variety and earnestness of these contributions, both in prose and verse, eloquently attest to the ambition of the young journalist formed and nourished in the quiet of the old printing shop. We can guess that the height of his ambition was to make himself a poet, a desire that he never quite relinquished. There is, however, little to suggest that during his years on the plantation he was storing his mind with keen observations of a way of life that within a decade was utterly to pass away, and that we can recreate only from his memories.

At this time he formed another ambition. He would not only break into the ranks of the recognized Southern poets; he would also compile an anthology of Southern poetry. For at least five years he worked on a projected collection to be entitled "Gems of Southern Poetry," in pursuance of which object he clipped the poetry columns of the exchanges which came to the *Countryman* office and entered into correspondence with verse writers of the region. In this way he got into communication with another literary journalist, James Wood Davidson, to whom he gave assistance in preparing *Living Writers of the South*. The publication of this volume in 1869 seems to have convinced young Harris that there was no need for his "Gems."

But before this time the tide of war had swept over Middle Georgia, impoverishing Mr. Turner and bringing the *Countryman* to its final number. Joe's apprenticeship was done. For a few months in 1866 he worked as typesetter on the Macon *Telegraph*. He left Macon to join the staff of the short-lived *Crescent Monthly* in New Orleans. He returned to Georgia and for three years edited a country weekly at Forsyth. In this newspaper, the *Monroe Advertiser*, he began to print humorous squibs, personal and political, which received such wide notice that in 1870 he was offered the position of associate editor on the Savannah *Morning News*. Here he speedily established his reputation as a humorous paragrapher and an all-round newspaper man, so that he was recognized as a personality in State editorial circles.

In spite of an innate shyness which caused him to make friends slowly and to move in a limited circle of his close acquaintance, in Savannah Joel Chandler Harris won his wife, Esther La Rose, the charming daughter of a French-Canadian sea captain, who lived in the same boarding house. When in 1876 the coast city was ravaged by an epidemic of yellow fever, the young husband sought safety inland for his wife and two babies. In Atlanta, Henry Grady, who had just been engaged by Captain Howell as editor of the *Constitution*, lost no time in offering the position of editorial paragrapher to his friend Harris. The latter was to serve on the staff of this increasingly influential newspaper until his retirement in 1900.

To the *Constitution* Mr. Harris regularly contributed humorous brevities which were quoted by newspapers throughout the State. He wrote political leaders, and made excursions into the informal essay for the Sunday edition. To the weekly edition, which had a large mail circulation, he contributed his first extended effort in fiction, *The Romance of Rockville*, which was published in instalments from April to September, 1878. Shortly after joining the newspaper he had begun the series of Negro dialect sketches for which he created the character of Uncle Remus, who was to reach his full stature as the teller of the folk tales of the old plantation with the publication of the original Tar-Baby story in July, 1879.

Uncle Remus caught on immediately. To many of the older generation he brought nostalgic memories of childhood friends in the quarters, house servants or field hands, who had told them long ago the tales of Brer Rabbit and Brer Fox in the very manner which Joel Chandler Harris had made his own. To the youngest generation he brought a story-telling art inexpressibly droll and irresistibly taking, which, while it avoided the Sunday-school morality of so much juvenile literature, yet was interpenetrated with an earthy wisdom that gave direction and force to fancy and humor.

It is not strange that as an Appleton scout traveled down through the South he should have heard constantly of the wit and wisdom of Uncle Remus, but it is greatly to his credit that when he reached Atlanta he did not falter in the moment of decision. *Uncle Remus, His Songs and His Sayings* was published in November, 1880 (though the title-page bears the date 1881). The book was an instantaneous success, as were the titles that followed in the series that gradually took form, *Nights with Uncle Remus* (1883) and *Uncle Remus and His Friends* (1892). The re-issue of the *Songs and Sayings* in 1895, with the inimitable drawings by A. B. Frost, caused a new wave of enthusiasm which has not ebbed. If *Uncle Remus* is not an American classic, then our literature has not yet produced one.

Mr. Harris insisted with a whimsical perversity on referring to himself as an "accidental author." He was ever zealous to point out that he told the tales of Uncle Remus as they were told to him; in insisting on their authenticity he showed no care for the recognition of his own creative role. Criticism has not, however, erred on that important point. As a matter of fact, a careful study of his career shows clearly enough that Joel Chandler Harris had from boyhood devoted himself to the self-discipline of learning to write. When the occasion offered, with sure tact he seized upon the materials that he had gathered and assimilated, even though unconsciously, and with them wrought out the ambition that had never flagged since he was the *Countryman's* devil.

Again he perverted the truth in referring to himself with humorous self-depreciation as a "cornfield journalist." In the era in which he wrote, the lines were drawn rather more loosely between journalist and man of letters than they are today. Mr. Harris's genuine modesty would not allow him to claim a style that was held with a self-conscious and aristocratic sense of separateness by certain members of the writing world in his day. In seeking to avoid snobbery, however, he denied his right to the title which posterity has forced upon him.

On the other hand it may be necessary to point out that by no means all of Joel Chandler Harris is to be found in his books. Harris of the *Constitution* was a force in Southern thought on political and social issues. In the anonymity of newspaper editorials on all the topics which concerned a quarter-century in which great constructive forces were at work on the social and economic order of the South, the creator of Uncle Remus never ceased to inform, exhort, warn, and occasionally reprimand his fellow citizens. The quality of his newspaper writing and something of the range of his comment may be seen in the volume by his daughter-in-law, Julia Collier Harris, *Joel Chandler Harris, Editor and Essayist*.

After *Nights with Uncle Remus* came *Mingo* (1884) and *Free Joe* (1887), in which he turned from folklore to original fiction. In these and in later "Georgian sketches" Mr. Harris showed a grasp of humble character, black and white, scarcely equalled in his generation. These books, and with them his stories of the war, are not much read just now, but they will not be forgotten. In the series begun with *Little Mr.*

Thimblefinger (1894) he gave free rein to his playful fancy for the delectation of children.

An active newspaper man who in his free time wrote volume after volume of various types of fiction, Mr. Harris found that home life in a quiet suburb of the growing city afforded him the relaxation and recreation that suited him best. He was almost an incorrigible family man. His greatest source of pride and pleasure was the rearing of six boys and girls, who have given a good account of the ideals of culture and service which were living forces in the West End household. J. C. H. left home as seldom as possible. Nevertheless a large correspondence with literary men in all sections of the country kept him from seeming quite a recluse, even to those who continually begged him to leave Atlanta to visit them in New York, or Hartford, or Indianapolis. Mr. Harris's meeting with Mark Twain in New Orleans was a notable episode in his life, although the acquaintance did not ripen into an intimate friendship. Intimacy was reserved for a lesser writer with a sunnier disposition. Perhaps Joel Chandler Harris rated the works of the celebrated raconteur and dialect poet, James Whitcomb Riley, above their true worth, but there was a genuine affection on both sides. Another friendship, springing from a just and mutual admiration, eventually brought Uncle Remus from his retirement to dine at the White House with President Theodore Roosevelt.

Mr. Harris had worked hard on the *Constitution* and even harder on his books. He had not been without reward in the high opinion of the home folks. At the Commencement of 1902, Emory College, at Oxford, not far from Eatonton, had conferred upon him the honorary degree of Doctor of Letters. When he retired from the newspaper in 1900, the press was filled with expressions of regard. Six years later his eldest son, Julian, formed plans for establishing a literary magazine in Atlanta to which his father should give his pen-name and the fruits of his long journalistic experience. *Uncle Remus's Magazine* was launched in 1907, and to its establishment on a strong footing Mr. Harris devoted the last months of his life. But he was worn out. He began visibly to decline in health during the spring of 1908; he did not regain his strength with the return of summer. On July third he died.

II

The memory of Joel Chandler Harris survives not merely in a row of books, though some of them have taken their place among our American classics. In his books and in his journalistic writings may be discovered a body of thought by which he did much to mold public opinion, North and South, in an age of transition. Perhaps no figure of his place and time more deserves that the body of his teaching be subjected to continued scrutiny, be seriously considered as a formative influence in an era that has not yet wrought out its destinies.

A living culture is a blend of past, present, and future. A living culture remembers the past and learns from it. It does not seek to cling to things that have gone by and are no more, for that would be to lose the sense of reality. But of all the data of experience it is the things of the past that most readily serve as instruments of comparison and measurement for the things of the present. A living culture lives intensely in the present, is fully responsive to the conditions of the present, yet is not cribbed, cabined, and confined by the most pressing and clamorous phenomena of the day that will pass. The future is just ahead; with it is inevitable change. If it may be, a living culture seeks to anticipate the changes of the future, or in any case to avoid putting up bars to their fortunate working out.

By this definition Joel Chandler Harris was the proponent of a living culture. He sought to preserve the memory of a gracious past, of all that possessed primary human values in the past of the South. He strove earnestly and intelligently for a solution of the pressing problems of his own day. He sought to lay deep the foundations of the future. It is perhaps true that his heart yearned for the simplicities of the past, Uncle Remus's "old farming days," but his mind sprang to meet the challenge of the complexities of the future. He was not afraid of progress. He was assured that all would be well with the world if only the human virtues of simplicity might be preserved even in the midst of complexity. There was nothing esoteric in Mr. Harris's philosophy:

> "It is a modest creed, and yet
> Pleasant, if one considers it."

Out of this creed flowed his achievements, both social and literary, though the one, as in much high endeavor, is sometimes scarcely distinguishable from the other. In the first place, though he came to the task late, he strove valiantly after a cruel war to perform the blessed labor of reconciliation. He endeavored to lead the Negro gently and kindly in the difficult ways of citizenship. While working with the builders of the New South, yet he sought to preserve the best part, the human part, of the Old South. Though he shared these tasks with others, his contribution was distinctive, and he deserves a full measure of credit for such successes in them as have been attained.

From the same source and by the same impulsion flowed his literary achievements. Mr. Harris's stories of the Civil War are animated by the zeal for reconciliation. This part of his literary output is probably less known today than his other books. It is unfortunate if this is so, for the best of his war stories anticipated the large national spirit of such later works as *John Brown's Body*. In his sketches of plantation and village life he preserved the memory of Georgia's pastoral age. There is much less of moonlight and roses in this than elsewhere in the fiction depicting the days "befo' de wah." The social historian will come to attach a high valuation to the homely realism of his best work in this kind.

Joel Chandler Harris's chief claim to fame must be that he interpreted the Negro to a generation to whom the Negro had almost ceased to be a person and had become chiefly a problem. It was not an accident that the plantation-trained boy became the great interpreter of the race. His opportunities for prolonged observation under the most favorable conditions had been exceptional, though it is one of the mysteries of genius that he should have gathered so large a body of literary materials before he came to realize that it *was* a body of literary materials. He knew the Negro as a person before he knew that he was a problem. His solution to that problem is implicit in his fiction and explicit in his journalism. He recommended the simple and sufficient principle of *noblesse oblige* over all the nostrums of all the reformers from both sides of Mason's and Dixon's Line.

Slavery was in its principle an inhuman system, but the works of man are seldom or never purely good or wholly evil. This evil thing, black slavery, had in it the possibility of adventitious good. Its redeeming feature is seen in the beauty of human relationships which, we may trust, not infrequently existed between white master and black servant. Mr. Harris seized upon the element which alone had made the institution of slavery tolerable, and argued that a renewed sense of the responsibility of position and privilege was the only humane and sure solution of the racial problem. No better yet has been proffered.

There is no lack of recognition of the part played by Mr. Harris as the channel by which was transmitted the repertory of folk tales that, with the spirituals, most fully represent the untutored genius of the Negro slave. The folk tales, with their store of racial wisdom and tang of racial genius, might have passed into oblivion had it not been that at a fortunate moment the body of traditional matter was recorded by one of another race whose ripe talents included in the highest degree both critical insight and sympathy. It is a fact too seldom insisted on that Uncle Remus is at least as great a creation as Brer Rabbit. Uncle Remus is great because he is a persuasive human figure in a recognizable background. The tales that he tells are great because in them we hear the tones of a human voice vibrant with the overtones and undertones of a rich personality.

Uncle Remus was not Mr. Harris's only creation, nor was all his best work devoted to rendering the Negro character. The sketches of Middle Georgia country and village life from which emerges the philosophic figure of Mr. Billy Sanders of Shady Dale, and the few but fine tales of the North Georgia mountaineers, have always had their admirers. These figures, white and black, of rural and humble life were the agents whom Joel Chandler Harris employed to preach his gospel of simplicity, the gospel which he profoundly sensed was best suited to America's awkward age.[1]

Notes

1. Ed. note: Part III, on the formation of the Uncle Remus Memorial Association and the establishment of the Harris Collection at Emory, has been omitted from this reprinting.

"Uncle Remus and the Malevolent Rabbit: 'Takes a Limber-Toe Gemmun fer ter Jump Jim Crow' "

Bernard Wolfe*

Aunt Jemima, Beulah, the Gold Dust Twins, "George" the Pullman-ad porter, Uncle Remus. . . . We like to picture the Negro as grinning at us. In Jack de Capitator, the bottle opener that looks like a gaping minstrel face, the grin is a kitchen utensil. At Mammy's Shack, the Seattle roadside inn built in the shape of a minstrel's head, you walk into the neon grin to get your hamburger. . . . And always the image of the Negro—as we create it—signifies some bounty—for us. Eternally the Negro gives—but (as they say in the theater) *really gives*—grinning from ear to ear.

Gifts without end, according to the billboards, movie screens, food labels, soap operas, magazine ads, singing commercials. Our daily bread: Cream O' Wheat, Uncle Ben's Rice, Wilson Ham ("The Ham What Am!"), those "happifyin' " Aunt Jemima pancakes for our "temptilatin' " breakfasts. Our daily drink, too: Carioca Puerto Rican Rum, Hiram Walker whiskey, Ballantine's Ale. Through McCallum and Propper, the Negro gives milady the new "dark Creole shades" in her sheer nylons; through the House of Vigny, her "grotesque," "fuzzy-wuzzy" bottles of Golliwogg colognes and perfumes. Shoeshines, snow-white laundry, comfortable lower berths, efficient handling of luggage; jazz, jive, jitterbugging, zoot, comedy, and the wonderful tales of Brer Rabbit to entrance the kiddies. Service with a smile. . . .

"The Negroes," writes Geoffrey Gorer, "are kept in their subservient position by the ultimate sanctions of fear and force, and this is well known to whites and Negroes alike. Nevertheless, the whites demand that the Negroes shall appear smiling, eager, and friendly in all their dealings with them."

But if the grin is extracted by force, may not the smiling face be a falseface—and just underneath is there not something else, often only half-hidden?

*Reprinted from *Commentary*, 8 (July 1949), 31–41, with the permission of the publisher. Mr. Wolfe is the author (with Mezz Mezzrow) of *Really the Blues* (1957) and other works on modern culture.

Uncle Remus—a kind of blackface Will Rogers, complete with standard minstrel dialect and plantation shuffle—has had remarkable staying power in our popular culture, much more than Daddy Long Legs, say, or even Uncle Tom. Within the past two years alone he has inspired a full-length Disney feature, three Hit Parade songs, a widely circulated album of recorded dialect stories, a best-selling juvenile picture book, a syndicated comic strip. And the wily hero of his animal fables, Brer Rabbit—to whom Bugs Bunny and perhaps even Harvey owe more than a little—is today a much bigger headliner than Bambi or Black Beauty, outclassing even Donald Duck.

For almost seventy years, Uncle Remus has been the prototype of the Negro grinner-giver. Nothing ever clouds the "beaming countenance" of the "venerable old darky"; nothing ever interrupts the flow of his "hearty," "mellow," "cheerful and good-humored" voice as, decade after decade, he presents his Brer Rabbit stories to the nation.

But Remus too is a white man's brainchild: he was created in the columns of the Atlanta *Constitution*, back in the early 1880's, by a neurotic young Southern journalist named Joel Chandler Harris (1848–1908).

When Remus grins, Harris is pulling the strings; when he "gives" his folk stories, he is the ventriloquist's dummy on Harris's knee.

The setting for these stories never varies: the little white boy, son of "Miss Sally" and "Mars John," the plantation owners, comes "hopping and skipping" into the old Negro's cabin down in back of the "big house" and the story-telling session gets under way. Remus's face "breaks up into little eddies of smiles"; he takes his admirer on his knee, "strokes the child's hair thoughtfully and caressingly," calls him "honey." The little boy "nestles closer" to his "sable patron" and listens with "open-eyed wonder."

No "sanctions of fear and force" here, Harris insists—the relationship between narrator and auditor is one of unmitigated tenderness. Remus "gives," with a "kindly beam" and a "most infectious chuckle"; the little boy receives with mingled "awe," "admiration," and "delight." But, if one looks more closely, within the magnanimous caress is an incredibly malevolent blow.

Of the several Remus collections published by Harris, the first and most famous is *Uncle Remus: His Songs and His Sayings*. Brer Rabbit appears twenty-six times in this book, encounters the Fox twenty times, soundly trounces him nineteen times. The Fox, on the other hand, achieves only two very minor triumphs—one over the Rabbit, another over the Sparrow. On only two other occasions is the Rabbit victimized even slightly, both times by animals as puny as himself (the Tarrypin, the Buzzard); but when he is pitted against adversaries as strong as the Fox (the Wolf, the Bear, once the whole Animal Kingdom) he emerges the unruffled winner. The Rabbit finally kills off all three of his powerful enemies. The Fox is made a thorough fool of by all the weakest animals—the Buzzard, the Tarrypin, the Bull-Frog.

All told, there are twenty-eight victories of the Weak over the Strong; ultimately all the Strong die violent deaths at the hands of the Weak; and there are, at most, two very insignificant victories of the Strong over the Weak. . . . Admittedly, folk symbols are seldom systematic, clean-cut, or specific; they are cultural shadows thrown by the unconscious, and the unconscious is not governed by the sharp-edged neatness of the filing cabinet. But still, on the basis of the tally-sheet alone, is it too far-fetched to take Brer Rabbit as a symbol—about as sharp as Southern sanctions would allow—of the Negro slave's festering hatred of the white man?

It depends, of course, on whether these are animals who maul and murder each other, or human beings disguised as animals. Here Harris and Remus seem to differ. "In dem days," Remus often starts, "de creeturs wuz santer'n 'roun' same like fokes." But for Harris—so he insists—this anthropomorphism is only incidental. What the stories depict, he tells us, is only the "roaring comedy of animal life."

Is it? These are very un-Aesopian creatures who speak a vaudeville dialect, hold candy-pulls, run for the legislature, fight and scheme over gold mines, compete for women in elaborate rituals of courtship and self-aggrandizement, sing plantation ditties about "Jim Crow," read the newspapers after supper, and kill and maim each other—not in gusts of endocrine Pavlov passion but coldbloodedly, for prestige, plotting their crafty moves in advance and often using accomplices. . . . Harris sees no malice in all this, even when heads roll. Brer Rabbit, he explains, is moved not by "malice, but mischievousness." But Brer Rabbit "mischievously" scalds the Wolf to death, makes the innocent Possum die in a fire to cover his own crimes, tortures and probably murders the Bear by setting a swarm of bees on him—and, after causing the fatal beating of the Fox, carries his victim's head to Mrs. Fox and her children, hoping to trick them into eating it in their soup. . . .

One dramatic tension in these stories seems to be a gastronomic one: *Will the communal meal ever take place in the "Animal" Kingdom?*

The food-sharing issue is posed in the very first story. "I seed Brer B'ar yistiddy," the Fox tells the Rabbit as the story opens, "en he sorter rake me over de coals kaze you en me ain't make frens en live naborly." He then invites the Rabbit to supper—intending that his guest will be the main course in this "joint" feast. Brer Rabbit solemnly accepts the invitation, shows up, makes the Fox look ridiculous, and blithely scampers off: "En Brer Fox ain't kotch 'im yit, en w'at's mo', honey, he ain't gwine ter." The Rabbit can get along very well without the communal meal; but, it soon develops, Brer Fox and his associates can't live without it.

Without food-sharing, no community. Open warfare breaks out immediately after the Fox's hypocritical invitation; and the Rabbit is invariably the victor in the gory skirmishes. And after he kills and skins the Wolf, his other enemies are so cowed that now the communal meal finally seems about to take place: "de animals en de creeturs, dey kep' on gittin' mo' en mo' familious wid wunner nudder—bunchin' der perwishuns tergidder in de same shanty" and "takin' a snack" together too.

But Brer Rabbit isn't taken in. Knowing that the others are sharing their food with him out of fear, not genuine communality, he remains the complete cynic and continues to raid the Fox's goober patch and the Bear's persimmon orchard. Not until the closing episode does the Fox make a genuine food-sharing gesture—he crawls inside Bookay the Cow with Brer Rabbit and gratuitously shows him how to hack out all the beef he can carry. But the communal overture comes too late. In an act of the most supreme malevolence, the Rabbit betrays his benefactor to the farmer and stands by, "makin' like he mighty sorry," while the Fox is beaten to death. . . . And now the meal which aborted in the beginning, because the Fox's friendliness was only a ruse, almost does take place—with the Fox as the main course. Having brutally destroyed his arch enemy, Brer Rabbit tries to make Mrs. Fox cook a soup with her husband's head, and almost succeeds.

Remus is not an anthropomorphist by accident. His theme is a *human* one—neighborliness—and the communal meal is a symbol for it. His moral? There are no good neighbors in the world, neither equality nor fraternity. But the moral has an underside: the Rabbit can never be trapped.

Another tension runs through the stories: *Who gets the women?* In sex, Brer Rabbit is at his most aggressive—and his most invincible. Throughout he is engaged in murderous competition with the Fox and the other animals for the favors of "Miss Meadows en de gals."

In their sexual competition the Rabbit never fails to humiliate the Fox viciously. "I'll show Miss Meadows en de gals dat I'm de boss er Brer Fox," he decides. And he does: through the most elaborate trickery he persuades the Fox to put on a saddle, then rides him past Miss Meadows' house, digging his spurs in vigorously. . . . And in sex, it would seem, there are no false distinctions between creatures—all differences in status are irrelevant. At Miss Meadows' the feuds of the work-a-day world must be suspended, "kaze Miss Meadows, she done put her foot down, she did, en say dat w'en dey come ter her place dey hatter hang up a flag er truce at de front gate en 'bide by it."

The truce is all to the Rabbit's advantage, because if the competitors start from scratch in the sexual battle the best man must win—and the best man is invariably Brer Rabbit. The women themselves want the best man to win. Miss Meadows decides to get some peace by holding a contest and letting the winner have his pick of the girls. The Rabbit mulls the problem over. He sings ironically,

> Make a bow ter de Buzzard en den ter de
>   Crow
> Takes a liber-toe gemmun fer ter jump
>   Jim Crow.

Then, through a tricky scheme, he proceeds to outshine all the stronger contestants.

Food-sharing, sex-sharing—the Remus stories read like a catalogue of Southern racial taboos, all standing on their heads. The South, wearing the blinders of stereotype, has always tried to see the Negro as a "roaringly comic" domestic animal. Understandably; for animals of the tame or domestic variety are not menacing—they are capable only of mischief, never of malice. But the Negro slave, through his anthropomorphic Rabbit stories, seems to be hinting that even the frailest and most humble of "animals" can let fly with the most bloodthirsty aggressions. And these aggressions take place in the two most sacrosanct areas of Southern racial etiquette: the gastronomic and the erotic.

The South, with its "sanctions of fear and force," forbids Negroes to eat at the same table with whites. But Brer Rabbit, through an act of murder, *forces* Brer Fox and all his associates to share their food with him. The South enjoins the Negro, under penalty of death, from coming near the white man's women—although the white man has free access to the Negro's women. But Brer Rabbit flauntingly demonstrates his sexual superiority over all the other animals and, as the undisputed victor in the sexual competition, gets his choice of *all* the women.

And yet, despite these food and sex taboos, for two solid centuries—for the Rabbit stories existed long before Harris put them on paper—Southerners chuckled at the way the Rabbit terrorized all the other animals into the communal meal, roared at the Rabbit's guile in winning the girls away from the Fox *by jumping Jim Crow*. And they were endlessly intrigued by the O. Henry spasm of the miraculous in the very last story, right after the Fox's death: "Some say dat . . . Brer Rabbit married ole Miss Fox. . . ."

An interesting denouement, considering the sexual fears which saturate the South's racial attitudes. Still more interesting that Southern whites should even have countenanced it, let alone revelled in it. . . ."

Significantly, the goal of eating and sex, as depicted in Uncle Remus, is not instinct-gratification. The overriding drive is for *prestige*—the South is a prestige-haunted land. And it is in that potent intangible that the Rabbit is always paid off most handsomely for his exploits. Throughout, as he terrorizes the Strong, the "sassy" Rabbit remains bland, unperturbed, sure of his invincibility. When he humiliates the Fox by turning him into a saddle-horse, he mounts him "same's ef he wuz king er de patter-rollers." ("Patter-rollers," Harris cheerfully points out, were the white patrols that terrorized Negro slaves so they wouldn't wander off the plantations.)

Brer Rabbit, in short, has all the jaunty topdog airs and attitudes which a slave can only dream of having. And, like the slave, he has a supremely cynical view of the social world, since he sees it from below. The South is the most etiquette-ridden region of the country; and the Rabbit sees all forms of etiquette as hypocritical and absurd. Creatures meet, address each other with unctuous politeness, inquire after each other's families, pass the time of day with oily clichés—and all the while they are plotting to humiliate, rob, and assassinate each other. The Rabbit sees through it all; if he is serene it is only because he can plot more rapidly and with more deadly efficiency than any of the others.

The world, in Brer Rabbit's wary eyes, is a jungle. Life is a battle-unto-the-death for food, sex, power, prestige, a battle without rules. There is only one reality in this life: who is on top? But Brer Rabbit wastes no time lamenting the mad unneighborly scramble for the top position. Because it is by no means ordained that the Weak can never take over. In his topsy-turvy world, to all practical purposes, the Weak *have* taken over. In one episode, the Rabbit falls down a well in a bucket. He can get back up only by enticing the Fox to climb into the other bucket. The Fox is duped: he drops down and the Rabbit rises, singing as he passes his enemy:

> Good-by, Brer Fox, take keer yo' close
> Fer dis is de way de worril goes
> Some goes up en some goes down
> You'll git ter de bottom all safe en soun'.

This is the theme song of the stories. The question remains, who sings it? The Rabbit is a creation of Uncle Remus's people; is it, then, Uncle Remus singing? But Uncle Remus is a creation of Joel Chandler Harris. . . .

There is a significant difference in ages—some hundreds of years—between Uncle Remus and Brer Rabbit. The Rabbit had been the hero of animal stories popular among Negroes from the early days of slavery; these were genuine folk tales told by Negroes to Negroes and handed down in oral form. Uncle Remus was added only when Harris, in packaging the stories—using the Negro grin for gift-wrapping—invented the Negro narrator to sustain the dialect.

Harris, then, fitted the hate-imbued folk materials into a framework, a white man's framework, of "love." He took over the animal characters and situations of the original stories and gave them a human setting: the loving and lovable Negro narrator, the adoring white auditor. Within this framework of love, the blow was heavily padded with caresses and the genuine folk was almost emasculated into the cute folksy.

Almost, but not quite. Harris all his life was torn between his furtive penchant for fiction and his profession of journalism. It was the would-be novelist in him who created Remus, the "giver" of interracial caresses, but the trained journalist in him, having too good an eye and ear, reported the energetic folk blow in the caress. Thus the curious tension in his versions between "human" form and "animal" content.

Before Harris, few Southerners had ever faced squarely the aggressive symbolism of Brer Rabbit, or the paradox of their delight in it. Of course: it was part of the Southerner's undissected myth—often shared by the Negroes—that his cherished childhood sessions in the slave quarters were bathed in two-way benevolence. But Harris, by writing the white South and its Negro tale-spinners into the stories, also wrote in its unfaced paradoxes. Thus his versions helped to rip open the racial myth—and, with it, the interracial grin.

What was the slippery rabbit-hero doing in these stories to begin with? Where did he come from? As soon as Harris wrote down the oral stories for mass consumption, these questions began to agitate many whites. The result was a whole literature devoted to proving the "un-American" genealogy of Brer Rabbit.

Why, one Southern writer asks, did the Negro pick the Rabbit for a hero? Could it be because the Rabbit was "symbolic of his own humble and helpless condition in comparison with his master the owner of the plantation"? Perhaps the Rabbit represents the Negro "in revolt at . . . his own subordinate and insignificant place in society"?

But no: if the Negro is capable of rebelling against society—American society—even symbolically, he is a menace. The Negro must be in revolt against *Nature*, against the "subordinate and insignificant place" assigned to him by biological fate, not America. The writer reassures himself: the Negro makes animals act "like a low order of human intelligence, such as the Negro himself [can] comprehend." The Negro naturally feels "more closely in touch with [the lower animals] than with the white man who [is] so superior to him in every respect." No threat in Brer Rabbit; his genealogy, having no *American* roots, is a technical matter for "the psychologist or the student of folklore."

However, uneasy questions were raised; and as they were raised they were directed at Harris. Readers sensed the symbolic taunts and threats in the Rabbit and insisted on knowing whether they were directed against white America—or against "Nature." Harris took refuge from this barrage of questions in two mutually contradictory formulas: (1) he was merely the "compiler" of these stories, a non-intellectual, a lowly humorist, ignorant of "folkloristic" matters; and (2) Brer Rabbit was most certainly, as Southerners intuited, an undiluted African.

"All that I know—all that we Southerners know—about it," Harris protested, "is that every old plantation mammy in the South is full of these stories." But, a sentence later, Harris decided there *was* one other thing he knew: "One thing is certain—the Negro did not get them from the whites; *probably they are of remote African origin*." And if they come from the Congo, they offer no symbolic blows to Americans; they are simply funny. So Harris warns the folklorists: "First let us have the folktales told as they were intended to be told, for the sake of amusement. . . ."

But if the folklorists *should* find in them something "of value to their pretensions"? Then "let it be picked out and preserved with as little cackling as possible."

The South wavered; it could not shake off the feeling that Brer Rabbit's overtones were more than just funny. And Harris, too, wavered. To a British folklorist editor he wrote, suddenly reversing himself, that the stories were "more important than humorous." And in the introduction to his book he explains that "however humorous it may be in effect, its intention is perfectly serious. . . . It seems to me that a volume written wholly in dialect must have its solemn, not to say melancholy features."

What was it that Harris sporadically found "important," "solemn," even "melancholy" here? It turns out to be the *Americanism* of Brer Rabbit: "it needs no scientific investigation," Harris continues in his introduction, "to show why he [the Negro] selects as his hero the weakest and most harmless of all animals. . . . It is not virtue that triumphs, but helplessness. . . . Indeed, the parallel between the case of the 'weakest' of all animals, who must, perforce, triumph through his shrewdness, and the humble condition of the slave raconteur, is not without its pathos."

A suggestive idea. But such a "parallel" could not have been worked out in the African jungle, before slavery; it implies that Brer Rabbit, after all, was born much closer to the Mississippi than to the Congo. . . . This crucial sentence does not occur in later editions. Instead we read: "It would be presumptious [*sic*] in me to offer an opinion as to the origins of these curious myth-stories; but, *if ethnologists should discover that they did not originate with the African, the proof to that effect should be accompanied with a good deal of persuasive eloquence.*"

In this pressing sentence we can see Harris's whole fragmented psyche mirrored. Like all the South, he was caught in a subjective tug-of-war: his intelligence groped for the venomous American slave crouching behind the Rabbit, but his beleaguered racial emotions, in self-defense, had to insist on the "Africanism" of Brer Rabbit—and of the Negro. Then Miss Sally and Mars John could relish his "quaint antics" without recognizing themselves as his targets.

Against the African origin of Brer Rabbit one may argue that he is an eloquent white folk-symbol too, closely related to the lamb as the epitome of Christian meekness (the Easter bunny). May not the Negro, in his conversion to Christianity, have learned the standard Christian animal symbols from the whites? Could not his constant tale-spinning about the Rabbit's malevolent triumphs somehow, in some devious way, suggest the ascent of Christ, the meekness that shall inherit the earth; suggest, even, that the meek may stop being meek and set about inheriting the earth without waiting on the Biblical timetable?

But, there *is* more definite evidence as to Brer Rabbit's non-African origins—skimpy, not conclusive, but highly suggestive. Folklore study indicates that if the Negro did have stories about a rabbit back in Africa, they were not these stories, and the rabbit was most decidedly not this rabbit. Brer Rabbit's truer ancestor, research suggests, hails from elsewhere.

"Most of these Negro stories," reported a Johns Hopkins ethnologist—one of the "cackling" folklorists—". . . bear a striking resemblance to the large body of animal stories made on European soil, of which the most extensive is that known as the *Roman de Renard*. The episodes which form the substance of this French version circulated in the Middle Ages on the Flemish border. . . . The principal actors . . . are the fox, who plays the jokes, and the wolf, most frequently the victim of the fox."

In incident after incident, the Brer Rabbit situations parallel the Reynard the Fox situations: the same props appear, the same set-to's, the same ruses, the same supporting characters, often the same dialogue. But there is one big difference: "In *Uncle Remus* the parts are somewhat changed. Here the rabbit, who scarcely appears (under the name Couard) in the *Renard*, is the chief trickster. His usual butt is the fox. . . ."

In Christian symbolism, then, the rabbit is the essence of meekness and innocence. And in an important part of white folk culture he stands for the impotent, the cowardly, as against the cunning fox. Suddenly, with the beginning of slavery, the Negro begins to tell stories in which the rabbit, now the epitome of belligerence and guile, crops up as the *hero*, mercilessly badgering the fox.

Could the Negroes have got the Reynard fables from the whites? Not impossible. The stories originated among the Flemish peasants. During the 12th century they were written down in French, Latin, and German, in a variety of rhymed forms. The many written versions were then widely circulated throughout Western Europe. And more than a few of the first Negro slaves were brought to France, Spain, and Portugal; and some of their descendants were transplanted to America. Also, many early slaves were brought to plantations owned by Frenchmen—whether in the Louisiana Territory, the Acadian-French sections of North Carolina, or the West Indies.

And many white masters, of French and other backgrounds, told these delightful fox tales to their children. And, from the beginning of the slave trade, many Negroes—who may or may not have had pre-Christian rabbit fables of their own back in Africa—could have listened, smiling amiably, slowly absorbing the raw materials for the grinning folk "gift" that would one day be immortalized by Joel Chandler Harris, Walt Disney, Tin Pan Alley, and the comics. . . .

The Harris research technique, we learn, was first-hand and direct. Seeing a group of Negroes, he approaches and asks if they know any Brer Rabbit stories. The Negroes seem not to understand. Offhandedly, and in rich dialect, Harris tells one himself—as often as not, the famous "Tar-Baby" story. The Negroes are transfixed; then, suddenly, they break out in peals of laughter, kick their heels together, slap their thighs. Before long they are swapping Rabbit yarns with the white man as though he were their lifelong "hail-feller." "Curiously enough," Harris notes, "I have found few Negroes who will acknowledge to a stranger that they know anything of these legends; and yet to relate one of the stories is the surest road to their confidence and esteem."

Why the sudden hilarity? What magic folk-key causes these wary, taciturn Negroes to open up? Harris claims to have won their "esteem"; but perhaps he only guaranteed them immunity. He thinks he disarmed the Negroes—he may only have demonstrated that he, the white boss-man, was disarmed.

And how much did the Negroes tell him when they "opened up"? Just how far did they really open up? Harris observes that "there are different versions of all the stories—the shrewd narrators of the mythology of the old plantation adapting themselves with ready tact to the years, tastes, and expectations of their juvenile audiences." But there seem to be gaps in Harris's own versions. At tantalizingly crucial points Uncle Remus will break off abruptly—"Some tells one tale en some tells nudder"—leaving the story dangling like a radio cliff-hanger. Did these gaps appear when the stories were told to Harris? When the slave is obliged to play the clown-entertainer and "give" his folk tales to his masters, young or old, his keen sense of the fitting might well delete the impermissible and blur the dubious—and more out of self-preservation than tact.

Of course, the original oral stories would not express the slave's aggressions straightforwardly either. A Negro slave who yielded his mind fully to his race hatreds in an absolutely white-dominated situation must go mad; and the function of such folk symbols as Brer Rabbit is precisely to prevent inner explosions by siphoning off these hatreds before they can completely possess consciousness. Folk tales, like so much of folk culture, are part of an elaborate psychic drainage system—they make it possible for Uncle Tom to retain his facade of grinning Tomism and even, to some degree, to believe in it himself. But the slave's venom, while subterranean, must nonetheless have been *thrillingly* close to the surface and its symbolic disguises flimsier, its attacks less roundabout. Accordingly his protective instincts, sensing the danger in too shallow symbolism, would have necessarily wielded a meticulous, if unconscious, blue pencil in the stories told to white audiences.

Harris tried hard to convince himself that Uncle Remus was a full-fledged, dyed-in-the-denim Uncle Tom—he describes the "venerable sable patron" as an ex-slave "who has nothing but pleasant memories of the discipline of slavery." But Harris could not completely exorcise the menace in the Meek. How often Remus steps out of his clown-role to deliver unmistakeable judgments on class, caste, and race! In those judgments the aggressions of this "white man's nigger" are astonishingly naked.

"Why the Negro Is Black" tells how the little boy makes the "curious" discovery that Remus's palms are white. The old man explains: "Dey wuz a time w'en all de w'ite folks 'us black—blacker dan me. . . . Niggers is

niggers now, but de time wuz w'en we 'uz all niggers tergedder. . . ."
How did some "niggers" get white? Simply by bathing in a pond which
washed their pigmentation off and using up most of the waters, so that the
latecomers could only dabble their hands and feet in it.

But the stragglers who were left with their dark skin tone are not
trapped—they may be able to wriggle out of it. In "A Plantation Witch,"
Remus, explaining that there are witches everywhere in the world that
"comes en conjus fokes," hints that these witches may be Negroes who
have slipped out of their skins. And these witches conjure white folks from
all sides, taking on the forms of owls, bats, dogs, cats—and rabbits.

And in "The Wonderful Tar-Baby Story"—advertised on the dust-
jacket as the most famous of all the Remus stories—Remus reverts to the
question of pigmentation. ("There are few negroes that will fail to respond" to this one, Harris advises one of his folklore "legmen.") The Fox
fashions a "baby" out of tar and places it on the side of the road; the
Rabbit comes along and addresses the figure. Not getting any answer, he
threatens: "Ef you don't take off dat hat en tell me howdy, I'm gwineter
bus' you wide open." (Here the Rabbit's bluster reads like a parody of the
white man's demand for the proper bowing-and-scraping etiquette from
the Negro; it is a reflection of the satiric mimicry of the whites which the
slaves often indulged in among themselves.) He hits the Tar-Baby—his
fist sticks in the gooey tar. He hits it with the other hand, then kicks
it—all four extremities are stuck.

This is "giving" in a new sense; tar, blackness, by its very yielding,
traps. Interesting symbol, in a land where the mere possession of a black
skin requires you, under penalty of death, to yield, to *give*, everywhere.
The mark of supreme impotence suddenly acquires the power to render
impotent, merely by its flaccidity, its inertness; it is almost a Gandhi-like
symbol. There is a puzzle here: it is the Rabbit who is trapped. But in a
later story, "How Mr. Rabbit Was Too Sharp for Mr. Fox," it turns out
that the Rabbit, through another cagey maneuver, gets the Fox to set him
free from the tar-trap and thus avoids being eaten by his enemy. The
Negro, in other words, is wily enough to escape from the engulfing pit of
blackness, although his opponents, who set the trap, do their level best to
keep him imprisoned in it. But it is not at all sure that anyone else who fell
victim to this treacherous black yieldingness—the Fox, say—would be
able to wriggle out so easily.

The story about "A Plantation Witch" frightens his young admirer so
much that Remus has to take him by the hand and lead him home to the
"big house." And for a long time the boy lies awake "expecting an
unseemly visitation from some mysterious source." Many of the other
stories, too, must have given him uneasy nights. For within the "gift" that
Uncle Remus gives to Miss Sally's little boy is a nightmare, a nightmare in
which whites are Negroes, the Weak torture and drown the Strong, mere
blackness becomes black magic—and Negroes cavort with cosmic forces

and the supernatural, zipping their skins off at will to prowl around the countryside terrorizing the whites, often in the guise of rabbits. . . .

Harris's career is one of the fabulous success stories of American literary history. Thanks to Uncle Remus, the obscure newspaperman was catapulted into the company of Mark Twain, Bret Harte, James Whitcomb Riley, and Petroleum V. Nasby; Andrew Carnegie and Theodore Roosevelt traveled to Atlanta to seek him out; he was quoted in Congress. And all the while he maintained—as in a letter to Twain—that "my book has no basis in literary merit to stand upon; I know it is the matter and not the manner that has attracted public attention . . . my relations towards Uncle Remus are similar to those that exist between an almanac-maker and the calendar. . . ."

But how was it that Harris could apply his saccharine manner to such matter, dress this malevolent material, these nightmares, in such sweetness and light? For one thing, of course, he was only recording the tottering racial myth of the post-bellum South, doing a paste-job on its fissioning falseface. As it happened, he was peculiarly suited for the job; for he was crammed full of pathological racial obsessions, over and above those that wrack the South and, to a lesser degree, all of white America.

Even Harris's worshipful biographer, his daughter-in-law, can't prevent his story from reading like a psychiatric recital of symptoms. The blush and the stammer were his whole way of life. From early childhood on, we are told, he was "painfully conscious of his social deficiencies" and his "lack of size"; he felt "handicapped by his tendency to stutter" and to "blush furiously," believed himself "much uglier than he really was"; in his own words, he had "an absolute horror of strangers."

During his induction into the typographical union, Harris stutters so badly that he has to be excused from the initiation ceremony; trapped in a room full of congenial strangers, he escapes by jumping out of the window. "What a coarse ungainly boor I am," he laments, "how poor, small and insignificant. . . ." He wonders if he is mad: "I am morbidly sensitive . . . it is an affliction—a disease . . . the slightest rebuff tortures me beyond expression. . . . It is worse than death itself. It is *horrible*." Again, he speculates about his "abnormal quality of mind . . . that lacks only vehemence to become downright insanity. . . ." Harris's life, it appears, was one long ballet of embarrassment.

"I am nursing a novel in my brain," Harris announced archly more than once. All along he was consumed with the desire to turn out some "long work" of fiction, but, except for two inept and badly received efforts (published after his forty-eighth year), he never succeeded. Over and over he complained bitterly of his grinding life in the journalistic salt mines—but when the Century Company offered him a handsome income if he would devote all his time to creative work, he refused. This refusal, according to his daughter-in-law, "can be explained only by his abnormal lack of confidence in himself as a 'literary man.' "

The urge to create was strong in Harris, so strong that it gave him no peace; and he could not create. That is the central fact in his biography: his creative impulses were trapped behind a block of congealed guilts, granite-strong; the works he produced were not real gushings of the subjective but only those driblets that were able to seep around the edges of the block.

Harris's stammer—his literal choking on words—was like a charade of the novelist *manqué* in him; his blush was the fitful glow of his smothered self, a tic of the guilty blood. And that smothered self had a name: Uncle Remus.

Accused of plagiarizing folk materials, Harris replies indignantly: "I shall not hestitate to draw on the oral stories I know for incidents. . . . The greatest literary men, if you will remember, were very poor inventors." Harris all his life was a very poor inventor; his career was built on a merciless, systematic plagiarizing of the folk-Negro. Small wonder, then, that the "plantation darky" was such a provocative symbol for him. For, ironically, this lowly Negro was, when viewed through the blinders of stereotype, almost the walking image of Harris's ego-ideal—the un-selfconscious, "natural," freeflowing, richly giving creator that Harris could never become. Indeed, for Harris, as for many another white American, the Negro *seemed* in every respect to be a negative print of his own uneasy self: "happy-go-lucky," socializing, orally expressive, muscularly relaxed, never bored or passive, unashamedly exhibitionistic, free from self-pity even in his situation of concentrated pain, emotionally fluid. And every time a Remus opened his mouth, every time he flashed a grin, he wrote effortlessly another novel that was strangled a-borning in Harris.

"I despise and detest those false forms of society that compel people to suppress their thoughts," Harris wrote. But he was himself the most inhibited and abashed of men. What fascinates him in the Rabbit stories, he confesses, is "the humor that lies between *what is perfectly decorous in appearance* and *what is wildly extravagant in suggestion.*" But, a thorough slave to decorum, he was incapable of the "wildly extravagant," whether in his love-making ("My love for you," he informs his future wife, "is . . . far removed from that wild passion that develops itself in young men in their teens . . . it is not at all wild or unreasoning") or in his writing.

Harris, then, was *awed* by Uncle Remus. It was the awe of the sophisticate before the spontaneous, the straitjacketed before the nimble. But was the Negro what Harris thought him to be? It is certainly open to question, for another irony of the South is that the white man, under his pretense of racial omniscience, actually knows the Negro not at all—he knows only the false-face which he has forced on the Negro. It is the white man who manufactures the Negro grin. The stereotype reflects the looker, his thwartings and yearnings, not the person looked at; it is born out of intense subjective need.

Harris's racial awe was only an offshoot of the problem that tormented him all his life: the problem of identifying himself. He was caught in the American who-am-I dilemma, one horn of which is white, the other often black. And there is abundant proof that, at least in one compartment of his being, Harris defined himself by identifying with the Negro.

As a child, Harris started the game of "Gully Minstrels" with his white playmates; and later in life, whenever he felt "blue" and wanted to relax, he would jump up and exclaim, "Let's have some fun—let's play minstrels!" Often, in letters and newspaper articles, and even in personal relations, he would *jokingly* refer to himself as "Uncle Remus," and when he started a one-man magazine, he decided to name it *Uncle Remus's Magazine* instead of *The Optimist*! Frequently he would lapse into a rich Negro dialect, to the delight of his admirers, from Andrew Carnegie down to the local trolley conductor. And, like Uncle Remus, he even toys with the idea that whites are only blanched Negroes: "Study a nigger right close," he has one of his characters say, "and you'll ketch a glimpse of how white folks would look and do without their trimmin's."

Harris seems to have been a man in permanent rebellion again his own skin. No wonder: for he was driven to "give," and it was impossible for him to give without first zipping out of his own decorous skin and slipping into Uncle Remus's. To him the artist and the Negro were synonymous.

And Harris virulently *hated* the Negro, too. "The colored people of Macon," he writes in his paper, "celebrated the birthday of Lincoln again on Wednesday. This is the third time since last October. . . ." And: "A negro pursued by an agile Macon policeman fell in a well the other day. He says he knocked the bottom out of the concern." Again: "There will have to be another amendment to the civil rights bill. A negro boy in Covington was attacked by a sow lately and narrowly escaped with his life. We will hear next that the sheep have banded together to mangle the downtrodden race."

The malice here is understandable. Can the frustrate—the "almanac-maker"—ever love unequivocally the incarnation of his own taboo self—the "calendar"? What stillborn novelist can be undilutedly tender towards the objectivization of his squelched alter-ego, whose oral stories he feels impelled to "draw on" all his life?

Most likely, at least in Harris, the love went deeper than the hate—the hate was, in some measure, a *defense* against the love. *"Some goes up en some goes down."* Who sings this theme song? A trio: the Rabbit, Remus, *and* Harris. Literally, it is only a rabbit and a fox who change places. Racially, the song symbolizes the ascent of the Negro "Weak" and the descent of the white "Strong."

But to Harris, on the deepest personal level, it must have meant: the collapse of the "perfectly decorous" (inhibition, etiquette, embarrassment, the love that is never wild, the uncreative journalist-compiler, the blush and the stammer) and the triumph of the "wildly extravagant" (spontaneity, "naturalness," the unleashed subjective, creativity, "Miss Meadows en de gals," exhibitionism, the folk-novelist). The song must have been *deliciously* funny to him. . . .

The Remus stories are a monument to the South's ambivalence. Harris, the archetypical Southerner, sought the Negro's love, and pretended he had received it (Remus's grin). But he sought the Negro's hate too (Brer Rabbit), and revelled in it in an unconscious orgy of masochism—punishing himself, possibly, for not being the Negro, the stereotypical Negro, the unstinting giver.

Harris's inner split—and the South's, and white America's—is mirrored in the fantastic disparity between Remus's beaming face and Brer Rabbit's acts. And such aggressive acts increasingly emanate from the grin, along with the hamburgers, the shoeshines, the "happifyin' " pancakes.

Today Negro attack and counter-attack becomes more straightforward. The NAACP submits a brief to the United Nations, demanding a redress of grievances suffered by the Negro people at the hands of white America. The election newsreels showed Henry Wallace addressing audiences that were heavily sprinkled with Negroes, protected by husky, alert, *deadpan* bodyguards—Negroes. New York Negroes voted for Truman—but only after Truman went to Harlem. The Gandhi-like "Tar-Baby" begins to stir: Grant Reynolds and A. Phillips Randolph, announcing to a Senate committee that they will refuse to be drafted in the next war, revealed, at the time, that many Negroes were joining their civil-disobedience organization—the first movement of passive resistance this country had seen.

Increasingly Negroes themselves reject the mediating smile of Remus, the indirection of the Rabbit. The present-day animated cartoon hero, Bugs Bunny, is, like Brer Rabbit, the meek suddenly grown cunning—but without Brer Rabbit's facade of politeness. "To pull a Bugs Bunny," meaning to spectacularly outwit someone, is an expression not infrequently heard in Harlem.

There is today on every level a mass repudiation of "Uncle Tomism." Significantly the Negro comedian is disappearing. For bad or good, the *Dark Laughter* that Sherwood Anderson heard all around white New Orleans is going or gone.

The grin is faltering, especially since the war. That may be one of the reasons why, once more, the beaming Negro butler and Pullman porter are making their amiable way across our billboards, food labels, and magazine ads—and Uncle Remus, "fetchin' a grin from year to year," is in the bigtime again.

[Satiric Allegory in the Uncle Remus Tales]

Ellen Douglass Leyburn*

One gift essential to the teller of satiric animal tales is the power to keep his reader conscious simultaneously of the human traits satirized and of the animals as animals. The moment he loses hold on resemblance and lets his protagonists become merely animals or merely people, his instrument has slipped in his hands and deflected his material away from satiric allegory into something like *Black Beauty* or *The Three Bears*. But if the writer of animal allegory can successfully sustain and play upon two levels of perception, making us feel that his animals are really animals and yet as human as ourselves, he can control the imaginative response. This doubleness of effect is the central power of great animal stories as different as the *Nun's Priest's Tale* and *The Tar Baby*. We delight in Chaunticleer and Pertelote and Brer Rabbit because they are at once real as people and real as animals. The climax of the Tar Baby story, "Bred en bawn in a brier-patch, Brer Fox—bred en bawn in a brier-patch!" reminds us inescapably that this creature is a rabbit exactly while it reminds us of his resemblance to the human being who by his wit can extricate himself from any difficulty. Uncle Remus concludes, "en wid dat he skip out des ez lively ez a cricket in de embers," and we find his liveliness irrestible because we see a real rabbit skipping off in a mood that we know as human. So with Chaucer's masterpiece: Pertelote's "Pekke hem up right as they growe and ete hem yn" is often cited as one of Chaucer's wittiest reductions to the animal level in all his mock-heroic scheme. Yet this remark, which reminds the readers with humorous felicity that a hen is speaking, conveys also the quintessence of Pertelote's wifely solicitude. It seems that when she is most a chicken, she is most full of the particular sort of femininity that Chaucer is placing beside masculine roosterishness for amused scrutiny.

*Reprinted with the permission of the author's estate and the publisher, from Ellen Douglass Leyburn, "Animal Stories," Ch. 4 of *Satiric Allegory: Mirror of Man* (New Haven: Yale Univ. Press, 1956), pp. 60–66. Professor Leyburn, Chairman of the English Department at Agnes Scott College at the time of her death in 1966, is the author of several articles as well as *Strange Alloy: The Relation of Comedy to Tragedy in the Fiction of Henry James* (1968).

Indeed, it is belief in these creatures as animals that accentuates and isolates the human trait singled out for laughing observation. The animal make-up from which the human characteristic emerges throws it into high light and sharpens perception, acting as a proper vehicle for the tenor. Thus the true animal allegory fulfills I.A. Richards' requirement: "the vehicle is not . . . a mere embellishment of a tenor which is otherwise unchanged but the vehicle and tenor in co-operation give a meaning of more varied powers than can be ascribed to either."[1]

Since the whole point of animal satire is to show up humanity by revealing human traits in nonhuman characters, it follows that the few human beings who appear must not be characterized at all lest they break into the allegorical scheme. At the end of the Uncle Remus stories we know no more about "Miss Meadows en de gals" than does the little boy when he first asks, "Who was Miss Meadows, Uncle Remus?" and gets the unenlightening response: "Don't ax me, honey. She wuz in de tale, Miss Meadows en de gals wuz, en de tale I give you like hi't wer' gun ter me." The characterization of Mr. Man is if possible even vaguer: "Des a man, honey. Dat's all."[2] In George Orwell's *Animal Farm*, where the notion of man as tyrannical master is necessary to the imaginative plan, the only human character who really figures after the ousting of Mr. Jones is Whymper, who as his name suggests has no personality at all, and he is never seen by the nonporcine animals from whose point of view the story is told. The *Nun's Priest's Tale* may seem an exception to this rule, for there is a good deal of circumstantial detail in the depicting of the widow who owns the fowls. But when we come to examine the treatment of her "sooty bower" and her "attempree diete," we find that all the attention is given to externals. As a person, the widow has no more identity than do the peasants who own Chaunticleer in Chaucer's sources. The realistic detail of her few possessions and her meager life is all used to sharpen the humor of the elaborate mock-heroic treatment of the cock and his lady. It seems safe to say that there does not exist anywhere a successful animal allegory which includes a vivid human character.

Another outgrowth of the choice of animal characters to throw human traits into bold relief is the concentration upon isolated human characteristics. The successful writer of animal allegory rarely gives his characters more than one human trait at a time. This concentrated singleness of attack might almost be laid down as a second law of the genre, as binding as the first that the animals shall stay both animal and human. It removes the possibility of very complex characterization. The complexity comes from the double consciousness of animal and human attributes; and the force of the tale is almost in proportion to the singleness and simplicity on the human level. This is true even of a fairly sustained piece such as Munro Leaf's *Ferdinand*. The increasingly funny repetition of the comment that Ferdinand just sat down quietly and smelled the flowers whenever he was expected to fight not only endears the bull to us in our belligerent world, but leaves the essence of his character indelibly fixed in our minds. This is all we know of him and all we need to know except that "He is very happy."

The same practice holds in aggregations of stories centered around one character such as the medieval beast epic of *Reynard the Fox*, where Reynard is always cruelly taking advantage of his neighbors, and the Uncle Remus stories, where Brer Rabbit always mischievously turns the tables on his stronger enemies. As Uncle Remus puts it, "Eve'y time I run over in my min' 'bout the pranks er Brer Rabbit . . . hit make me laugh mo' en mo'. He mos' allers come out on top, yit dey wuz times w'en he hatter be mighty spry."[3] His invention is boundless, but he is always himself.

> I 'speck dat 'uz de reas'n w'at make ole Brer Rabbit git 'long so well, kaze he aint copy atter none er de yuther creeturs. . . . W'en he make his disappearance 'fo' um, hit 'uz allers in some bran new place. Dey aint know wharbouts fer ter watch out fer 'im. He wuz de funniest creetur er de whole gang. Some folks moughter call him lucky, en yit, w'en he git in bad luck, hit look lak he mos' allers come out on top. Hit look mighty kuse now, but 't wa'n't kuse in dem days, kaze hit 'uz done gun up dat, strike 'im w'en you might en whar you would, Brer Rabbit wuz de soopless creetur gwine. (pp. 21–22.)

The essence of his character revealed in story after story Uncle Remus summarizes: "dey w'a'n't no man 'mungs de creeturs w'at kin stan' right flat-footed en wuk he min' quick lak Brer Rabbit" (p. 129). What most stimulates his intelligence is being in a tight place: "Brer Rabbit 'gun ter git skeer'd, en w'en dat creetur git skeer'd, he min' wuk lak one er deze yer flutter-mills" (p. 220).

A corollary of the focus upon single human traits in animal tales is brevity. The swiftness with which the narrative reaches its climax sharpens the concentrated effect of the flashing out of the human motive. Uncle Remus's comment on his hero's character gives the clue to the simple plot of most of his stories, which without ever seeming monotonous repeatedly show Brer Rabbit "monst'us busy . . . sailin' 'roun' fixin' up his tricks" (p. 63) to outdo the other animals who have it in for him: "dem t'er creeturs. Dey wuz allers a-layin' traps fer Brer Rabbit en gittin' cotch in um deyse'f" (p. 119). Though he is usually extricating himself from a difficulty, he sometimes initiates pranks from sheer love of mischief. He is always alert for fun. "Brer Rabbit, he one er deze yer kinder mens w'at sleep wid der eye wide open" (p. 93). The illustrations of his ingenuity as it makes the plots for the tales are endless: he gets Mr. Fox, who has come to fetch him for revenge, to serve as his "ridin' hoss" by pretending to be too ill to accompany Brer Fox on foot; he gets Miss Cow stuck fast by the horns in the persimmon tree so that he and all his family can milk her by

promising her a feast of persimmons that she is to shake down by butting
the tree; he scalds Mr. Wolf, who runs into his chest for protection from
the dogs; he gets the bag after Mr. Fox's hunt by playing dead and tempting Brer Fox to add the rabbit to his game; on two occasions he nibbles up
the butter and manages to let the 'possum and the weasel have the blame;
he saves the meat of his own cow, takes Mr. Man's cow from Brer Fox,
and steals Mr. Man's meat and money by a series of ruses; he often persuades other animals to take his place in traps by appealing to their greed;
he escapes from the hawk by begging to be allowed to grow big enough to
make a full meal and from the embrace of the wildcat by offering to tell
him how to get turkey meat; he turns the tables on other enemies by appealing to their perversity in many variations on the Tar Baby story.
Always Brer Rabbit is equal to the emergency. His own ruses succeed and
those to outwit him fail. Only the Terrapin and the Crow ever best him,
never any of the stronger animals like the Fox, the Bear, and the Lion.
After the account of his exploits, Uncle Remus's judgment seems a model
of understatement: "Bless yo' soul, honey, Brer Rabbit mought er bin
kinder fibble in de legs, but he w'a'n't no ways cripple und' de hat" (p.
208).

Just as the hero of these stories represents always mischievous fooling,
so he confronts only one trait in his antagonist in each story. The singleness of impression, which enforces the sharpness, is never violated. But
one source of variety from story to story is the range of human traits
singled out in the other creatures for Brer Rabbit's laughter. To be sure,
laughter is the quality of his prankish intelligence. "Well . . . you know
w'at kinder man Brer Rabbit is. He des went off some 'ers by he own-
alone se'f en tuck a big laugh" (p. 214). Uncle Remus's adjective for him is
"sassy." But the very story of his Laughing Place is another illustration
that the weaknesses of the other creatures give him ample scope to exercise
his ingenuity in besting them for his own amusement. Here it is Brer Fox's
curiosity that makes him the victim. The stories already mentioned show
Brer Rabbit playing upon greed, vanity, eagerness for revenge, or sheer
cruelty in his more imposing neighbors. The stories of his frightening the
other and bigger animals, even the Lion, by playing upon their natural
timorousness are especially striking in view of his own physical
helplessness. The Lion lets Brer Rabbit tie him to a tree to save him from
being blown away by a nonexistent wind; the animals all run from Brer
Rabbit when he appears bedecked in leaves; he scares them from the
house they have built by saying that the cannon is his sneeze and the pail
of water his spit; he sets a stampede in motion by simply running past and
saying he has heard a big noise; and he outdoes himself in frightening the
others by the clatter he makes dressed up in the tin plates they are waiting
to steal from him:

Brer Rabbit got right on um 'fo dey kin git away. He holler
out, he did:

"Gimme room! Tu'n me loose! I'm ole man Spewter-Splutter
wid long claws, en scales on my back! I'm snaggle-toofed en
double-jinted! Gimme room!"

Eve'y time he'd fetch a whoop, he'd rattle de cups en slap de
platters tergedder—*rickety, rackety, slambang*! En I let you
know w'en dem creeturs got dey lim's tergedder dey split de
win', dey did dat. Ole Brer B'ar, he struck a stump w'at stan' in
de way, en I ain't gwine tell you how he to' it up 'kaze you
won't b'leeve me, but de nex' mawnin' Brer Rabbit en his
chilluns went back dar, dey did, en dey got nuff splinters fer
ter make um kin'lin' wood all de winter. (p. 123)

The human bully is probably the character most roundly mocked by Brer
Rabbit.

In Caxton's version of the medieval stories of Reynard, on the other
hand, the hero is the bully. Surely from the folklorist's viewpoint one of
the most interesting aspects of animal stories is the relationships among
the various groups. The story of Brer Rabbit's rising from the well by getting the fox to leap into the other well bucket, for instance, is identical
with the story that Erswynd, wife of Isegrim the Wulf, tells of her being
tricked into the well bucket by Reynard. A plot that is repeated with different characters in both sets of stories is that of the creature delivered and
turning on his deliverer, only to be re-imprisoned by the judgment of a
third party. Rukenaw tells in Caxton the story of the man's freeing the ser-
pent, who then turns on the man, with Reynard as the judge who refuses
advice until he sees the contestants in their original positions. In the Uncle
Remus version, the creature under the rock is the wolf, who is freed by
Brer Rabbit, and the judge is Brer Tarrypin (always Brer Rabbit's ally except when he outruns his speedier friend in the Uncle Remus variant of
the story of the Tortoise and the Hare) who says: "I hates might'ly fer ter
put you all gents ter so much trouble; yit, dey aint no two ways, I'll hatter
see des how Brer Wolf was kotch, en des how de rock wuz layin' 'pun top
un 'im" (p. 278). Then of course the wolf is left pinned under the rock just
as is the snake in the other story.

The intricate ramifications of interrelations of sources for both sets of
stories lie beyond the scope of this study, which is concerned with the artistry of the telling. But the subject of the representation of the heroes is
an aesthetic problem which is curiously linked with the larger an-
thropological relation. It is hard to resist the impression that somewhere
in the course of the development of the two groups of tales, one hero was
set up in deliberate response to the other. Both are extremely clever; and
both triumph over the other animals by deceits. But the feeling created by
the two is totally different. When Uncle Remus says, "dat seetful Brer
Rabbit done fool ole Brer Fox" (p. 89), we laugh with the rabbit. When
Erswynd says, "Ache feele reynart/noman can kepe hym self fro the[e]/
thou canst so wel vttre thy wordes and thy falsenes and reson sette
forth,"[4] our sympathy is all with the duped she-wolf. Instead of rejoicing

at Reynard's triumphs, the reader shudders at the cruelty of his tricks, which grow in evil from his making Bruin lose "his scalp, ears, and forepaws," in his bloody escape "nearly dead" from the cloven tree, through his preparing for his false pilgrimage by securing a square foot of Bruin's hide for his scrip and two shoes from each by ripping off the pawskins of Isegrim and Erswynd, through his cold-blooded devouring of Cuwart, the Hare, to the horrors of the final fight in which he slips his shaved and oiled body always out of Isegrim's grasp while he blinds the wolf by slapping his face with the tail befouled according to Rukenaw's suggestion, kicking sand into Isegrim's eyes, and treating him with every sort of indignity until he wins with his ugly stratagem leaving Isegrim mutilated and half dead. Parallel to the mounting cruelty of his deeds is the increasing baseness of his false speeches. His deceits instead of tickling the fancy like those of Brer Rabbit make their treachery abhorrent. There is serious hatred of Reynard and serious reason for it:

> Alle the beestis both poure and riche were alle stylle when the foxe spak so stoutly/the cony laprel and the roek were so sore aferde that they durste not speke but pyked and stryked them out of the court bothe two. and whan they were a room fer in the playne they saide. god graunte that this felle murderare may fare euyl. he can bywrappe and couere his falshede. that his wordes seme as trewe as the gospel herof knoweth noman than we. how shold we brynge wytnesse. it is better that we wyke and departe. than we sholde holde a felde and fyghte with hym. he is so shrewde. ye[a] thaugh ther of vs were fyue we coude not defende vs. but he shold sle vs alle.

While the narrative management in *Reynard the Fox*, as in other groups of animal stories, is episodic, Caxton's version of the epic has decided organization toward a climax. The increasing tension is craftily arranged. Reynard's first false defense is filled with consummate treachery; but his villainy is greater in his second hoodwinking of the king. When honors are finally heaped upon him after his foul play to Isegrim, perfidy is left triumphant. If we turn from such a spectacle of evil to the merry pranks of Brer Rabbit, we are bound to feel some slight restoring of poetic justice in the fact that Brer Fox is always defeated in his efforts to outwit Brer Rabbit. Nothing can bring to life the hens and pigeons and other helpless creatures, even Cuwart the Hare himself, whom Reynard has foully murdered; but it is hard to resist the feeling that the sly Brer Fox is suffering some retribution for the sins of Reynard.

This strong difference in response to the two protagonists suggests a third criterion by which to judge the satirist using animal tales for his allegory. The kinds of smartness displayed by Reynard and Brer Rabbit are, of course, different; but much of the difference in the feeling about them is determined by the attitude toward them displayed in the stories. The establishing of a clear point of view toward the animal characters seems as important a requisite for the successful animal tale as does the focusing on a single dominant trait in the animal. The rejoicing of Uncle Remus and his various hearers in the exploits of Brer Rabbit is an incalculable aid to Harris in communicating the same attitude to the reader; but as he repeatedly says in the introductions to his various volumes, he did not create Uncle Remus's point of view. Brer Rabbit is the hero, in the full admiring sense of the word, of the stories as Harris heard them told by Negro after Negro. To be sure, he is a hero that can be laughed at; but the gay satire is directed at the human foibles of the other animals which lead them into Brer Rabbit's traps. In the stories of Reynard, on the other hand, while there is some mockery of the animals who are Reynard's dupes, the appalling comment on human character comes in Reynard himself. Modern experience of the rise of tyrants through cruelty and lies must intensify response to the revelation of iniquity in Reynard; but there can be no doubt that Caxton intends Reynard to be regarded as a villain. We see that Isegrim is as simpleminded as Brer Wolf; but instead of feeling that his stupidity is mocked, we resent the violence done him. We are conscious of the greed of Bruin and Tybert which helps make them prey to Reynard's wiles; Bellin's desire for importance is directly responsible for his being killed as Cuwart's murderer; and Nobel seems a very unsuspecting monarch indeed to be taken in by Reynard's flattery. But many of the fox's victims have no other weakness than physical helplessness. The revealing light of the allegorical satire is turned most searchingly upon the villainous hero himself; and when he is allowed to go off triumphant in the end, the feeling is that the wicked ways of the world have been convincingly displayed.

Notes

1. *The Philosophy of Rhetoric* (New York: Oxford Univ. Press, 1936), p. 100.

2. *Uncle Remus: His Songs and His Sayings* (New York: Appleton, 1921), pp. 25, 143.

3. *Nights with Uncle Remus* (Boston: Houghton Mifflin, 1911), p. 311. All further quotations from *Uncle Remus* are from this edition.

4. Quotations are from *The History of Reynard the Fox*, translated and printed by William Caxton, ed. Edward Arber (London: 1880), pp. 96 and 71.

"Joel Chandler Harris and the Cornfield Journalist"

Jay Martin*

Visiting the South in 1887, Charles Dudley Warner pronounced it "wide awake to business."[1] A group that centered around the publicity and oratory of Henry Grady had helped to create this condition. Among Grady's friends and co-workers, Joel Chandler Harris was the one most largely responsible for the editorial defense of the New South in Grady's *Atlanta Constitution*. From 1876 until the first decade of the twentieth century, Harris was the editorial paragrapher and then chief editorial writer for this paper. When Grady died in 1889, Harris wrote his biography. Grady was, Harris insisted, "the very embodiment of the Spirit that he aptly named 'the New South' . . . that, reverently remembering and emulating the virtues of the old . . . turns its face to the future."[2] Harris, too, seemed to have turned his face to the future, along with the stock speculators, railroad interests, and textile manufacturers who had wrested control of the state from the planting aristocracy and were bent on keeping it from the rural population. From 1876 until Grady died in 1889, Harris's editorials, widely reprinted in the North, spread an unalloyed gospel of the New South.

One of Harris's closest editorial advisers in the North, Walter Hines Page, spoke of the difference he felt between "Joe Harris" the journalist, and "Joel Chandler Harris" the author.[3] He was sure that the journalist did not appreciate what the author had achieved. Certainly it is true that Harris spoke consistently of his *Uncle Remus* stories as "accidents" and even as "the 'Remus' trash." He claimed in public print that he was merely the editor of the tales he gathered, although he had written and rewritten some of them as many as sixteen times.[4] He seemed uncomfortable with the stories he had written. Although he wrote to J.W. Burlinghame, editor of *Scribner's*, "I wish I were out of newspaper work so I

*Reprinted with the permission of the author from Jay Martin, "Paradises Lost," Ch. 3 of *Harvests of Change: American Literature 1865-1914* (Englewood Cliffs: Prentice-Hall, 1967), pp. 96–100. Professor Martin is Leo S. Bing Professor of Literature at the University of Southern California. He is also a Research Psychoanalyst and Associate of the Southern California Psychoanalytic Institute and member of the faculty of the University of California, Irvine Medical School. His most recent books are *Always Merry and Bright: The Life of Henry Miller* (1978) and *Winter Dreams* (1979).

could devote my whole time to stories and magazine work," he turned down an offer from Gilder and The Century Company whereby he would have received a fixed and adequate income for creative work.[5]

He himself was well, even painfully, aware of the distinction between his two selves. Alluding to the unexpected popularity of his novel *Sister Jane: Her Friends and Acquaintances* (1896), which he considered "poor stuff," he attributed it to the appeal of "the brother" in the book, William Wornum. "No doubt," he wrote,

> that's because the brother represents my inner—my inner—oh well! my inner spezerinktum; I can't think of the other word. It isn't 'self' and it isn't—oh, yes, it's the other fellow inside of me, the fellow who does all my literary work while I get the reputation, being really nothing but a cornfield journalist.[6]

Editors were continually irritated by his doubts—those of the skeptical practical cornfield journalist—of the literary work that the "other fellow" had submitted; on occasion Harris even withdrew work that had already been accepted. In a letter of 1898 to his daughters he again took up the theme of the double self:

> As for myself—though you could hardly call me a real, sure enough author—I never have anything but the vaguest ideas of what I am going to write; but when I take my pen in my hand, the dust clears away and the "other fellow" takes charge. You know all of us have two entities, or personalities. . . . I have often asked my "other fellow" where he gets all his information, and how he can remember, in the nick of time, things that I have forgotten long ago; but he never satisfies my curiousity. He is simply a spectator of my folly until I seize a pen, and then he comes forward and takes charge.
>
> Sometimes I laugh heartily at what he writes. . . . [It] is not my writing at all; it is my "other fellow" doing the work and I am getting all the credit for it. Now, I'll admit that I write the editorials for the paper. The "other fellow" has nothing to do with them, and, so far as I am able to get his views on the subject, he regards them with scorn and contempt.[7]

Much like Edgar Watson Howe, Harris the jovial cornfield journalist kept a firm hand on his literary self, allowing him only the nights, after a day's work had tired the journalist, for his creative riot. He regularly avoided discussions of literary matters. Asked by an editor, for instance, to contribute to a symposium on the historical novel, he characteristically replied: "Now, if you had asked me something about the different brands of pot-liquor, whether that made from collards has a finer flavor than that made from cabbages, . . . you would have found me at home, as the saying is."[8] Lionized in New York in 1882, he refused to make speeches, and even ran into his hotel in a panic. Not long thereafter he would refuse—at the last moment—an offer of $10,000 to lecture with Mark Twain. He was never known to read his Uncle Remus tales in public. Indeed, he even refused to read them to his children. Throughout life, he stuttered or was speechless in the presence of strangers. Characteristically of the psychic complex that underlies stuttering, he avoided novel situations, even (like Charles Lamb, also a stutterer) refusing to change the style of his clothes as he grew older, and so coming to appear slightly antiquated.[9]

But the "other fellow" took his revenge on the journalist of the New South by insisting upon his own, autonomous vision. Gradually—and particularly after the death of Henry Grady, an alter-ego support for the journalist—the publicist of the New South, the journalist himself, was transformed by the insistent energy of his literary self. This transformation came in the Uncle Remus tales, beginning in the late '70s, while Harris was deeply involved in spreading Grady's vision of the New South. In the December 1877 issue of *Lippincott's* Harris had read an article on Negro folklore which, he later said, "gave me my cue, and the legends told by Uncle Remus are the result."[10] Only a few days later he wrote an essay on "The Old Plantation," the myth stirred up in association with the folktales. Here he declared that "the memory of the old plantation will remain green and gracious forever."[11] The Ideal began to encroach upon the Real. This was the work of the "other fellow," and it resulted three years later in *Uncle Remus: His Songs and Sayings: The Folklore of the Old Plantation* (1880). For the next decade the journalist and the writer would run side by side. During the week the journalist celebrated the industrial, progressive New South; but in Harris's tales, songs, and legends, and in the rural, pastoral Nature editorials which regularly appeared on Sundays, the "other fellow" celebrated the epic of the primitive, Edenic world of Uncle Remus.

Announcing in the preface to *Uncle Remus* that his book was to be catalogued with humorous publications, Harris also insisted, contrariwise, that his intention was "perfectly serious": "to give to the whole a genuine flavor of the old plantation" as a "sympathetic supplement" to Harriet Beecher Stowe's *Uncle Tom's Cabin*. Uncle Remus—having "nothing but pleasant memories"[12] of the discipline of slavery—replaces Uncle Tom, as dream replaces reality and the Old South replaces the New. In the stories Uncle Remus—the Negro who serves as a father-figure—initiates the white child—who is the product of the postwar "practical reconstruction"—into "the mysteries of plantation lore," revealing the secret mysteries and rituals of an age now passed. The image of initiation appears regularly. In "The Night Before Christmas," the last and one of the best stories in *Nights with Uncle Remus: Myths and Legends of the Old Plantation* (1883), Uncle Remus takes the boy to the Negro cabins and, in a marvelously ambiguous rite, like a priest announces: "Less go back ter ole times":

"Now, den," Uncle Remus went on, "dey's a little chap yer dat you'll all come ter know mighty well one er deze odd-come-shorts, en dish yer littel chap ain't got so mighty long fer ter set up 'long wid us. Dat bein' de case we oughter take'n put de bes' foot fo'mus fer ter commence wid."

He then leads a hundred voices in a Christmas dance song from the old times, keeping time by striking his breast; and as the little boy drifts into sleep "the song seemed to melt and mingle" into his dreams. It is Christmas day and he has been born anew.[13]

The world into which the boy is initiated is, of course, far from comic. It has the seriousness of the ideal. When one character complains that Uncle Remus never smiles, he replies "with unusual emphasis": "Well, I tell you dis, Sis Tempy, . . . ef deze yer tales wuz des fun, fun, fun, en giggle, giggle, giggle, I let you know I'd done drapt um long ago. Yasser, w'en it come down ter gigglin' you kin des count ole Remus out."[14] Furthermore, in the world of Uncle Remus, ordinary values are transformed. The weak Brer Rabbit regularly wins over the strong fox, wolf, cow, and bear; ultimately all the strong animals die violent deaths: the rabbit ruthlessly murders the wolf, for instance, early in the series. Harris had hinted in his preface to *Uncle Remus* that it was "to a certain extent allegorical" that "it is not virtue that triumphs, but helplessness; it is not malice, but mischievousness."[15] Certainly it is clear that the stories are largely allegorical assertions of the superiority of the weak against the strong—of the power of the Old Plantation against the New Industry; of the primacy of the primitive over the modern, of wisdom over power. "The Story of the Deluge," which Uncle Remus tells, rejects the Noah myth and insists that in a congress of animals the crayfishes became so angry when the elephant stepped on two of their family that they bored down until they made holes for the fountains of the earth to "squirt out" and flood the earth. The weakest animals always, these tales assert, have primary strength. Such tales, of course, originally gave the slave society particular satisfaction by implicitly asserting the superiority of the weak slave over his powerful master. In them Harris found a subtle way of expressing his psychic need to rebel against the industrial program to which, as a journalist, he had been committed by Grady.

After Grady's death, new characters emerged in Harris's world. The persona that Harris the journalist first adopted, Billy Sanders—the "philosopher of Shady Dale"—is a rustic critic of the industrial politics that Grady had promoted. In "Mark and Mack, and the Philosophy of Trusts" (1900), Billy satirizes the way McKinley and Hanna have promoted big business. He dislikes reformers, editors, railroad men, and in general "the scramble after the bright dollar."[16] Another persona, "the Sage of Snap-Bean Farm"—a new Horace, reviving the pastoral Sabine Farm—also emphasizes the kind of agrarian rejection of the new industrialism that was being voiced politically by Tom Watson. Harris's friend and leader of the Southern Populists, Watson had been violently criticized by Grady and the *Atlanta Constitution*. But as the Sage of Snap-Bean Farm, Harris takes Watson's ground. The Farmer refuses to regard science seriously, and insists that "all the political principles that are worth remembering . . . could be placed on one page of a very small book."[17] One of his most critical disquisitions is entitled "The Philosophy of Failure." In this piece, the Sage, finding the modern standards of commercial success unsatisfactory, elevates "the old Colonel, whose history is in decided contrast to everything that stands for . . . success," above the modern businessman, and so implicitly rejects the new industrial values.[18] As in *Uncle Remus*, the primitive conquers the modern, the failure becomes the true success, the weak is the only strong. It is appropriate, then, that Billy Sanders, the Sage, and the old Negro all appeared together as various personae for Harris in *Uncle Remus's Magazine*, which he wrote for the last two years of his life. At last, his other self had become his only self. Defending "things unseen" in his last Christmas editorial, Harris wrote that he "hopes that Santa Claus will come to [children] while they sleep, and that real Fairies will dance in their innocent dreams!"[19] He was living in the world of the "other fellow's" fantasies. Just before he sank into a final unconsciousness preceding death, Harris was asked how he felt. "I am about the extent of a tenth of a gnat's eyebrow better," he replied.[20] No cornfield journalist would have said that. It was the final triumph of the "other fellow."

Perhaps, then, Harris's "other fellow" had indeed been his true self and had taken on the guise of the liberal progressive merely as a mask, in order to continue writing in a South where the literal satirist might be in physical danger. Harris was well aware of the tender sensibilities of his Southern audience. A writer such as Thackeray, Harris wrote in an essay entitled "As to Southern Literature" (1879), "took liberties with the people of his own blood and time that would have led him hurriedly in the direction of bodily discomfort if he had lived in the South."[21] Masked as a cornfield journalist, a harmless darky, and a jovial farmer, Harris satirized the South emerging in his time by questioning all of the values it was developing. Fearing the results of writing direct satire, he adopted personae who could transmute and suppress the satirical into the allegorical impulse.

Notes

1. Warner's visit was in 1887, and the quotation is taken from an article, "The South Revisited," *Harper's*, 74 (March 1887), 638. It was later reprinted in *Studies in the South and West . . .* (1889), in *The Complete Writings of Charles Dudley Warner* (Hartford: American Publishing Co., 1904), Vol. VIII, p. 123.

2. *The Life of Henry W. Grady*, [. . .] *Edited by Joel Chandler Harris (Uncle Remus)* (New York: Cassell Publishing Co., 1890), p. 59.

3. Page's remarks in an interview, "The New South," in the *Boston Post*, 28 (September 1881, quoted in Julia Collier Harris, *The Life and Letters of Joel Chandler Harris* (Boston and New York: Houghton Mifflin, 1918), pp. 177–78.

4. It is interesting to note that one of Theodore Roosevelt's uncles had earlier taken down some Brer Rabbit stories from an old Negress's dictation, and published these verbatim in *Harper's* where, as Roosevelt testifies, "they fell flat." Only with much labor did Harris give them permanent life.

5. *Life and Letters*, pp. 310, 214.

6. *Life and Letters*, p. 345.

7. *Life and Letters*, pp. 384–85.

8. *Life and Letters*, pp. 565–66.

9. *Life and Letters*, pp. 57–58, 178.

10. "An Accidental Author," *Lippincott's*, N.S. 11 (April 1886), 419.

11. The quotations from Harris's essays in this chapter are in *Joel Chandler Harris: Editor and Essayist*, ed. Julia Collier Harris (Chapel Hill: Univ. of North Carolina Press, 1931). This quotation, from "The Old Plantation," is found on p. 91.

12. "Introduction" to *Uncle Remus: His Songs and His Sayings* (New York: D. Appleton, 1880), p. vi.

13. "The Night Before Christmas," in *Nights with Uncle Remus* (Boston and New York: James R. Osgood, 1883), pp. 412, 413, 415.

14. *Nights*, p. 338.

15. "Introduction" to *Uncle Remus: His Songs and His Sayings*, p. xiv.

16. "Mr. Billy Sanders Discourses on the Negro Problem" in *Joel Chandler Harris: Editor and Essayist*, p. 216.

17. "Shakespeare of Modern Business" in *Joel Chandler Harris: Editor and Essayist*, p. 389.

18. "The Philosophy of Failure," in *Joel Chandler Harris: Editor and Essayist*, p. 300.

19. "Santa Claus and the Fairies" in *Joel Chandler Harris: Editor and Essayist*, p. 335.

20. *Life and Letters*, p. 588.

21. *Joel Chandler Harris: Editor and Essayist*, p. 44.

[Duplicity and Cynicism in Harris's Humor]

Jesse Bier*

A little later [than the era of Charles Henry Smith's "Bill Arp"], in the case of Joel Chander Harris (no relation to G[eorge]W[ashington] Harris), we face at once the most fetching and deep-leveled cynical inversions in the entire period and perhaps in the whole of American humor. He achieves his fame by turning traditional values inside out for a regional but dubious triumph, the true character of which he does not fully measure. The violent Uncle Remus tales are given a duplicitous framework of gentle and charming interlocution between the boy and the old Negro retainer, and the fables themselves engagingly teach the wildest chicanery. The stories propound a cynical ethic of success at any cost, placing the rabbit (the wily, unreconstructed south) against the fox (the predatory north), allowing Brer Rabbit any means to the end of survival. There is no question of giving even lip service to an older code, acknowledging that outwitting, cheating, or tricking are bad form. The rule is: Don't be outwitted, cheated, or tricked. And this con-man defensiveness is easily converted into defensive aggression; he laughs last who outwits best. The Negro dialect is but a supreme ruse, as a superficial device one of the great implicit jokes in the history of American humor. The blackface mask and voice were taken in earnest by the south, and Uncle Remus' partisanship for the rabbit, who joyously and cunningly outtricks his oppressors, was Harris' own.

If might does not make right, guile does, as the Negro learned for whatever good it might have done him. Like the Freudian dream work, the frequent mechanics of humor are bizarre displacement and witful substitution, and the motive is wish fulfillment. Thus a history of American comedy turns comic itself, tracing the spiral-like inversions of value; our insights flash from brackets within parentheses set in digressionary

*Reprinted from Jesse Bier, " 'The Literary Comedians': The Civil War and Reconstruction," Ch. III of *The Rise and Fall of American Humor* (New York, Chicago, San Francisco: Holt, Rinehart and Winston, 1968), pp. 80–82, 92–95. Copyright ©1968 by Jesse Bier. Reprinted by permission of the author and Holt, Rinehart and Winston, Publishers. Jesse Bier has been Professor of American Literature at the University of Montana for fifteen years, although he has held visiting positions elsewhere, including the Chair of American Literature at the University of Lausanne, Switzerland. He has written four books and published articles in *The Humanist*, *American Literature*, *Virginia Quarterly Review*, *Esquire*, and other journals.

passages more in context than the text. We see the enslaving south twice enslaved itself, first by the vindictive north and then by Negro psychology, whose subversiveness it uses to be free of the other. Further, the Negro, later in Faulkner, as in actual experience, will have to appropriate the old imperturbability of the white south to aid him in a resurgence of his own from southern reconquest. If the re-emergence of white supremacy comes in great part from the seriocomic lesson of Negro psychology, the endurance of the Negroes is relearned in equal part from the example of deviousness and flexibility in the reorganized southern psyche. In the end, it is a matter of which resiliency will win—and a comic dumb show beneath directs a violent drama above. It is the American subtlety under all the overt American action and mayhem.

Meanwhile, with our normal modern sensibilities, we tend to be amused and gratified at the spectacle of literal black slaves and ex-slaves seizing any psychologic means to their end. But we do not grant the ex-slave owners the same means to their renewed ends, and are scandalized when we penetrate the heavy disguise of Harris and the enormous but unconscious deception of his cynicism. If we are also partly amused, that is because we seek general, annihilatory laughter as a way to explode the con-man confusion that stems from Harris' brilliant added inspiration, probably suggested to him by previous southwest example.

But the north was not without its newly prevalent ethic or non-ethic of success. Artemus Ward's blatant cynicism becomes a kind of national aphorism, though Browne's aim was direct exposé: "You scratch my back and Ile scratch your back." Connivance at any cost and at the expense of any person is the target that figures in Browne's most critical humor, more realistic than extravagant by now, as exemplified in *Artemus Ward: His Travels* (1865).

> "Say, Bill, wot you done with that air sorrel mare of yourn?"
> "Sold her," said William with a smile of satisfaction.
> "Wot'd you git?"
> "Hund'd an fifty dollars, cash deown!"
> "Show! Hund'd an' fifty for that kickin' spavin'd critter? Who'd you sell her to?"
> "Sold her to mother!"
> "Wot!" exclaimed brother No. 1, "did you railly sell that kickin' spavin'd critter to mother? Wall, you *air* a shrewd one!"

The difference between [Henry Wheeler] Shaw and Browne, on one side, and Joel Chandler Harris, on the other, lies in their overview. But our attention is directed in either case to a pervasive amoralism abroad in the land, which furnishes capital for either humorous exposé or propaganda. And so we dare conclude again that humor, like literature in general, is an index to mentality, probably the swiftest register of changing value in the recesses of national mind.

In his depths, Joel Chandler Harris takes a basically antithetical position toward inherited and mouthed values: "Proudness in a man don't count none if his head is cold." In the Aesopian guise of the freed slave, he sets himself against the old southern code of gentility, honor, and pride and against northern victory and rapacity. As for Charles Henry Smith, the attitude of his Bill Arp is unreconstructed antagonism, although he generally avoids being mordant [. . . .]

[Following a discussion of grotesquerie in humor and an allusion to Eugene Field's "grotesque and mischievous sadism" in the *Denver Tribune*, Bier again turns to Harris:]

And we may advert topically again to Joel Chandler Harris. The instances of reciprocal cruelty and incessant grotesque revenge that accompany the tactics of witting and outwitting in the fables are legion. In a gleeful cannibalistic climax Brer Rabbit brings home the fox's head to Mrs. Rabbit for a triumphant broth. And everyone knows the catalogue of inexpressible deaths that the captive rabbit guesses is on the fox's mind in "The Wonderful Tar-Baby Story."

> "'En who stuck you up dar whar you iz? Nobody in de roun' worril. You des tuck 'en jam yo'se'f on dat Tar-Baby widout waitin' fer enny invite', ses Brer Fox, sezee, 'en dar you is, en dar' you'll stay twel I fixes up a bresh-pile and fires her up, kaze I'm gwineter bobbycue you dis day, sho', sez Brer Fox, sezee.
> "Den Brer Rabbit talk mighty 'umble.
> " 'I don't keer w'at you do wid me, Brer Fox,' sezee, 'so you don't fling me in dat brier-patch. Roas' me, Brer Fox,' sezee, 'but don't fling me in dat brier-patch,' sezee.
> " 'Hit's so much trouble fer ter kindle a fier,' sez Brer Fox, sezee, 'dat I speck I'll hatter hang you,' sezee.
> "Hang me dez ez high as you please, Brer Fox,' sez Brer Rabbit, sezee, 'but do fer de Lord's sake don't fling me in dat brier-patch,' sezee.
> " 'I ain't got no string,' sez Brer Fox, sezee, 'en now I speck I'll hatter drown you,' sezee.
> " 'Drown me dez ez deep ez you please, Brer Fox,' sez Brer Rabbit, sezee, 'but don't fling me in dat brier-patch,' sezee.
> " 'Dey ain't no water nigh,' sez Brer Fox, sezee, 'en now I speck I'll hatter skin you,' sezee.
> " 'Skin me, Brer Fox,' sez Brer Rabbit, sezee, 'snatch out my eyeballs, t'ar out my years by de roots, en cut off my legs,' sezee, 'but do please, Brer Fox, don't fling me in dat brier-patch,' sezee."

And the possible roasting, hanging, drowning, skinning, and dismemberment all make Brer Rabbit's blows, kicks and headbuttings on the stubbornly reticent Tar-Baby look like positively gentle assaults—assaults (which the fox had counted on in the nature of things) for the Tar-Baby's not saying good morning at the start of the tale. In a still later work, "Brother Rabbit's Laughing Place," Brer Fox is led to a secret grove that happens to contain a hidden hornet's nest. From judiciously chosen sidelines the rabbit laughs "fit to kill" at the fox's yowling among those thickets and vines and hornets. He explains at the last that all he had promised was to show "*my* laughing place."

There is, unmistakably, a high quantum of aggression, gratuitous and personal, that informs all the levels and regional settings of the humor of the period. There is no coyness, and there are few indirections when it occurs. The thrusts of cruelty are naked, the revelations of sadism frank, and the grotesquerie of violent or morbid action insistent.

The conspiracy of cruelty and the fantasy of amoralism intimately shared by the little plantation white boy and Uncle Remus light up a subsidiary question in American literature and race relations. Critics whose unorthodoxy has become standard by now have seen piquant suggestions of homosexuality and expiation in relationships similar to that of Harris' framework characters, in Twain's Huck and Jim and Faulkner's Chick and Lucius Beauchamps or Lucius Priest and Uncle Ned later on, or indeed Cooper's Leatherstocking and Chingochook [sic] and Melville's Ishmael and Queequeg in classic American literature before Joel Chandler Harris. But from our vantage point, we are not so sure of the accuracy or exclusive relevance of such factors, as particularly expounded by the literary critic, Leslie Fiedler. Kenneth Lynn's insight, especially into the comic pairs of racial protagonists, gives another dimension to the issue. He infers a theme of common alienation, in which the white hero joins the colored in voluntary rejection of prevailing injustices or absurdities. Quite operative, then, is a democratic inclination toward a broader human solidarity of the oppressed and disaffected, a comic and rebellious companionship. It is no accident that most of these relationships have something of an extravagant minstrel unity and revelry as their basis. Furthermore, at least half of Melville's, Twain's, and Faulkner's juxtapositions are conceived as comic characterizations in themselves as well as indirect and humane criticisms of society. To suggest that the power of Eros, especially in companionable revolt, can transcend the usual psychoanalytic classifications may strike an old-fashioned note nowadays. But it is no more vulnerable as an explanation than to suggest that Nigger Jim's address of "honey" to Huck Finn was no regional southernism, natural in their fugitive camaraderie, but a sort of pre-Freudian slip of the tongue.[1] We need not argue the fact that in the famous relationship portrayed by Twain, Jim, who is much older than Huck, was separated from his own children and that he naturally displaced, but did not misplace, his paternal affections on the fourteen-year-old boy. In these matters rigorous psychoanalysts will not necessarily accept paternal regard as an irreducible emotion. How they might dispose

of the relation (other than to ignore it very hard, as they have done) between decrepit Uncle Remus and his young interlocutor, between a
manifest grandfather figure and a boy in the classic stage of latency, remains a puzzle.

Clearly there is another factor involved, and the comic pairing of the
races which Harris gives us is a significant clue. First of all, the conjunction of the two suggests, as in other standard cases, that the very pairing
of the races is a renunciation of the culture's artificial separation of them
and is comic reduction of arbitrary superiority. It is true that some
American comedians, from Browne to W.C. Fields, are touched by racial
prejudice, and even Twain had his blindness about Indians. We cannot
avoid human variety and bias even among comedians. But in those cases
where sympathetic racial pairing does exist, the gross antithetical function of the humor in our WASP culture is obvious. We overlook it only
because our infatuation with subtlety intervenes. Moreover, as in the
minstrel background of such pairings, the very mixture itself is broadly
comic, as well as blasphemous, by virtue of unlikely contrast and of the
outlandish comic harmony unexpectedly derived from it. These are factors that must be put together with whatever is tenable theory about
homosexual undercurrent and expiation, especially with respect to clearly
comic intentions and to those relationships, like Joel Chandler Harris',
which are purged of all sexuality and inferred guilt.

In such a relationship as Harris depicts, the second infancy of Uncle
Remus and the primary one of the lad conspire, in an insulated free fantasy, to give us parables of the purest comic amorality, rising from the
deepest wishes of the new south and of the author himself. We may be
taught that the superego is as devious and as manifold as the id. And we
are reminded to frame our judgments in the widest and most appropriate
cultural settings as well as in nether regions of the hidden heart.

Notes

1. At the 1966 Senate Committee Hearings on the plight of the urban Negro, Senator
Ribicoff was addressed by the New York Negro writer, Claude Brown, who was responding
to Ribicoff's unfeigned sympathy, in this manner: ". . . you are beautiful, Baby." Harlemese
is a repository of the older southernisms and, in fact, is the chief contemporary means for rein-
fusing comic, and therefore unabashed, affectionate expression into our slang, song lyrics,
and everyday speech.

"Harris' Achievement"

Paul M. Cousins*

The death of Joel Chandler Harris at the age of fifty-nine was widely and deeply mourned. Messages of sympathy came to his family from all parts of the country, the first of which was from President Roosevelt. Editorials in the press were also warmly appreciative both of the man himself and of the significance of his work as an author. In its evening edition of the day before his death, the Atlanta *Journal* wrote of the artless skill with which he had taken the folklore of the antebellum Negro and opened up a new vein in the literature of the Southern people. It said that as a man and a citizen, as well as an ornament to the world of letters, he was needed to leaven the crude materialism of the times. Clark Howell, editor of the *Constitution*, who had known Harris more intimately than any other man in Atlanta since the death of his father Evan P. Howell, wrote of him as follows in the *Constitution* in its edition the day after his death:

> From all of his studied unobtrusiveness, the man wrought himself a broad and firm place in the spiritual history and traditions of his people; and it is from things spiritual that the things of substance take their color and substance. . . . His reputation is worldwide because he was the articulate voice of that humble race, whose every mood and tense he knew with complete comprehension. His mission was—and is—broader. For his folklore and his novels, his short stories and his poems breathe consistently a distinguished philosophy. It was the creed of optimism, of mutual trust, and of tolerance of all living things, of common sense and of idealism that is worthwhile because it fits the unvarnished duty of every hour.

The editors of newspapers and magazines outside Atlanta who had known Harris only through his literary work also wrote of him with a particular emphasis on the value of his contributions to America's literature. The Philadelphia *Inquirer* declared that no man since Abraham Lincoln

*Reprinted by permission of the author and Louisiana State University Press from Paul M. Cousins, Ch. 12 of *Joel Chandler Harris: A Biography* (Baton Rouge: Louisiana State Univ. Press, ©1968 by Louisiana State University Press), pp. 219–24. Dr. Cousins, formerly President of Shorter College, Rome, Ga., is a retired Professor of English at Mercer University.

had got nearer to the hearts of the whole people than Harris had succeeded in doing.[1] The Boston *Herald* said that it would be hard to say whether the North or the South would mourn more sincerely the death of Joel Chandler Harris or the more keenly feel his loss. His stories were familiar to the South, it said, but to the North they were a revelation of little-known characters and conditions of life, which were all the more delightful because they were foreign to anything of which the North had had personal experience. His stories, the Washington *Star* asserted, had done more to make the life of the Old South familiar and charming to Northern readers than had the work of any other Southern writer, and that they must be counted as one of those potent influences which, during the last two decades, had so greatly influenced and softened Northern opinion of the South.[2]

These and other expressions of regret over the death of Harris merely confirmed a feeling which had long existed that Harris was the most beloved author in America during his lifetime. If, however, he had lived for more years and had continued to write, he would probably have added nothing new or original to what he had already written. This conclusion is justified by the pleasing but mediocre quality of the essays, poems, stories, and book reviews which he wrote for *Uncle Remus's Magazine*. He was physically weary and his genius was no longer inspired or creative. By 1908, the plantation South had already become a remote period in the rapidly evolving history of the South. By then, too, the South which Harris had known during four years of civil war and the even more tragic years of poverty and civic strife that had immediately followed was now well on its way to a new social and economic order. It had resumed its place in a reunion of the states, and its younger generation looked toward the future with glowing faith in their destiny. Since his genius as a writer was primarily nostalgic, it was fitting that Southern authors younger than he should survey the various aspects of an emerging new Southern culture and that hands other than his should reflect them in their work.

Harris had not been a giant among the writers of American fiction. He had never written a short story with the precision of technique as Poe had done, nor had he composed a novel which compared with the sombre Puritan tragedy of Hawthorne's *The Scarlet Letter*, or with the conflict between the destructive forces of evil in Melville's *Moby-Dick*, or with the psychological penetration and meticulous attention to style and structure that had characterized Henry James's novels. He had never become severely critical of the human race and its institutions of government and church as Mark Twain had done after the publication of his *Huckleberry Finn*. He had, however, within the limitations of his own ability as a literary technician done his work well. In Uncle Remus he had created an immortal character in American fiction, and his stories of fantasy and fact in a setting of the Old South had brought pleasure to countless readers both young and old over a period of twenty-five years and earned for him a respected place among his contemporary American writers.

It has often been the fate, however, of an author who was greatly beloved, widely read, and highly honored in his own day to be lightly considered by a succeeding generation if changing times produced a new culture. However, Harris' stories of both the Old and the New South had a lasting interest to readers even in the midst of the social and literary changes which were taking place both in the South and in America as a whole between 1880 and 1908. The republication of the folklore tales attests the current interest in them. In 1946 Walt Disney Productions brought out Disney's *Uncle Remus Stories*, with the dialect somewhat modernized, an edition with colored illustrations of fourteen of the legends from *Told by Uncle Remus* and *Uncle Remus and his Friends* upon which was based the successful motion picture, "The Song of the South." A letter from Houghton Mifflin Company, Boston, on February 2, 1966, stated that their edition of *Favorite Uncle Remus* in 1948 had had a total of nine printings with a sale of 43,000 copies, and that their edition of *The Complete Tales of Uncle Remus* in a single volume in 1955 had gone through five printings of 32,000 copies as of that date. No listing of the characters of the most permanent appeal in American fiction would be complete unless it contained Uncle Remus, nor would any anthology of the most representative stories of the Old South be fully authentic that did not include some of the folklore tales told by Uncle Remus.

No complete edition of the works of Harris has yet been issued, and the volumes of his non-folklore stories have been allowed to go out of print. It remains true, however, that the social and the literary historians of the South before 1908, the students of the English language in America, the scientific folklorists, and the general reader who may be interested in a trustworthy presentation in fictional form of the plantation and early industrial South will find in them a dependable source of information and an ample reward for the time spent in reading them.

In these stories Harris created many memorable characters who were as indigenous to the South as was Uncle Remus but who were overshadowed by him. The list is a long and worthy one. It contains, among others, Miss Sally and the first Little Boy, Mingo, Blue Dave, Mink, African Jack, Sis Tempy, Daddy Jake, Free Joe, Ananias, Aunt Minervy Ann, Mrs. Feratia Bivins, Sister Jane, Grandsir Johnny Roach, Uncle Jimmy Cosby, Gabriel Tolliver, Major Tumlin Perdue, and Billy Sanders. Harris endowed each of them with life, and in the stories through which they moved he recaptured and preserved for subsequent generations the various features of the old plantation culture.

Harris loved the South with a genuine devotion. He knew its people with a comprehensive understanding of their faults and virtues as no other Southern author of his day knew them, and he strongly felt that the antebellum writers of Southern fiction had given a distorted picture of their culture by overemphasizing its romantic features and by including its sectional politics. It was his major purpose in his own fiction to correct that misrepresentation, and in his effort to do so he revealed the Southern mores in both their romantic and realistic features in the belief that factual knowledge brings understanding. He asserted that there was little fundamental difference between James Russell Lowell's Hosea Bigelow and William Tappan Thompson's Major Joseph Jones. The end result was that through his stories he became the apostle of reconciliation between the North and the South.

Southern writers of the twentieth century are therefore indebted to Harris for his pioneer leadership in moving Southern literature from ultraromanticism to realism. Howard W. Odum, in his *An American Epoch*, appraised Harris' work as that of a "vigorous realist, in which he never forgot the tragedies of the South, the poor white man, the darker aspects of slavery, the separation of families, and the hypocrisies reflected in sentimentality and religiosity." He said that Harris had picked out from a mass of Southern ruins what had been considered to be inchoate materials and that through clear delineation, a new and effective form, admirable proportions, rhythm and sympathy, he had developed an art that was at once harmonious and beautiful. Odum concluded his analysis of Harris' realistic treatment of life in the South by characterizing him as an essentially modern Southerner crying in the wilderness as a forerunner of those who in the first quarter of the twentieth century had turned the searchlight upon the Southern scene.[3]

In his political affiliation, Harris was a Democrat, but he was liberal in his views and he never used his stories for the propagation of sectional politics. He was openminded and held the welfare of the nation as a whole above that of any section of it. Although his genius as an author shone to best advantage in his interpretation of the South's past, his vision for its future extended beyond cultural and political boundaries. He roundly condemned the radical politicians for the emergence of the Negro problem after the war, and he greatly admired the constructive contribution which Booker T. Washington was making toward the improvement of the lot of Negroes in the South as the president of Tuskegee Institute in Alabama. In an editorial in the *Constitution* on September 20, 1895, he praised the address which Washington had given in Atlanta the day before at the Cotton States and International Exposition as the most remarkable address ever delivered by a Negro in Atlanta. The speech stamped him, Harris said, as a wise counsellor and a safe leader. In turn, Washington later commended Harris for his sane discussion of the problem in the articles which he had contributed to the *Saturday Evening Post*, January 2, January 30, and February 2, 1904. The bugaboo of social equality never frightened Harris. He believed that the problem could be solved through the patient and constructive cooperation of both the whites and the Negroes in the South if the radical politicians would not interfere. The responsibility, he said, for a successful solution must be shared by both races with an intelligent leadership.

Although the South has made remarkable advances in every phase of its culture since Harris' death in 1908, his contribution toward its advancement was a significant and permanent one. He will be remembered by those who, like him, place loyalty to their common country above a blind and emotional loyalty to any one section of it, by those who in private and public life take their stand for simple justice to all men irrespective of their race or creed, by those who respect the dignity of the individual without regard to his social, economic, political, or color status, and by those, who out of their generosity of mind, spirit, and wholesome humor, help to soften the blows that afflict erring humanity.

The man and his work were one. Painfully shy, extremely sensitive, and perhaps always conscious—who shall say—of the circumstances of his humble origin, he exhibited in both his life and literature a cheerful philosophy of goodwill and reconciliation that was not born of any shallow optimism. Along the road which he traveled from the poverty and obscurity of his childhood to international fame as an author in his mature years, he wrestled at times in the loneliness of his own soul with personal problems which could have defeated him, but he overthrew them without any erosion of his gentle, genial, and compassionate nature.

Notes

1. Reprinted in the *Atlanta Journal*, 4 July 1908.
2. *Boston Herald*, 5 July 1908.
3. Howard W. Odum, *An American Epoch* (New York: Henry Holt, 1930), pp. 299, 300.

"Joel Chandler Harris in the Currents of Change"

Arlin Turner*

Joel Chandler Harris insisted that he was not a literary author, but a "paragrapher," a "cornfield journalist." At his retirement in 1900, he could look back on thirty-five years in journalism, the last twenty-four years with the Atlanta *Constitution*. During those years he was able to take up his literary pen only after a day at the newspaper office, and he claimed no more lofty origin for what he wrote than the Wren's Nest, Snap-Bean Farm, Shady Dale, or a slave cabin. These claims are consistent with the characterization of Harris which Paul M. Cousins presents in his new biography, that he was uncommonly modest and shy, and was ever fearful of being enticed out of his retirement.

He traveled to New Orleans to meet Mark Twain and George W. Cable; he later visited the White House to have dinner with President Theodore Roosevelt. Though he ventured away from home now and then on lesser occasions than these, it was no small matter for him to leave Atlanta. Following a banquet at the Tile Club in New York in 1882 he gave no ground when he was urged to speak; he "suffered the agony of the damned twice over," he wrote afterward. Another day he packed hastily and took the train for Atlanta, rather than risk having the experience repeated at another banquet he had agreed to attend. Five years later an invitation to lecture at Nashville drew his reply: "I could not do so though you were to offer me $100,000,000. I never appeared before a public audience in my life, and the very thought of such a thing is horrifying." Even a small private audience was horrifying. In New Orleans, Harris could not be persuaded to read an Uncle Remus story for the children who had gathered at Cable's house to see him. "After days of intimacy," Mark Twain found Harris's shyness "in about as strong force as ever," but he

*A review-essay on Paul M. Cousins, *Joel Chandler Harris: A Biography* (1968), reprinted with the permission of the author and the publisher from *Southern Literary Journal*, 1 (Autumn 1968), 105–111. Arlin Turner (1909–1980) was James B. Duke Professor of English Emeritus at Duke University and Therese Kayser Lindsey Professor of Literature at Southwest Texas State University. He served as visiting professor in Australia, Canada, England, and India. His publications include articles and reviews in several scholarly journals and a number of books, including *George W. Cable: A Biography* (1956) and the definitive *Nathaniel Hawthorne: A Biography* (1980).

added, "There is a fine and beautiful nature hidden behind it." The consensus of those who knew Harris was to endorse Mark Twain's statement.

Harris laid claim to only a small domain, middle Georgia. On that region he spoke with the assurance of one who knew it well; on others he normally spoke with diffidence. In the rare instances when he broke his normal practice, he stood ready to draw back, acknowledging that it was risky to generalize from his own Putnam and surrounding counties. The Banjo War resulted, for example, when he wrote in the *Critic* that he had heard plantation Negroes play several different instruments but never the banjo. Readers came forward with testimony that the banjo was common on plantations in many parts of the South. Harris of course undertook to speak only for middle Georgia.

Soon after the first book of Uncle Remus tales appeared in 1880, an erudite essay in the *Popular Science Monthly* of April, 1881, viewed the folklore of Harris's tales in comparison with the lore of Europe, Africa, and Asia. Prompted by this and other comparisons, Harris set about the study of international folklore and incorporated his findings in an introduction to his second collection, *Nights with Uncle Remus*, 1883. Even in the introduction he was half-apologetic, however, and noted that in these no less than the earlier tales his main purpose was to capture something of plantation life in the old days. At a later date he mentioned this discussion of folklore and remarked that the author "is willing to make an affidavit that he knows no more on the subject than a blind horse knows about Sunday."

Middle Georgia was a large enough lump of earth for Harris, as Nathaniel Hawthorne once said about his native New England. In 1893 Harris declared, without equivocation: "Middle Georgia was and is the center of the most unique—the most individual—civilization the Republic has produced." To his mind the region represented by Eatonton and Putnam County was beyond compare in kindness and generosity. His mother, unwed and abandoned by his father, had found the community friendly and willing to furnish the work she needed to support herself and her son. Then the apprenticeship he began as a boy of twelve on Turnwold plantation offered him ideal opportunities. When Harris called his middle Georgia thoroughly democratic, as he often did, he seems to have had reference less to politics than to the sort of kindness he and his mother received from those in position to help them.

This past moved irretrievably away from Harris, and with distance it became encased in a mellow glow. Leaving Turnwold at the end of the war, he worked in several Georgia towns and went as far as New Orleans before settling, not in Putnam County, but in Atlanta. More important still, Harris's middle Georgia was caught up in change—the immediate change produced by military defeat and emancipation, and the continuing change required for reshaping the Southern social and economic structure.

The new biography by Paul M. Cousins draws a clear and sympathetic picture of Harris: a warm human being, kindly, optimistic, and staunchly convinced of man's goodness. Mr. Cousins presents Harris against the land, the people, and the time which produced him. He writes from within Harris and his contemporaries, showing how Harris viewed himself and his works, and how he and others viewed the South of their time and earlier. The most convincing and most detailed recreation is the Joseph Addison Turner plantation, where the young Harris read in the plantation library, began his career as a journalist, and observed plantation life in transition from the stability of the slave era to the uncertainty and threat which followed the war. The tone of the book echoes Harris's backward look, his nostalgia for an era he continued to see in the freshness of an expanding boyhood. This quality of intimacy and sympathy was the biographer's goal, and it is the great merit of the book.

It was this past, so relished by Harris and so successfully recreated by his biographer, that gave Harris his most distinctive work—the Uncle Remus tales. An editorial Harris wrote on "The Old Plantation" for the *Constitution* of December 9, 1877, suggests the way in which the past of his youth remained with him. After recalling the days and the nights on the plantation, he concludes:

> But alas! all these are gone. The moon pursues her pathway as serenely as of old, but she no longer looks down upon the scenes that were familiar to your youth. The old homestead and the barn are given up to decay, and the songs of the negroes have been hushed into silence by the necessities of a new dispensation. The old plantation, itself, is gone. It has passed away, but the hand of time, inexorable, yet tender, has woven about it the sweet suggestions of poetry and romance, memorials that neither death nor decay can destroy.

The tales Harris put into the mouth of Uncle Remus came to him from the slave quarters, he reported, many of them from tellers he had heard at the Turner plantation and others relayed to him after his first tales had been published. Although Harris declared that he was no more than a re-teller, adding nothing of his own, Mark Twain protested that "the stories are only alligator pears—one eats them merely for the sake of the dressing." That dressing contains the ingredients of Harris's genius: his understanding of the subtle relations existing in the plantation society among the owners, the household slaves, the field hands, and the poor-whites; his view of motives and morality simplified to elemental terms; and his faith that a saving balance prevails, with the weak protected by compensating qualities and by their weakness itself.

Uncle Remus spins his yarns from a mind turned backward, to an unchanging era in Putnam County, when creatures and things were "monstus stout." "In dem days," Uncle Remus says, "Miss Meadows's bed-cord would a hilt a mule." Affairs of a later time appear only as they are caught in the periphery of the backward glance. But Harris's newspaper career of course held his focus on daily topics, at a time when America was engulfed in change, and particularly in the deep South the economic, political, and social foundations were awash. He did not initiate or encourage reform, as George W. Cable did, nor did he join those who dreamed of returning to an impossible past. Rather, he was a pragmatist and a meliorist, with an overriding faith in mankind. In editorials, essays, and fiction his plea was for acceptance, for making the best of things, as a way of lessening strife and pain. After the close of the Civil War, he urged reconciliation of the sections. The story "Aunt Fountain's Prisoner" brings a Union soldier back to the South after the surrender to marry and settle down and to furnish the narrator "a practical illustration of the fact that one may be a Yankee and a Southerner too, simply by being a large-hearted, whole-souled American." With emancipation a reality, Harris offered no defense of slavery. He more than once, in fact, dwelt on the evils of slavery, with stress on the suffering of the slaves and comparable stress on inhumanity among the whites. The story "Where's Duncan?" reaches an eerie resolution in the death by fire of the three principals in an affair which is more hinted than recounted: a plantation owner, a mulatto slave woman, and the son of theirs whom the father sold as a child long ago. Another story, "Mom Bi," turns on less dramatic but subtler elements in the slave-master relations. When the Union soldiers have brought freedom to Mom Bi, she sets out in search of a child who was sold away from her years before. To the question whether she will not say goodbye to the owner's family, she replies only, "I done been fergive you." She forgave them, she says, when she saw them give up their son to death in the war.

In "Free Joe and the Rest of the World" Spite Calderwood is a heartless, vindictive slaveowner; the pathetic Free Joe illustrates the fate of the free Negro in slave times and suggests also the pitiable estate Harris saw the freedmen slipping into after emancipation. The greatest mistake of the Southern whites after the Civil War, Harris wrote in an editorial for the *Constitution*, was in not taking the Negroes into economic and political partnership, instead of allowing them to fall into the hands of others ready to exploit them. As this statement suggests, Harris believed the former slaves were so dependent on the whites that their future in America could be only what the white society would allow. But Harris saw no basis for protest here. For he assumed the Southern whites would be generous and kindly. He said next to nothing of the freedmen's rights; he did not think of them as citizens. For all his sympathy, he could see the Negroes only from a distance, the distance inevitable to one member of a society looking at members on another level above or below.

Harris's views on the freedmen in America during the forty-three years he lived after Appomattox were largely the views held by moderate Southerners who were conservative in outlook. Accepting the outcome of the war, he spoke out for reunion. Recognizing that the sectionalism produced by slavery in the Old South and its aftermath in the New South caused a variety of ills, he asked for tolerance and freedom from sectional demands. He spoke with special force in urging that literary authors be liberated from all requirements to support a sectional point of view. Believing that the ex-slaves would have basic rights as American citizens, he urged the Negroes to prepare themselves for citizenship and urged the whites to accept them in their new status. Harris joined others in approving Booker T. Washington's program for the Negroes—to seek advancement in the areas open to them, while postponing until later the troublesome question of public rights. In a letter of April 2, 1880, he called himself "an uncompromising state rights democrat." In keeping with his shy nature, his faith in human goodness, and his distrust of rapid change, he believed that best solutions to the race problem, as with others, would be found close to home.

As legal restrictions were imposed on the rights of Negroes, most notably the state laws on segregation and voting qualifications passed in the 1890's, Harris could accept them; for he thought the forces of melioration would thus be more effective. Since dissatisfaction with the new restrictions was voiced occasionally (by Cable, for one, and some spokesmen for the Negroes), and since there was still some possibility of national interference, Harris in effect reversed the position he had taken earlier. Whereas he formerly exhorted white Southerners to accept the Negroes in their post-war role, which he assumed would be permanent, he now justified the new policies of restriction and encouraged the Negroes to accept the new dispensation and strive for the kind of improvement it envisaged. The change in Harris's purpose can be illustrated by comparing his early editorials, in both content and tone, with the three essays on the Negro question he wrote for the *Saturday Evening Post* in 1904. His humanitarian nature had not changed, nor his wish to meliorate the conditions of both whites and blacks. But laws and public outlook had changed, and the requirements for peace and improvement were no longer the ones Harris had recognized in the two decades after the Civil War.

The new definition of the Negro's position in American life pleased Harris because it promised immediate dividends in peace and well-being for both races. (He gave less weight to the compromise with right and equality.) Moreover it reduced the threat of disruptive change, which had grown more and more distasteful to him as he grew older, and had driven him to look more and more into the past.

"Daddy Joel Harris and His Old-Time Darkies"

Darwin T. Turner*

Most readers identify Joel Chandler Harris with only one Negro—Uncle Remus, who blends wisdom and childishness in proportions which have endeared him to generations of white and black American readers. To presume that Uncle Remus is Harris's archetypal Negro, however, is to misunderstand Harris's use of Remus and to minimize the powers of observation of an author who recognized and reproduced physical, mental, and emotional differences in slaves and freedmen.

For example, Aaron, the Arab (*The Story of Aaron*, 1896, and *Aaron in the Wildwoods*, 1897), has a well-shaped head, sharp black eyes, thin lips, a prominent nose, and thick, wavy hair. Descended from a tribe of brown-skinned dwarfs, who "were always at war with the blacks,"[1] Tasma Tid, who has straight, glossy black hair, is "far above the average negro in intelligence, in courage and in cunning, . . . as obstinate as a mule, . . . uncanny when she chose to be, outspoken, vicious, and tenderhearted."[2] Blue Dave ("Blue Dave," *Mingo and Other Sketches in Black and White*, 1884) is blue-black whereas tall-gaunt Mom Bi ("Mom Bi: Her Friends and Enemies," *Balaam and his Master and Other Sketches and Stories*, 1891) is jet-black, but her lips are not thick and her nose is not flat. Small, wiry Qua (*Qua, A Story of the Revolution*[3]), an African prince, is comical but brave. In contrast, Drusilla (*The Story of Aaron*, 1896), a child, is comical and timid. Whereas Blue Dave refused to obey his first master, Randall (*The Bishop and the Boogerman*, 1909), a freedman, is polite, even obsequious, although he distrusts white people. Uncle Remus approximates the dialect of Virginian slaves, but African Daddy Jack (*Nights with Uncle Remus*, 1883) speaks the Gullah of the Sea Island blacks.

*Reprinted with the permission of the author and the publisher from *Southern Literary Journal*, 1 (Autumn 1968), 20–41. Darwin T. Turner is Professor of English and Chair of Afro-American Studies at the University of Iowa. He has published many articles on literature, drama, and the English profession in *College English*, *CLA Journal*, and other journals. He has written or edited several books, including *Black American Literature: Essays, Poetry, Fiction, Drama* (1970), *In a Minor Chord: Three Afro-American Writers and Their Search for Identity* (1971), *Responding: Five* (1973), and *The Wayward and the Seeking: Selected Writings of Jean Toomer* (1979).

To see clearly the Negro characters created by Joel Chandler Harris, one must probe through the haze of memory and desire which blurred Harris's vision of reality. A fatherless, impoverished youth from a small town in Georgia, thirteen-year-old Joel Chandler Harris moved to Turnwold plantation in 1862 to set type for *The Countryman*, a periodical written and published by Joseph Addison Turner, who was recognized regionally for his love of literature, his defense of Southern ideals, and his humane treatment of slaves.[4] In 1866, when Turner ceased publishing *The Countryman*, Harris left Turnwold, but he never forgot his life there. As passing years and nostalgia dimmed and distorted memory, Harris was haunted by the dream of a world in which "old-time" slaves, particularly African slaves, worshipped their aristocratic Anglo-Saxon masters.

Harris perceived that the dream could not become reality, for legalized slavery had been abolished and would not—should not—be restored. With Henry Grady, a fellow editor on the Atlanta *Constitution*, Harris encouraged and proclaimed a new, industrialized, urban South, rising like a Phoenix from Sherman's flames, renouncing its spurious and sentimental sectionalism, and speeding toward reunion with the North. Neither the mythic, "old-time" Negro nor his aristocratic master had a place in the new, postbellum society.

Nevertheless, reason and reality could not dispel Harris's dream. Abandoned by a father whom he had never known, Harris projected a utopia in which each deserving Anglo-Saxon American is satiated with love from childhood to death. As a child, he is entertained, comforted, and advised by a devoted black nurse or a slave playmate who is more faithful than a pet hound. As an adult, he is attended by servants who, like dutiful genies, live only for his pleasure while he, like an indulgent father, protects them and supervises their growth. Such a utopia had existed, or had been possible, Harris imagined, on plantations before the Civil War.

Unable to resist the hypnotic enticements of his dream of love and godly power, Harris, for more than thirty-five years as a professional writer, shaped reality to conform to his dream: While he introduced American readers to African myths about Brer Rabbit, Brer Wolf, and Brer Bear, simultaneously he developed and popularized an Anglo-Saxon myth about the "old-time" Negroes and their benevolent masters.

The difficulty of analyzing and appraising the Negro characters in Harris's work is intensified by the fact that Harris was neither a Negrophobe nor a conventional romancer of antebellum days.

Unlike Thomas Dixon, for example, Harris neither hated nor feared Negroes. To the contrary, he frequently praised them. Qua (*Qua, A Story of the Revolution*) proves his bravery as a soldier during the Revolution, and Whistling Jim (*A Little Union Scout*, 1904) earns grudging respect from General Forrest, who presumes cowardice to be inherent in Africans. The Reverend Randall (*The Bishop and the Boogerman*, 1909) is eloquent, intelligent, and industrious, "a pattern, a model, for the men of his race, and indeed, for the men of any race, for there was never a moment when he was idle."[5] Harris did not restrict his praise to slaves. He commended the educability of Negroes and compared their progress favorably with the probable progress of the early Britons in the years immediately following their release from service to foreign conquerors.[6] He even judged Negroes to be industrious and more temperate than whites.[7]

Harris's defense of the actions of slaves frequently seems surprisingly tolerant and perceptive. He implied respect for Daddy Jake ("Daddy Jake, the Runaway," *Daddy Jake the Runaway and Short Stories Told After Dark*, 1889), who runs away rather than perform a chore outside his accustomed duties. Harris ridiculed the terrifying rumors about escaped slaves. Although mere mention of his name frightens women and children, Blue Dave ("Blue Dave," *Mingo*, 1884) actually is kind and gentle. Harris justified the slaves' hatred of white men: "Hamp never got over the idea . . . that his old master had been judged to be crazy simply because he was unusually kind to his negroes, especially the little ones."[8] Harris even justified the restlessness of the newly freed blacks:

> He [Gabriel Tolliver] thought that the restless and uneasy movements of the negroes were perfectly natural. They had suddenly come to the knowledge that they were free, and they were testing the nature and limits of their freedom. They desired to find out its length and breadth. So much was clear to Gabriel, but it was not clear to his elders. And what a pity that it was not: How many mistakes would have been avoided! What a dreadful tangle and turmoil would have been prevented if these grown children could have been judged from Gabriel's point of view! For the boy's interpretation of the restlessness and uneasiness of the blacks was the correct one. Your historians will tell you that the situation was extraordinary and full of peril. Well, extraordinary, if you will, but not perilous. Gabriel could never be brought to believe that there was anything to be dreaded in the attitude of the blacks.[9]

Harris exonerated the Freedmen from many evils attributed to them during Reconstruction; instead, he castigated the Radical Republicans, the carpetbaggers, and the scalawags, who abused the ignorant Freedmen and used their votes.

As he was not a Negrophobe, so Harris was not a conventional romancer of the antebellum myth. Repeatedly, he scolded Southern writers for clinging to romantic delusions about the perfection of Southern civilization. Repeatedly, he called for a Southern writer sufficiently bold to present and even to ridicule the actualities of Southern life, and he challenged Southern readers to accept such criticism.[10]

In his own fiction, Harris revealed some destructive delusions of the masters. In "The Old Bascom Place" (*Balaam and His Master*, 1891), for instance, Judge Bascom loses his mind brooding over ways to regain his estate. Harris revealed even more frequently the cruelties of masters. Hamp, for example, "received small share of kindness, as well as scrimped rations, from the majority of those who hired him."[11] Free Joe ("Free Joe," *Free Joe and Other Georgian Sketches*, 1887), is denied permission to visit his slave wife. The daughter of Mom Bi was sold to a man living far from the plantation where Mom Bi worked. Crazy Sue (*Daddy Jake the Runaway*, 1889) lost her child because, sent to the fields to work, she could not nurse the baby. In "Where's Duncan?" (*Balaam and His Master*), a slave kills the master who sold their mulatto son to a slave speculator.

Despite his fondness for Negroes and his awareness of weaknesses of Southern life, despite his perception that the South must relinquish the past and move into the present, Harris, however, clung philosophically and emotionally to the dream of a utopian plantation society. As early as 1877, three years before the first published collection of Remus tales, Harris extolled the system which he judged responsible for the civilization which had produced "the genius of such men as Washington, Jefferson, Patrick Henry, Taney, Marshall, Calhoun, Stephens, Toombs and all the greatest leaders of political thought and opinion from the days of the Revolution to the beginning of the Civil War. . . ."[12]
Harris concluded:

> It [the old plantation] has passed away, but the hand of time . . . has woven about it the sweet suggestions of poetry and romance, memorials that neither death nor decay can destroy.[13]

Twenty-five years later, writing for a national audience instead of the more limited and homogenous circulation of *The Constitution*, Harris continued to exalt the old plantation, "the brightest and pleasantest of all the dreams we have."[14]

The romance of the plantation, Harris asserted, was first described by Harriet Beecher Stowe, whose artistic genius compelled her to show that "all the worthy and beautiful characters [of *Uncle Tom's Cabin*] . . . are products of the system the text of the book is all the time condemning . . . [whereas] the cruelest and most brutal character she depicts . . . is a Northerner, the product of a State from which slavery had long been banished."[15] Harris continued,

> The real moral that Mrs. Stowe's book teaches is that the possibilities of slavery anywhere and everywhere are shocking to the imagination, while the realities, under the best and happiest conditions, possess a romantic beauty all their own; and it has so happened in the course of time that this romantic feature . . . has become the essence, and almost the substance, of the old plantation as we remember it.[16]

The "romantic feature" of the plantation is the tender relationship between kind masters and devoted "old-time darkies," who were tactful, conservative, practical, energetic, humble but not servile, unobtrusive, faithful, firm but goodnatured, discreet, hospitable, gentlemanly, proud of the family but not obsessed by pride in self, affable, and gently dignified.[17]

One wishes to believe Harris was teasing his Northern readers in this eulogy to slavery and to the old-time Negro. One does not want to presume that a man as intelligent as Harris could seriously advance the bizarre notion that the idealized virtues of Tom and Eva and St. Clair existed because of slavery rather than despite it. Knowing Harris's talent for satire, one wants to credit him with awareness that the exhaustive catalogue of angelic virtues ascribed to the Negroes is sufficient proof that Harris expected his readers to discern his ironic chiding of Southerners who, by romantically clinging to a myth of what never was and never could have been, prescribed unattainable standards for twentieth-century Negroes.

Nevertheless, it is difficult to defend an ironic reading, for Harris supported his eulogy to old-time Negroes by reciting incidents proving their virtues. Moreover, despite their apparent variety in appearance and personality, Harris's memorable Negroes, in general, fit comfortably into the familiar stereotypes of the plantation myth: the wise, venerable old-time Negro, the devoted slave, the mammy, the comic darky, and the pathetic freedman.

The archetypal family retainer in Harris's works is, of course, Uncle Remus. But Remus transcends the stereotype. As Stella Brewer Brookes has written, "Among the immortal 'real folks' of literature Uncle Remus' place is secure . . . Uncle Remus is an individual—a distinctive personality. . . ."[18] The individualizing, however, does not result from a single portrait in any work. It is, instead, a composite drawn from many works in which Harris used Remus variously—as a comic narrator, as the prototype of the old-time Negro, as a literary substitute for the father whom he never knew, and as a spokesman for his own ideas.

In the earliest stories,[19] Remus, a kind, aged story-teller, is almost maternal in his relationship with the seven-year old son of Miss Sally. He dandles the boy on his knee, caresses his hair, scolds him gently, fusses with him, entertains him with stories, and offers the love which young "Joe" Harris never experienced from a man. Not yet having assumed a mythic stature, Remus is made realistic by small but significant details. He wears spectacles, suffers from rheumatism, eats yams, performs minor chores, and occasionally exhibits irritability.

Perceiving that Remus was as popular as the African tales themselves, Harris expanded Remus's character in the next stories.[20] In many, particularly in those in which he and the boy are the only human characters, Remus is merely a stereotyped old-time Negro: He praises Miss Sally, recalls the virtues of "ole Miss," worries about Miss Sally's attitude towards him, comforts the little boy, contrasts plantation owners' affection for Negroes with the hostility of whites who own no slaves, and warns the little boy against imitating his impoverished neighbors, the Favers:

> Yo' pa, he got the idee dat some folks is good ez yuther folks; but Miss Sally, she know better. She know dat dey ain't no Favers 'pon de top side er de yeth w'at kin hol' der han' wid de Abercrombies in p'int er breedin' en raising.[21]

In his relationships with other Negroes, however, Remus appears as an individual subject to human frailties. He is superstitious, petulant, hypocritical, vain, and jealous. Although he is hospitable to the Negro companions who enter his cabin to listen to his stories, he treats the housegirl 'Tildy superciliously, criticizes African Daddy Jack, expresses his contempt for the Negro fieldhands, and jealously but silently contests with Aunt Tempy for the position of supreme slave on the plantation.

In years immediately following, Harris developed Remus into the master portrait of the old-time Negro, whom he described explicitly in *Daddy Jake the Runaway and Short Stories Told After Dark*, 1889:

> Uncle Remus was not a "field hand"; that is to say, he was not required to plow and hoe and engage in the rough work on the plantation.
>
> It was his business to keep matters and things straight about the house, and to drive the carriage when necessary. He was the confidential family servant, his attitude and his actions showing that he considered himself a partner in the various interests of the plantation. He did no great amount of work, but he was never wholly idle. He tanned leather, he made shoes, he manufactured horse-collars, fish-baskets, foot-mats, scouring-mops, and ax-handles for sale; he had his own watermelon and cotton-patches; he fed the hogs, looked after the cows and sheep, and in short, was the busiest person on the plantation.
>
> He was reasonably vain of his importance, and the other Negroes treated him with great consideration. They found it to their advantage to do so, for Uncle Remus was not without influence with his master and mistress. It would be difficult to describe, to the satisfaction of those not familiar with some of the developments of slavery in the South, the peculiar relations existing between Uncle Remus and his mistress, whom he called "Miss Sally." He had taken care of her when she was a child, and he still regarded her as a child.
>
> He was dictatorial, overbearing and quarrelsome. These words do not describe Uncle Remus's attitude, but no other words will do. Though he was dictatorial, overbearing and quarrelsome, he was not even grim. Beneath everything he said there was a current of respect and affection that was

thoroughly understood and appreciated. All his quarrels with his mistress were about trifles, and his dictatorial bearing was inconsequential. The old man's disputes with his "Miss Sally" were thoroughly amusing to his master, and the latter, when appealed to, generally gave a decision favorable to Uncle Remus.[22]

In later stories, Harris, with increasing frequency, projected his own ideas through Uncle Remus. Using the tales as *exempla* in his sermons, Remus, for instance, teaches Miss Sally's son that success does not depend upon physical size, that a confident man does not boast, that one should seek his fortune at home, and that the love of money is sinful. In the stories collected into *Told by Uncle Remus*, 1905, Remus voices the aging Harris's yearning for the past and his displeasure with the urbanized South. Above all else, Remus disapproves of the new standards for rearing children: the excessive emphasis upon discipline and cleanliness, the insistence upon early maturity and practicality, and the restriction or elimination of imagination and fantasizing.

More fully delineated than any other character in Harris's works, Uncle Remus transcends the stereotype of the "old-time darky." Negroes who appear less frequently more obviously conform to the stereotype. Despite their varied physiques and personalities, they are identical in their unquestioning, undeviating devotion to their masters.

For instance, Mingo is proud to belong to such aristocratic masters as the Bushrods. As a slave, he is happy, an essential consideration in the myth of the contented slave. As "his condition was no restraint on his spirits,"[23] so it did not diminish his self-respect: "when he bent his head, and dropped his eyes upon the ground, his dignity was strengthened and fortified rather than compromised." Emancipation provides the opportunity to leave the plantation and a new mistress who hates Negroes, but Mingo remains because he believes that his dead mistress, in a dream, has asked him to protect her child.

Reared together, Balaam ("Balaam and His Master," *Balaam and His Master*, 1891) and Berrien Cozart, his master, love each other. Berrien protects Balaam from punishment by the whites, and Balaam tries to guard Berrien against his own wildness. When Berrien is expelled from school and barred from his home, Balaam accompanies him. When Berrien, having lost everything gambling, proposes to sell Balaam, Balaam threatens to run away from the new master. Together, they devise a fraudulent scheme to raise money without disrupting the relationship. After being sold, Balaam will return to Berrien, who then will have the money and his slave. Balaam's devotion continues until death. After Berrien has been arrested for murder, Balaam breaks *into* prison, where he discovers his master's dead body.

The most incredibly devoted of all is Ananias ("Ananias," *Balaam and His Master*, 1891). Repulsive in countenance and manner, Ananias never gains his master's trust. When Sherman's troops steal livestock from the plantation, Ananias, who has attempted to stop them, is accused of helping them. Unable to articulate a defense, he accompanies the soldiers, expecting to receive money which he can give to his master. When he learns that he will not be paid, he returns to his master. Ananias not only continues to work happily for a master who pays him nothing and who distrusts him, but he also supports the master with money which he earns by working for others. Unable to provide sufficiently for the master's family, however, Ananias steals food, is caught, and is imprisoned because his master refuses to stand his bond. After the trial reveals how Ananias helped the family, the master forgives him, the master's daughter praises him, and Ananias cries with happiness.

If any of Harris's readers presumed that that fairy tale might be the standard for a significant number of human beings, they must have been distressed when emancipated Negroes refused to emulate Ananias. Undoubtedly, many readers sympathized with and echoed Mrs. Haley: "Prince use to be a mighty good nigger before freedom come out, but now he ain't much better'n the balance of 'em. . . . Folks is got so they has to be mighty perlite to niggers sence the war."[24] Nevertheless, Harris argued that old-time Negroes continued to exist even after Emancipation. Uncle Plato (*Gabriel Tolliver*, 1902) provokes his fellow freedmen because, rejecting the persuasions of carpetbaggers, he insists that Negroes should not become involved in government. After Emancipation, Jess adopts Briscoe Bascom as a master because he respects the aristocracy of the Bascom family. He even begs from his former master, Major Jim Bass, so that the Bascoms will not be forced to eat food "too common and cheap for the representatives of such a grand family."[25]

Equal in importance to the "old-time darky" is the "mammy," for whom Harris expressed special fondness:

> But the old black mammy—she was never anything but herself from first to last; sharp-tongued, tempestuous in her wrath, violent in her likes and dislikes, she was wholly and completely human. At a word she was ready to cry or quarrel, but those who knew and appreciated her worth knew that a good deal of her temper and all her shrewdness were merely assumed to conceal the tenderness that was ready to overflow with every beat of her pulse.[26]

Like the "old-time darkies," the mammies are diversified in appearance but identical in character. In the Remus stories, the mammy is Aunt Tempy,

> a fat, middle-aged woman, who always wore a head-handkerchief, and kept her sleeves rolled up. . . . She never hesitated to exercise her authority, and the younger Negroes on the place regarded her as a tyrant; but in spite of her loud voice

and brusque manners she was thoroughly good-natured, usually good-humored, and always trustworthy.[27]

Because Remus himself assumes the role of maternal adviser and comforter, Tempy lacks opportunity to display the devotion characteristically identified with the mammy stereotype.

Such selfless devotion is illustrated, however, by Mom Bi. Tall and gaunt, rather than plump, the kerchief-capped Mom Bi rules the Waynecroft family aggressively and caustically. Unbroken in spirit despite slavery, she quarrels with her masters, prevents insolence from the other servants, terrifies visitors and strangers, and evokes respect and devotion from the family. Like Remus, she proudly presumes "her" family to be superior to the impoverished whites, the "sandhillers." When the Civil War begins, she protests bitterly against Gabriel Waynecroft's enlisting to fight beside sandhillers. After the youth has been killed, she becomes surly, irritable, and violent, and she leaves the plantation. She says that Gabriel's death has caused her to forgive her master's having sold her daughter but that nothing will cause her to forgive his sending his son into the army.

Less incredibly devoted is Lucindy (*The Bishop and the Boogerman*, 1909), who, despite a thoughtless master, finds happiness in caring for a child and the child's invisible playmate. When the child becomes ill, Lucindy, jealous of a potential rival, refuses to consent to the hiring of a Negro nurse; instead, she performs her own chores during the day and watches the sick child during the night.

Emancipation did not weaken a mammy's devotion. In *Gabriel Tolliver*, Harris described Rhody, Silas Tomlin's cook and housekeeper:

> She was very willing for Silas Tomlin to be drawn through a hackle; she was willing to see murder done if the whites were to be victims; but Paul—well, according to her view, Paul was one of a thousand. She had given him suck; she had fretted and worried about him for twenty years; and she couldn't break off her old habits all at once. She has listened to and indorsed [sic] the incendiary doctrines of the radical emissary who pretended to be representing the government; she had wept and shouted over the strenuous pleadings of the Rev. Jeremiah; but all these things were wholly apart from Paul. And if she had had the remotest idea that they affected his interest or his future, she would have risen in the church and denounced the carpetbagger and his scalawag associates, and likewise the Reverend Jeremiah.[28]

According to Harris, a mammy's devotion was equalled only by her aggressiveness. Although Wimberly Driscoll possesses the "worst temper ever seen in a white man," Mammy Kitty belittles and abuses him. The Southern narrator of the tale comments, "Ef one of your Northern fellows could 'a' hern 'er, you'd 'a' got a bran' new idea in regards to the oppressed colored people."[29] Wimberly, however, ignores the abuse because he knows how much Mammy Kitty loves him.

The temper and the devotion are evident also in Aunt Minervy Ann, great-granddaughter of an African princess:

> She had a bad temper, and was both fierce and fearless when it was aroused; but it was accompanied by a heart as tender and a devotion as unselfish as any mortal ever possessed or displayed. Her temper was more widely advertised than her tenderness, and her independence more clearly in evidence than her unselfish devotion, except to those who knew her well or intimately.[30]

The requisite quality in both the old-time darky and the mammy was asexual devotion to a master. The mammies lack the normal maternal outlets. Lucindy and Mom Bi have offspring, but even these are adult. Lucindy's son, Randall, is a minister; Mom Bi's daughter has children of her own. Childless, the mammies lavish a mother's love upon the white children of the plantation. The old-time male darkies are sexless. Uncle Remus is ancient. After tending Miss Sally when she was a child, he is nurse and companion for Miss Sally's son and grandson. Uncle Plato and Hamp Perdue have wives, but romance and sensuality cannot be associated with their marriages. Among the Negro men, only aging Daddy Jack courts a woman, but his flirtation with teen-aged 'Tildy suggests comedy rather than romance. Whether young or old, Harris's Negro men give their love only to their masters.

By emphasizing the slaves' devotion, Harris may have hoped to excuse slavocracy. Appreciating literature's usefulness as propaganda, Harris implied that slavery, in its ideal state in the South, was no more brutal than a typical patriarchal family structure, for the slaves were chained only by love, which they gave only to deserving individuals. Although she resents her master, Mom Bi continues to serve the family because she loves the master's son. Having run away from an unjust overseer, Daddy Jake returns at the bidding of the master's children.

Harris's most dramatic presentation of this amazing argument is "Blue Dave" (*Mingo*, 1884). Women and children in Georgia are terrified by the thought of Blue Dave, an unmanageable slave, who has run away. One night, however, Dave risks freedom to ask Kitty Kendrick to warn George Denham against crossing rain-swollen Murder Creek after dark. Denying that he is a "bad nigger," Dave also reveals his desire to be Denham's slave. Later, after George fails to receive the message, Dave again risks freedom to warn him. When George ignores the warning, Dave follows him, rescues him from the creek, carries him bodily to the Kendrick home, and walks four miles to inform Denham's family. After the Denhams reward Dave by buying him, Dave works industriously and expresses his new-found happiness by singing and dancing frequently.

It is interesting to speculate whether Harris's emphasis upon the devoted slaves may have reflected his own emotional needs, his fantasying about the kind of world in which a Joel Chandler Harris might be happy. One who never has known his father's family might imagine aristocratic lineage to be essential to Utopia. Similarly, one deserted by his father might dream of a world centered on familial love.

In Harris's proposed Utopia, a slave's devotion was returned by a wise master, who understood the interdependence which Harris explained best in a letter from a mother to her son:

> My Dear Son: I write this letter to commend the negro Shade to your special care and protection. He will need your protection most when it comes into your hand. I have told him that in the hour when you read these lines he may surely depend on you. No human being could be more devoted to my interests and yours than he has been. Whatever may have been his duty, he has gone far beyond it. But for him, the estate and even the homestead would have gone to the sheriff's block long ago. The fact that the mortgages have been paid is due to his devotion and his judgment. I am grateful to him, and I want my gratitude to protect him as long as he shall live. I have tried to make this plain in my will, but there may come a time when he will especially need your protection, as he has frequently needed mine. When that times comes I want you to do as I would do. I want you to stand by him as he has stood by us. To this hour he has never failed to do more than his duty where your interests and mine were concerned. It will never be necessary for him to give you this letter while I am alive; it will come to you as a message from the grave. God bless you and keep you in the wish of your
>
> Mother.[31]

Harris, however, obviously was not proposing interdependence of equals. Instead, he presumed a society of interdependent masters and slaves or aristocrats and freedmen. Although he endorsed Negroes' rights to equal protection by the laws of America, he believed nineteenth-century Negroes to be intellectually and socially inferior to the nineteenth-century Anglo-Saxons. This idea, even more than the plantation dream, vitiated his capability of depicting Negroes authentically. Emotionally unable to accept them as equals despite his rational respect for such exceptional individuals as Booker T. Washington, Harris invariably saw his Negro characters as comical, pathetic, or humbly aware of their inferiority.

Most often he emphasized the comical appearances, personalities, and behavior, for he believed Negroes to be amusing and easily amused. As he explained in "Daddy Jake, the Runaway," whenever Negroes have filled their stomachs, "dey bleege to holler."

At an extreme he stereotyped Comic Darkies—ignorant, easily

frightened minor figures who are memorable only because they are ludicrous. These are such characters as Drusilla (*The Story of Aaron*, 1896, and *Aaron in the Wildwoods*, 1897) or ten-year-old William (*Free Joe*, 1887), who expects learning to run from his school book if he holds it upside down.

More irritating than his farcical use of comic stereotypes is his demeaning portraiture of many major characters, who appear well-intentioned but comical by nature. Even Remus suffers this patronizing treatment, particularly in *Nights with Uncle Remus*. As the master laughs at Remus's quarrels with "Miss Sally," so the reader laughs at Remus's vanity and childish petulance.

Aunt Minervy Ann, Harris's most colorful mammy, falters farcically at her noblest moments. Her boast to protect her husband dissipates into frightened stutters and flight when she learns that the "Kukluckers" have threatened him. When she defends her master, her courage is obscured by the vivid picture of her "frailing" the attackers. Blindly trusting her master, she promises to help him by persuading her husband to introduce a favorable legislative bill. During the incident, she comically retrieves Hamp from two female admirers and, from the gallery, farcically chastizes Hamp and disputes with the legislators. Heroic Qua looks comical. Mingo, Daddy Jake, and Blue Dave, like court jesters, enjoy entertaining the master and his family even if it necessitates making themselves the subject of the humor. All the mammies, except Mom Bi, elicit laughter rather than terror when they rage. Even Randall, the most idealized of Harris's Negroes, appears comical when he relates his determined but unsuccessful efforts to educate himself.

Feeling as he did, Harris could not fear Negroes. Consequently, it is neither surprising nor creditable that Harris defended Negroes against allegations that they were objects of terror. One does not hate or fear a child or a pet, even when he misbehaves.

Persuaded of the intellectual inferiority of Negroes, however, Harris harshly ridiculed freedmen who assumed the right to help govern the South. Disregarding the fact that many Negroes in Southern legislatures during Reconstruction had received formal education superior to that of their white fellow legislators,[32] Harris pictured them as vain and stupid people. For instance, Hamp Perdue (*The Chronicles of Aunt Minervy Ann*), who gave himself the name "Perdue" because his wife thought it pretty, decides to run for the legislature even though he is ignorant and uneducated. When the "Kukluckers" threaten him, he cowers comically while his wife's former master protects him. Having become a member of the legislature, he moves into a new house, to appease his vanity; parades pompously before his female admirers in Atlanta; takes unauthorized vacations from legislative sessions; ignorantly attempts to discuss "principles" of the Republican Party; and behaves sensibly, according to Harris, only when Aunt Minervy Ann tells him what to do.

Assisted by a vain and ignorant wife, Jeremiah Tomlin is even more ludicrous:

> In common with the great majority of his race—in common, perhaps with the men of all races—he was eaten up by a desire to become prominent, to make himself conspicuous. Generations of civilization (as it is called) have gone far to tone down this desire in the whites, and they manage to control it to some extent, though now and then we see it crop out in individuals. But there had been no toning down of the Rev. Jeremiah's egotism; on the contrary, it had been fed by the flattery of his congregation until it was gross and rank.
>
> It was natural, therefore, under all the circumstances, that the Rev. Jeremiah should become the willing tool of the politicians and adventurers who had accepted the implied invitation of the radical leaders of the Republican Party to assist in the spoliation of the South. The Rev. Jeremiah, once he had been patted on the back, and addressed as Mr. Tomlin by a white man, and that man a representative of the Government, was quite ready to believe anything he was told by his new friends, and quite as ready to aid them in carrying out any scheme that their hatred of the South and their natural rapacity could suggest or invent.[33]

Harris did not presume that all Negroes are comical. Most of the others, however, appeared pathetic to him, especially when they lived outside the paternalistic system which he judged essential to their well being. Prior to emancipation and his "ridiculous" career as a legislator, Hamp Perdue was pathetic because, hired by many men, he never experienced the kind treatment he would have received from a single master. Formerly a proud and happy slave, Mingo is a melancholy free man. Mulatto Mary Ellen (*The Chronicles of Aunt Minervy Ann*) lives unhappily on the border of two worlds until, assisted by education, she identifies herself only with the white world. The most pathetic of all is Free Joe, who, protected by no master, becomes the slave of all white men. Being outside the normal social structure, he is alienated even from members of his own race, who despise him.

Between the comic and the pathetic, Harris envisaged only a few, whom he judged admirably humble. Harris's worthy Negroes acknowledge their inferiority. Ananias confesses to a white man that Negroes cannot articulate their ideas clearly to white men; ironically, Ananias has no difficulty explaining his inability to explain. Harris applauds the dignity of Mingo, who lowers his eyes whenever he talks with white people. The most humble of all is Randall, Harris's model for Negro freedmen. Although he is an intelligent, self-educated property owner, Randall distinguishes his dignity from that of a white man. After he polishes the shoes of his mother's former master, he says that he would do so even if he were a bishop, for such an act, possibly beneath the dignity of a white man in a comparable position, is not beneath the dignity of a Negro. Harris added the comment that Randall spoke sincerely. Harris thus assured his readers that, regardless of his accomplishments, a black man should consider it his responsibility to obey the whim of any member of Southern "aristocracy."

It is not easy to organize Harris's images of Negroes into a coherent pattern because Harris himself responded to divergent magnets. For instance, even though he extended pity for the emotional abuses in slavery, he ignored physical maltreatment. His slaves suffer only from unjust orders or food restrictions or separation from their families. Not once in Harris's works does a slave or freedman feel the sting of a whip.

Although he professed pleasure that slavery had ended, he contended that white masters, and especially their wives, had suffered more than the slaves. The masters had been responsible for feeding, clothing, protecting, and managing the slaves. In contrast, the slaves benefited from a system which "under providence, grew into a university in which millions of savages served an apprenticeship to religion and civilization, and out of which they graduated into American citizens."[34] It is ironic to use the term "university" to describe the practices of a system which legally prohibited the formal education of slaves. It is presumptuous to praise slavery for giving religion to the Africans, who observed a religious faith long before they became American slaves. Such praise seems especially reprehensible because the new religion, Christianity, was not used to help the slaves but to encourage them to submit to eternal bondage. It is irrational to praise slavery for graduating slaves into American citizens when slave holders, by every means in their power, attempted to deny citizenship to Negroes both before and after emancipation. Nonetheless, Harris believed these ideas, or at least persuaded his readers to accept them.

Harris wanted to place Negroes properly in the postbellum world; but, believing them ideally suited for domestic and farm labor, he could not determine satisfactory alternatives. Even though he affirmed their educability, he remained vague about the practical or immediate uses of that education. If it seemed absurd for a cobbler to learn Latin,[35] Harris, nonetheless, defended a cobbler's right to study what he pleased. Harris did not propose to exclude Negroes from professions—except for ministry and law—but he reminded readers of the limited demand for the services of Negro professional men. Harris, however, urged Negroes to restrict the numbers entering the ministry and to forbid any to enter law. It seems irrational to argue the importance of Christianity to Negroes while suggesting that fewer Negroes should be Christian ministers. It seems contradictory to suppose that an Uncle Remus is sufficiently wise to advise Miss Sally's daughter-in-law about rearing children but is too ignorant to serve in a legislative body. Nevertheless, Harris did not attempt to modify the inconsistencies in his position.

The most obvious distortion of fact is Harris's presentation of political events during Reconstruction. For part of that period, Harris was a newspaper editor, who should have had access to accurate information about politics in Georgia. Repeatedly, however, Harris charged that emancipated Negroes were deluded by carpetbaggers' allegations that the South intended to re-establish slavery. Such intentions may very well have seemed credible, especially in Georgia, where the legislature in 1865 excluded Negroes from their proposal for public education, rejected the Fourteenth Amendment in 1866, expelled its Negro members in 1868, and rejected the Fifteenth Amendment in 1869.

In *Gabriel Tolliver*, Harris, repudiating the constitutional convention of 1867–1868, asserted that it was composed of political adventurers from the Northern states and "boasted a majority composed of ignorant negroes and criminals,"[36] that the Governor of Georgia was discharged because he refused to pay the convention from state funds, and that fraudulent means were proposed for the adoption of the new constitution. According to Harris, these unwarranted conditions inspired a need satisfied by the Knights of the White Camellia.

Actually, however, in Georgia's constitutional convention of 1867–1868, only thirty-three delegates were Negroes. Nine were Northern whites, and 128, or 74%, were white Georgians.[37] Rather than being controlled by Negroes, the convention struck from the constitution the statement guaranteeing every voter the right to hold office. In 1868, only three members of the Georgia Senate were Negro; thirty-three were white. Twenty-nine members in the House were Negro; 106 were white. This "Negro-dominated" body in 1868 forced the resignation of one Negro senator, and expelled the other two senators and twenty-five of the twenty-nine Negro members of the House. Historian John Hope Franklin insists that the other four remained only "because their fair complexion made it impossible to prove that they were Negro."[38]

Such a wanton disregard of facts irritates any reader who wishes to give Harris the benefit of the doubt, to suppose that clouded memory or compulsive fancy caused him to misconstrue the characters of Negroes. Nevertheless, in respect for Uncle Remus, the judgment about his creator should be favorable: A Caucasian, born in Georgia and reared during the Civil War and Reconstruction, Harris could not escape from the attitudes instilled by his culture. Believing in the black man and wanting to help him, Harris, like Kipling, felt superior to the black man.

He saw Negroes, especially when he collected stories from them. He observed their reticence in their relationship with whites, and inferred an innate shyness. He saw their humility in their relationship to whites; and, ignoring the fact that the humility had been enforced through three hundred years of custom and physical abuse, he attached dignity to it. The alternatives—that the Negro was servile, or was merely feigning respect—did not conform to his ideal. Undoubtedly, Harris also knew hostile Negroes and educated, independent Negroes, but he preferred to write about those who fit into his myth of the devoted servant who, regardless of circumstance, instinctively dedicates his life to nursing, amusing, consoling, and worshiping his master.

As Africans modified real foxes and rabbits into Brer Fox and Brer Rabbit for Negro folk myths, so Joel Chandler Harris in his fiction molded actual Negroes into the old-time slaves essential to the romantic myth of a utopian plantation, governed by a kingly and paternal master. All too soon, this Anglo-Saxon myth became more popular than the African tales. Harris's modified realities assumed the dimension of a new and false Reality, and the never-was, the never-could-be was assumed to be the once-was. Thus, Joel Chandler Harris, the collector of tales became "Daddy Joe," the father of a myth.

Notes

1. *Gabriel Tolliver: A Story of Reconstruction* (New York: McClure, Phillips, 1902), p. 10.

2. *Gabriel Tolliver*, p. 11.

3. Not published during Harris's lifetime.

4. Paul M. Cousins, *Joel Chandler Harris: A Biography* (Baton Rogue: Louisiana State Univ. Press, 1968), pp. 40–44.

5. *The Bishop and the Boogerman* (New York: Doubleday, Page, 1909), p. 139.

6. See "The Negro of Today: His Prospects and His Discouragements," *Saturday Evening Post*, 30 January 1904, and "The Negro Problem: Can the South Solve It—and How?" *Saturday Evening Post*, 27 February 1904, both reprinted in Julia C. Harris, ed., *Joel Chandler Harris: Editor and Essayist* (Chapel Hill: Univ. of North Carolina Press, 1931), pp. 130–46, 146–59.

7. "The Negro of Today, p. 145.

8. *The Chronicles of Aunt Minervy Ann* (New York: Charles Scribner's Sons, 1899), p. 5.

9. *Gabriel Tolliver*, pp. 114–15.

10. See editorials in the *Atlanta Constitution*, 3 November and 30 November 1879, reprinted in *Editor and Essayist*, pp. 43–47.

11. *The Chronicles of Aunt Minervy Ann*, p. 5.

12. "The Old Plantation," *Atlanta Constitution*, 9 December 1877, reprinted in *Editor and Essayist*, p. 90.

13. "The Old Plantation," p. 90.

14. "The Negro as the South Sees Him," *Saturday Evening Post*, 2 January 1904, reprinted in *Editor and Essayist*, p. 115.

15. "The Negro as the South Sees Him," pp. 116–17.

16. "The Negro as the South Sees Him," p. 117.

17. "The Negro as the South Sees Him," pp. 119–21.

18. "Introduction," *Uncle Remus: His Songs and His Sayings* (New York: Schocken, 1965), p. vii.

19. Collected in *Uncle Remus: His Songs and His Sayings* (New York: D. Appleton, 1880).

20. Collected in *Nights with Uncle Remus: Myths and Legends of the Old Plantation* (New York: James R. Osgood, 1883).

21. "How Brother Fox Was Too Smart," in Richard Chase, ed., *The Complete Tales of Uncle Remus* (Boston: Houghton Mifflin, 1955), p. 130.

22. "How the Birds Talk," *Complete Tales*, pp. 449–50.

23. "Mingo," *Mingo and Other Sketches in Black and White* (Boston: James R. Osgood, 1884), p. 6.

24. "Azalia," *Free Joe and Other Georgian Sketches* (New York: Charles Scribner's Sons, 1887), p. 207.

25. "The Old Bascom Place," *Balaam and His Master* (Boston: Houghton, Mifflin, 1891), p. 254.

26. "The Negro as the South Sees Him," p. 29.

27. "Brother Wolf Says Grace," *Complete Tales*, pp. 224–25.

28. *Gabriel Tolliver*, p. 228.

29. *The Shadow Between His Shoulder-Blades* (Boston: Small, Maynard, 1909), p. 12. Ironically, despite his denial that Southerners oppress Negroes, the narrator, a few pages later, abuses a Negro youth merely because the boy is frightened.

30. *Chronicles of Aunt Minervy Ann*, p. 3.

31. "The Colonel's 'Nigger Dog,' " *Tales of the Home Folks in Peace and War* (Boston: Houghton, Mifflin, 1898), pp. 66–67.

32. See John Hope Franklin, *Reconstruction after the Civil War* (Chicago: Univ. of Chicago Press, 1961), pp. 88–89.

33. *Gabriel Tolliver*, pp. 162–63.

34. "Observations from New England," *Atlanta Constitution*, September 1883, reprinted in *Editor and Essayist*, p. 166. See also repetitions of the same idea in "Azalia," p. 164, and *Aaron in the Wildwoods* (Boston: Houghton, Mifflin, 1897), pp. 152–53.

35. "The Negro of Today," p. 141.

36. *Gabriel Tolliver*, p. 243.

37. Franklin, *Reconstruction after the Civil War*, p. 102.

38. Franklin, *Reconstruction after the Civil War*, p. 131.

"The Oral Tradition"

Robert Bone*

Joel Chandler Harris is in bad odor among the younger generation of literary men. The blacks, who tend to equate Uncle Remus with Uncle Tom—sometimes, one suspects, without having read either Harris or Stowe—reject the Uncle Remus books out of hand. And sympathetic whites, who hope thereby to ingratiate themselves with the black militants, are fond of giving Harris a gratuitous kick in the shins. Both responses are regrettable, for they blind their victims to the archetypal figure of Brer Rabbit, who is not only a major triumph of the Afro-American imagination, but also the most subversive folk hero this side of Stagolee.

Harris did not invent the animal fables that constitute the imaginative center of the Uncle Remus books. But he did transpose them to the written page, thus saving them from possible oblivion. It was through Harris that a major figure in the pantheon of American folk heroes saw the light of day. Brer Rabbit, who has kindled the imagination of black writers for almost a century, came loping into view in 1880. But Clio, a muse of history, is no respecter of race. It was a white man of the deep South who forged the missing link between the Afro-American folktale and the Afro-American short story.

The rehabilitation of Joel Chandler Harris was no part of my original intent. As a journalist, after all, he was an active propagandist in the cause of white supremacy, and as a literary man, a leading proponent of the plantation myth. Still less did I intend—nor do I now propose—to serve as an apologist for Uncle Remus, who is principally a figment of the white imagination. But the Brer Rabbit tales themselves are something else again. A product of the Afro-American oral tradition, these magnificent folktales must not be allowed to languish simply on the grounds that a white Georgian was the first to write them down.

*Reprinted by permission of the author and G. P. Putnam's Sons from Ch. 2 of Robert Bone, *Down Home: A History of Afro-American Short Fiction from Its Beginnings to the End of the Harlem Renaissance* (New York: G. P. Putnam's Sons, 1975), pp. 19–41. Copyright © 1975 by Robert Bone. Robert Bone is Professor of English at Teachers College, Columbia University. He has published essays in *American Quarterly*, *Tri-Quarterly*, *The Nation*, *Change Magazine*, and elsewhere. He has also written *The Negro Novel in America* (1965) and *Richard Wright* (1969).

So perhaps some modest effort at rehabilitation will be tolerated by the young. Out of simple justice, then, let it be entered on the record that, whatever else he was, Joel Chandler Harris was a complicated man, full of neurotic conflicts and self-deceiving ways; a Southern maverick, capable of stubborn orthodoxies and equally tenacious heresies where black people were concerned; an admirer of black folklore, and an ethnologist of strict integrity, to whom black Americans owe a considerable debt for the preservation of their folk heritage; and a catalytic agent of prime importance in the history of the Afro-American short story.

Our final judgment of this man and his work cannot be a simple one. If the Uncle Remus books perpetuate the pro-slavery myths of the plantation tradition, they also contain one of the sharpest indictments of the institution in American literature. Perhaps we cannot improve on the formulation of William Stanley Braithwaite, who wrote in 1925, ". . . in the Uncle Remus stories the race was its own artist, lacking only in its illiteracy the power to record its speech. In the perspective of time and fair judgment the credit will be divided, and Joel Chandler Harris regarded as a sort of providentially provided amanuensis for preserving the folk tales and legends of a race."[1]

The Afro-American Folktale

Modern folklorists, both black and white, have attested to the storytelling powers of the folk Negro. A large body of material has been collected in the field, and a good deal is known about its scope and variety.[2] The repertory includes animal fables, trickster tales (e.g., the John-and-ole-Marster cycle), conjure stories, preacher tales, jokes, proverbs, anecdotes, and plantation lore of every description. Wonder tales, horror stories, voodoo legends, and what Zora Hurston calls "just plain lies" have passed from mouth to mouth in the black community for generations.

The origins of the Afro-American folktale may be traced to West Africa, where a rich tradition of storytelling flourished for centuries. Especially prominent in this repertory was a large body of animal fables. But what precisely is the relationship of the Brer Rabbit tales to the animal legends of West Africa? Do the folktales of the American Negro represent a survival of African culture in the New World? Joel Chandler Harris was inclined to think so. Basing his opinion on the latest findings of contemporary scholarship, he wrote of the animal tales, "One thing is certain—the Negroes did not get them from the whites: probably they are of remote African origin."[3]

At the same time, Harris recognized that some Afro-American folktales were more African than others. He knew, for example, that the stories told on the cotton plantations of central Georgia were strikingly different from those recounted in the rice-growing districts of the Georgia coast. To accommodate these differences in his fiction he invented Daddy Jack, a narrator who came straight from Africa and told his tales in Gullah dialect. By creating a coastal counterpart of Uncle Remus, Harris anticipated, if only at the level of artistic intuition, some of the conundrums that have yet to be resolved by modern scholars.

Scientific folklorists are divided on the issue. Melville Herskovits leans to the theory of African origins while Stith Thompson points to the existence of European cognates. Richard Dorson argues that the tales are drawn from multiple sources which include Africa, Europe, the West Indies, and white American folk traditions. After weighing the available evidence he concludes that "the New World Negro repertoire falls into two groups of stories, one pointing toward Africa and one pointing toward Europe and Anglo-America."[4] Northeastern South America, the Caribbean and Atlantic islands, and the Gullah districts of the Georgia and Carolina coast produced the first group; the plantation states of the American South the second.

What seems beyond dispute is that a very ancient African tradition survived the middle passage, and served as a basis for renewed creative efforts in the Western Hemisphere. At the same time, we must insist that the Brer Rabbit tales were conceived not by Africans, but Afro-Americans. For these tales reflect the social conditions and historical experience of black slaves on the continent of North America. They represent the first attempt of black Americans to define themselves through the art of storytelling; a heroic effort on the part of chattel slaves to transmute the raw materials of their experience into the forms of fiction.

Chesnutt and Dunbar were of course exposed, personally and directly, to this folk tradition. Teaching as a young man in the Freedman's Bureau schools of North Carolina, Chesnutt was fascinated by the conjure stories of emancipated slaves. Dunbar heard stories of plantation life from his own mother, who had been a house servant in a prominent Kentucky family. But for the most part their knowledge of the Afro-American folktale was vicarious and literary. Like other middle-class Americans of their time and place, they came to know the power of the folk imagination through the Uncle Remus books. It was Joel Chandler Harris who aroused their emulation by demonstrating the potential of the folktale as a literary form.

There was nothing unusual in this cultural dialectic. The postwar era was one of widespread interest in Afro-American folklore, popularized for the most part by white authors. As early as 1867, Thomas Wentworth Higginson contributed an essay on the spirituals to the *Atlantic Monthly*, and that same year W. F. Allen published his still valuable *Slave Songs of the United States*. In 1877 William Owens wrote an article for *Lippincott's* entitled "Folklore of the Southern Negroes," which inspired Harris to undertake the Uncle Remus books. It therefore seems historically appropriate that we, like Chesnutt and Dunbar themselves, should approach the archetypal figure of Brer Rabbit through the mediating vision of Joel Chandler Harris.

The problem of authenticity will instantly arise. How faithful was Harris to his folk sources? In the process of writing down the animal fables, and providing them with a narrative frame, to what extent did he impose his own values and point of view as a white Southerner? At this point, a crucial distinction must be drawn between the kernel and its husk. It is undeniable that the external wrappings of the Brer Rabbit tales function to perpetuate the plantation myth. But the tales themselves were never tampered with. As a conscientious if amateur ethnologist, Harris respected their integrity.

Harris himself vouches for their authenticity. In his introduction to *Nights with Uncle Remus* (1883) he asserts that "The thirty-four legends in the first volume were merely selections from the large body of plantation folk-lore familiar to the author since his childhood. . . ." No tale, he continues, was included without being verified, either by his own extensive practice of yarn-swapping with the blacks, or by correspondence with other folklorists. He insists, moreover, on his fidelity to the originals: "Not one of them is cooked, and not one nor any part of one is an invention of mine. They are all genuine folk-tales."[5]

These claims to authenticity have been fully substantiated by modern scholarship. J. Mason Brewer, a Negro folklorist, confirms in his *American Negro Folklore* (1968) that "The first, and still the most significant and authentic volume of Negro animal tales is Joel Chandler Harris' *Uncle Remus: His Songs and His Sayings.* . . ." Richard Dorson, a white scholar, and former president of the American Folklore Society, offers evidence of a more objective kind. In *American Negro Folktales* (1967), Dorson has collected 1,000 stories, tape-recorded on field trips to Michigan, Arkansas, and Mississippi in the early 1950's. Of his thirty-four animal tales, nine are variants closely related to the Harris versions.

There is lastly the internal evidence of the Brer Rabbit tales themselves. They depict, as we shall see, the master-slave relation from the slave's point of view. Their central emotion is hostility toward the powerful and strong. Their moral code is that of an oppressed people; their hidden motives are such as no white man could entertain. The world of Brer Rabbit, in short, is an unmistakable projection of the black imagination. The adjacent and enfolding world of Uncle Remus is something else again. The moment that we move from the folktale to its narrative frame, we enter a fictive world entirely of the white man's making.

Afro-American animal tales belong to the genre of the beast fable, which is a species of satiric allegory.[6] They are allegorical by virtue of their veiled presentation of the slave's situation through images drawn from the animal world. They are satirical by virtue of their veiled attack on ole Massa. To attribute human traits to animals is one of those devices of indirection which are the trademark of the satirist. This indirection springs, in all literatures, from the fear of censorship, suppression, or retaliation from the high and mighty. Never was this fear more justified than in the case of the chattel slave, who found himself in the absolute power of his owner.

The Brer Rabbit tales have been widely misconstrued, for the good and sufficient reason that they constitute a secret code. The slaves who created these remarkable fictions were under the life-and-death necessity of masking in the presence of white power. To express openly the subversive sentiments concealed in these animal tales would have invited instant retaliation from the Big House. The bitter truths of the slave's existence were too dangerous to acknowledge in the master's presence, and too painful to acknowledge even to the conscious self. The result was a set of fables notable for their subliminal method of communication.

It was a white critic who first noted the subversive character of the Brer Rabbit tales. In a brilliant essay called "Uncle Remus and the Malevolent Rabbit,"[7] Bernard Wolfe has shown that these animal fables, far from being harmless children's tales, and still farther from being a defense of Southern orthodoxy, constitute a covert assault on white power. Brer Rabbit, according to Wolfe, is a projection of the slave's festering hatred of his master, a means of giving vent to his aggressive impulses. The animal tales are a type of masquerade: what they reveal to posterity is "the venomous American slave crouching behind the Rabbit."

Brer Rabbit is a symbol of covert resistance to white power. As the crimes of slavery were manifold, so the modes of resistance were many. The heroism of the slave revolt is not that of the underground railroad, and neither encompasses the brand of heroism that stands its ground and fights the system from within. The trickster-hero represents a mode of resistance, not submission or accommodation. To neglect the Brer Rabbit tales because a white man was the first to write them down is to betray the black man's folk tradition. For the American Negro's heritage from slavery times is neither negative nor negligible, and one of its most precious features is precisely the figure of Brer Rabbit.

From a literary point of view, the importance of the animal fables lies in the outlaw code that they espouse. This code of conduct, embodied in the figure of Brer Rabbit, was forged in the crucible of slavery, and cannot be understood apart from the brutalities that gave it shape. Living in the shadow of lash and gun, black storytellers had no choice but to formulate an outlaw code. For a master's sense of right and wrong is hardly suited to a slave. A man on short rations is bound to steal chickens. The only moral code he can afford to entertain is one that helps him to survive.

The Brer Rabbit tales are a celebration of this survival code. Stressing such qualities as slickness, deceit, evasiveness, and ruthless self-interest, the code is profoundly anti-Christian. It is this feature that makes the animal tales a more authentic product of the slave imagination than the more familiar spirituals. For the spirituals embody the official morality to which the bondsmen formally subscribed, while the folktales have immortalized the survival ethic that they actually practiced. If this code ran counter to Christian values, that was because the slave system which gave it birth was itself demonic.

The black man's folktales are his Handbook of Survival. Everything that he has been compelled to hide—his anger and resentment, his hatred and malevolence, his scheming and duplicity, his male aggressiveness and sexuality, his yearning for revenge—has been projected into the mythic world of the Brer Rabbit tales. Through the ritual of storytelling these illicit feelings have been safely drained away. At the same time the tales define a stance, a posture, a model of behavior, a means of preserving one's integrity even in the face of overwhelming odds. This role model is embodied in the figure of Brer Rabbit, the trickster-hero of an enslaved people.

The trickster-hero, based on the archetypal figure of Brer Rabbit, reappears in the short fiction of Charles Chesnutt and Paul Dunbar. Chesnutt's Uncle Julius, the narrator of his conjure tales, is such a hero. Uncle Julius might be described as Uncle Remus revamped according to the specifications of the Afro-American oral tradition. Dunbar too has produced a handful of trickster tales of which one, "The Scapegoat," is his best story. Both writers have thus been responsive, although in varying degrees, to their folk tradition, and both have been inspired by an oral literature whose crowning glory was the creation of the Brer Rabbit tales.

Of crucial importance to the present study is the point in time when this oral tradition surfaced, transcended its folk origins, and became incorporated into the literary culture of nineteenth-century America. That moment occurred in 1880, with the publication of the first book of Uncle Remus tales. Because of the cultural significance of this event, as well as its neglect by literary men, the remainder of this chapter will be devoted to a close inspection of *Uncle Remus: His Songs and His Sayings*. While this effort will involve us briefly with the life and career of Joel Chandler Harris, our primary aim is to illuminate the storytelling genius of the black slave.

Mask and Countermask

Joel Chandler Harris (1848–1908) was born in Putnam County, central Georgia. According to Jay Hubbell, "His mother, Mary Harris, had fallen in love with an Irish day laborer and in spite of strong family opposition had gone off to live with him. When he deserted her and their child, she settled in Eatonton with her mother and earned her living by sewing."[8] Harris attended school irregularly until the age of thirteen when [. . .] he undertook an apprenticeship in the printing trades at the

Turner plantation. The boy who grew to manhood at Turnwold was lonely, shy, and insecure. Something of an outcast by virtue of his bastardy, he turned for solace to the Negro slaves.

This emotional attachment to a pariah class was to manifest itself in his writings as a strange ambivalence. On the one hand he is the conscientious ethnologist who presents "uncooked" folktales to the world. On the other, he is perfectly capable of using Uncle Remus, in the columns of the *Atlanta Constitution*, as a counter in the white man's game of Reconstruction politics. So deep is this fissure in his personality that it is not extravagant to speak of schizoid tendencies. Harris acknowledges as much in a letter to his daughter: "You know all of us have two entities or personalities."[9] Only a split personality can account for an author who juxtaposes such antithetical images of Negro life as Uncle Remus and Brer Rabbit!

In 1865 the *Countryman* went under, and Harris was forced to leave Turnwold. For the next ten years he knocked about the South, working as a typesetter and journalist in Macon, New Orleans, and Forsyth, Georgia. In 1876, having married a woman of French Canadian antecedents, he settled in Atlanta, where he joined the staff of the *Atlanta Constitution*. As early as January 1877, Harris printed songs in Negro dialect in his regular column. During the next two years he published character sketches of Uncle Remus and an occasional animal tale. In 1880 he selected from the *Constitution* files the proverbs, songs, and stories which comprise the first of his Uncle Remus books.

Uncle Remus: His Songs and His Sayings (1880) was an instantaneous popular success. Within a matter of months the book passed through four editions. It was soon followed by a second volume, *Nights with Uncle Remus* (1883). Six such books eventually appeared, whose impact on American culture has yet to be properly assessed. Harris had established a new literary mode whose first fruits included Charles Chesnutt's *The Conjure Woman* (1899) and Don Marquis' *The Lives and Times of Archie and Mehitabel* (1916). Later works in the same line of descent would include William Faulkner's *The Sound and the Fury* (1929), Ralph Ellison's *Invisible Man* (1952), and John Updike's *Rabbit Redux* (1971).

Uncle Remus: His Songs and His Sayings was the book that launched the plantation revival of the 1880's. It was, in point of fact, the first major literary statement of the New South. As such, it bore the historic burden of revealing to the nation the current state of the Southern soul. Was the defeated South in a repentant frame of mind, or unregenerate in its defense of slavery? The answer, when it came, seemed unequivocal. The new generation of Southern writers, by their revival of the plantation myth, seemed determined to idealize the old regime, mitigate its harshness, cloak it in a haze of nostalgia, and thereby justify the restoration of white supremacy.

Joel Chandler Harris, who was, after all, a political commentator for a major Southern newspaper, was entirely orthodox in this respect. There is nothing in his characterization of Uncle Remus that violates the spirit of the plantation myth. On the contrary, it is the author's avowed purpose to create a sympathetic, nostalgic, and untroubled portrait of plantation life before the war. The point of view, he tells us frankly, will be that of an old Negro "who has nothing but pleasant memories of the discipline of slavery—and who has all the prejudices of caste and pride of family that were the natural results of the system. . . ."[10]

Harris' unconscious motivations were something else again. Guilt is an elusive state of mind, whether in a man or nation. Seldom appearing to the conscious mind in its own guise, it assumes a thousand Protean shapes and forms. Dramas of the soul involving guilt are more likely to be enacted in the dark than before the bright glare of television cameras. Hence Harris' fascination with the subliminal world of the black folktale. Folktales are allied to dream states, and possess something of the magical fluidity of dreams. Precisely because they deal with buried feelings, they confront us with blurred outlines, veiled analogies, hints and correspondences. They thus permit us to know and not to know at the same time.

At some deeper level of artistic intuition, Harris must have known that Uncle Remus was not the whole story, and perhaps not even the true story, of slavery times. Through the character of Uncle Remus he gave form to the white man's fantasy of being loved by his slaves. But there was another perspective from which to view chattel slavery, as Harris was well aware from his lonely adolescent years at Turnwold. That was the black slave's point of view, as embodied in his folklore. Try as he would, Harris could not bring himself to suppress it. This ghost is present in the Uncle Remus books, just as inescapably as it is buried in the nation's consciousness.

Whatever the intentions—conscious or unconscious—of Joel Chandler Harris, the Uncle Remus tales confront us with two distinct, and ultimately irreconcilable, versions of reality. One is white, the other black, and they are embedded in a two-tier or split-level structure consisting of (1) a narrative frame, and (2) an animal tale. Dramatically, the tales shift from the human to the animal plane; from Uncle Remus and the little boy to Brer Rabbit and the other woodland creatures. Linguistically, they shift from standard English to Negro dialect, so that the very texture of the prose announces unmistakably the transition from a white to a Negro world.

The two fictive worlds of the Uncle Remus tales are in fact the divided worlds of the American South. They are the segregated and yet curiously interlocking worlds of the two races, of the Big House and the slave quarters, of Euro-American and Afro-American culture. Their uneasy coexistence in the Uncle Remus books is a tribute to the capacity of the human mind for self-deception. For if the one world is nostalgic and sentimental, the other is utterly subversive; if the one is steeped in fantasy and wish-fulfillment, the other is immersed in the harsh realities of American slavery. On the literary plane, these tensions are reflected in the conventions of pastoral and antipastoral.

Consider the tableau that sets the tone of the Uncle Remus books. The figures of Uncle Remus and Miss Sally's little boy cling to one another in pastoral innocence and peace. The boy rests with his head against the old man's arm or sits on his knee, as Uncle Remus strokes and caresses the child's hair. It is a picture of utter confidence and trust, mutual tenderness and love. In a word, the scene is idyllic. What it proclaims to the reader is this: "There is nothing to be afraid of, or even upset by, in these animal fables; they are merely quaint legends or harmless children's stories."

Now consider the central images of the folktales themselves. Far from creating an atmosphere of tranquility and love, they convey a world of unrelieved hostility and danger, violence and cruelty, terror and revenge. In one tale, Brer Rabbit lures Brer Wolf into a large wooden chest, bores holes in the top, and scalds him to death with boiling water. In another, he persuades the animals whom he has robbed to submit to an ordeal by fire, and as a consequence, the innocent Brer Possum is killed. In a third, having caused Brer Fox to be beaten to death, Brer Rabbit attempts to serve up his enemy's head in a stew to his wife and children.

The tales are full of beatings, tortures, savage assaults, and deadly ambushes. They reproduce, in their jagged images of violence, the emotional universe of the Negro slave. How else should the black imagination respond to the brutalities of the American slave system? What other images would be commensurate with its inhumanity? If the flagrant sadism of the Brer Rabbit tales offends, it is well to remind ourselves that violence and cruelty were the mainstays of the institution. If the white imagination is content to linger over the smiling aspects of the slave estate, it would be strange indeed if the black storyteller should follow suit.

The Brer Rabbit tales preserve not so much the dramatic features as the moral atmosphere of slavery. What they are about, in the last analysis, is the black slave's resistance to white power. Hence the effort to "contain" this subversive theme in a pastoral frame. But in the tales themselves, an unrelenting state of war obtains between Brer Rabbit and his powerful antagonists. It is a war to the knife, without truce or quarter or forgiveness. The moral vision projected in these tales is that of men who have been brutalized, degraded, rendered powerless—and yet who manage to survive by dint of their superior endurance and mother wit, their cunning artifice and sheer effrontery.

The world of Brer Rabbit is a pathological world, both emotionally and morally. There is nothing normal about being a slave, and nothing normal about the black man's response to an intolerable situation. Absolute power produces absolute desperation; all moral scruples are discarded in a fierce effort to survive. This is the explanation for the code of conduct that is celebrated in these tales. Deceit and trickery, theft and betrayal, murder and mayhem are endorsed as appropriate responses to the slave condition. Such are the ruthless expedients of Brer Rabbit, who can survive in Hell by outsmarting the Devil. Having been raised in a brier patch, he is one tough bunny.

Uncle Remus and Brer Rabbit stand in the relationship of mask to countermask. Uncle Remus, the creation of Joel Chandler Harris, is one of many masks employed by the Plantation School to justify the restoration of white supremacy. But Brer Rabbit, the creation of anonymous black slaves, may be thought of as a countermask which contravenes the pastoral charade and exposes the harsh reality. A closer look at the first book of Uncle Remus tales will serve to substantiate this claim. An exhaustive survey of the Uncle Remus books would be beyond the scope of this study. A suggestive treatment of selected tales is our intent, and for this purpose a generous sampling of the first volume should suffice.

The Brer Rabbit Tales

Slavery was first of all a system of compulsory labor. A number of the animal fables are thus devoted to methods of survival which include shirking and malingering, "going fishing," and similar evasions of brutal toil in the hot sun. In one tale the animals are clearing new ground that they intend to plant in corn. Feigning an injury, Brer Rabbit slips off to take a nap in the shade. In another, they are patching up the leaky roof of their communal storehouse. On the pretext that his wife is ill, Brer Rabbit deserts the scene, steals down to the spring house, and consumes the community's entire supply of butter.

The most impressive of the work tales is "A Story About the Little Rabbits." Brer Fox drops in on Brer Rabbit and finds no one at home except the rabbit children. His mouth waters in anticipation, but some sort of pretext is required before he can devour them. He imposes three unreasonable tasks, which he expects to be beyond their strength or capacity. They are ordered to break a piece of sugar cane, carry water in a sieve, and put an enormous log on the fire. Each time a little bird instructs them in the art of the impossible:

> Sifter hold water same ez a tray
> Ef you fill it wid moss en dab it wid clay.
> De Fox git madder de longer you stay—
> Fill it wid moss en dab it wid clay.[11]

This tale is a parable of survival under a forced labor system. Brer Fox is assigned the role of tyrannous overseer, working his charges to the point of exhaustion: "Hurry up dar, Rabs! I'm a waitin' on you." To survive in such a situation, the slave had to be capable of accomplishing the impossible. If the externally imposed conditions of work were cruel and unalterable, then the only recourse was to alter one's own attitude. That is the burden of the little bird's song about the huge log:

Spit in yo' hans en tug it en toll it
En git behine it, en push it, en pole it;
Spit in yo' hans en r'ar back en roll it. (110)

Chronic undernourishment of the labor force was a common feature of the slave economy. For the closer a planter could drive his slaves to the margin of subsistence, the faster he could grow rich. If the Brer Rabbit tales are any indication, a constant hunger stalked the slave's imagination, producing what amounts to an obsession with images of food. In many of the tales, the action is devoted to the acquisition of a supplemental food supply, sometimes through hunting or fishing but more often through stealing. The theft of food was the archetypal plantation crime; its penalty was customarily exacted by the lash. Savage beatings thus provide the dominant images of several tales.

Typical of this crime-and-punishment motif is the tale "Mr. Fox Gets Into Serious Business." The story opens with an unmistakable delineation of the master-slave relationship:

"Hit turn out one time dat Brer Rabbit make so free wid de man's collard patch dat de man he tuck'n sot a trap fer ole Brer Rabbit."
"Which man was that, Uncle Remus?" asked the little boy.
"Des a man, honey. Dat's all." (140–41)

When the little boy persists, Uncle Remus parries with the comment, "Now den, less des call 'im Mr. Man en let 'im go at dat."

Having trapped the culprit in a snare, Mr. Man goes off into the brush to cut himself some switches. In his absence, Brer Fox passes by. Through an involved maneuver that plays on his victim's sexual appetites, Brer Rabbit tricks Brer Fox into taking his place in the noose. When Mr. Man returns he is astonished at the change that has overtaken his captive, but he proceeds with the whipping on general principles: "en wid dat he lit inter Brer Fox wid de hick'ries, en de way he play rap-jacket wuz a caution ter de naberhood." No doubt it was often thus in slavery times, when the guilty party escaped his punishment by tricking an innocent bystander into assuming the scapegoat role.[12]

Before proceeding it may be well to enlarge our cast of characters. While resisting the temptation to allegorize, we may yet observe that the animals can be divided into two distinct groups. In addition to the wily Rabbit, Brer Possum and Brer Terrapin may be regarded as folk heroes. Brer Fox and Brer Wolf, on the other hand, are a constant source of fear to the sympathetic characters. It is clear that the former group would offer many possibilities of identification to a slave audience, while the latter would tend to be regarded as dangerous foes or menacing authority figures.

Brer Possum, that artful dodger, is a symbol of survival-by-illusion. In the story "Why Mr. Possum Loves Peace," Mr. Dog attacks Brer Coon and Brer Possum. Brer Coon, who "wuz cut out fer dat kinder bizness," puts up a pretty stiff fight, but Brer Possum plays dead. He embodies the slave's knowledge that he cannot hope to offer a frontal challenge to white power. But by "playing possum," or in other words *by creating a fiction*, he can escape the worst excesses of that power. Fiction, in short, is perceived as a mode of survival. With this perception, we are very close to the sources of the black man's storytelling art.

Brer Terrapin is a symbol of survival-by-endurance. With his notoriously long life and his impenetrable armor, he represents the slave's ability to outlast trouble:

> "Tuck a walk de udder day, en man come 'long en sot de fiel
> a-fier. Lor', Brer Fox, you dunner w'at trubble is," sez Brer
> Tarrypin, sezee.
> "How you git out de fier, Brer Tarrypin?" sez Brer Fox,
> sezee.
> "Sot en tuck it, Brer Fox," sez Brer Tarrypin, sezee.
> "Sot en tuck it, en de smoke sif' in my eye, en de fier scorch
> my back," sez Brer Tarrypin, sezee. (60)

Short in stature and slow of foot, Brer Terrapin compensates for his lack of size or speed by clever stratagems. In a race with Brer Rabbit, he places wife and children at every marker and successfully carries off the impersonation. (All us Terrapins look alike!) In a contest of strength with Brer B'ar, he challenges his opponent to pull him out of the branch with a long cord. Diving to the bottom, he ties the cord to a husky tree root and humiliates the bear. The object lesson of these tales is clear: the slave is not a passive victim. He can survive and even prevail by learning to overcome his handicaps and limitations.

What of the figures of the Fox and Wolf? Beasts of prey, carnivores endowed with an appropriate strength and ferocity, they are exteriorizations of the slave's sense of danger. It is tempting to conclude that they are symbols of white power: certainly they become the principal targets of aggression and revenge. It may be closer to the truth, however, to suggest that slavery creates a situation where every black man is a wolf to his neighbor. For slavery abrogates community, destroys solidarity, and pits each slave against his fellows in a fierce struggle to survive. Hence the atmosphere of distrust and suspicion of which these tales are a projection.

Brer Fox and Brer Wolf, it is worth noting, are tricksters in their own right. They are forever trying to "put up a game on Brer Rabbit." In the tale "Mr. Wolf Makes a Failure," they attempt to lure him into the house of Brer Fox:

> "How you gwine git 'im dar?" sez Brer Fox, sezee.
> "Fool 'im dar," sez Brer Wolf, sezee.
> "Who gwine do de foolin'?" sez Brer Fox, sezee.
> "I'll do de foolin'," sez Brer Wolf, sezee, "ef you'll do de
> gamin'," sezee. (54–55)

The game consists of a scheme to trap Brer Rabbit by persuading him that Brer Fox is dead. The intended victim spoils the game, however, by inventing a countergame that penetrates his enemy's disguise.

Games and countergames, jokes and counterjokes, masks and countermasks: these are the stock-in-trade of the Brer Rabbit tales. To what cultural reality do these literary devices correspond? Once again we must turn to Ralph Ellison's comment that "America is a land of masking jokers." As if it were not enough for the slave to contend with raw white power, he finds himself controlled and manipulated, disarmed and disoriented, by white hypocrisy. Ellison has of course devoted an entire novel to the subject. Suffice it to observe of the Brer Rabbit tales that the white man's disingenuous treatment of the black supplies the delicious motive of the masker unmasked, the deceiver deceived.

In the deadly game of masking and countermasking, the slave's most powerful defense is a knowledge of his master's weaknesses. Like all tricksters, Brer Rabbit exploits the vices of his victims: their pride and vanity, greed and lust. Through studying the foibles of his masters, the slave becomes a natural satirist, as the dance form of the cakewalk demonstrates. Armed with this secret weapon he employs a kind of spiritual judo, whereby the white man's own momentum can be used against him. Prevented from asserting his own will, the slave learns to manipulate his master's to his own advantage.

This spiritual judo is the subject of the story "Mr. Rabbit Grossly Deceives Mr. Fox." Brer Fox invites Brer Rabbit to a party, where he intends to humiliate him in front of "Miss Meadows en de gals." But Brer Rabbit, scenting trouble, insists that he is too sick to attend. After much negotiation he agrees to go, but only if Brer Fox will tote him on his back, fully equipped with saddle and bridle. Brer Fox, intent on establishing his reputation with the ladies, readily submits. In an ironic reversal typical of the Brer Rabbit tales, it is Brer Fox, spurred mercilessly by the triumphant Rabbit, who is humiliated in the end.

The linguistic mode of the Brer Rabbit tales is derived from the principle of masquerade. That mode is irony, a form of verbal masking. In the world of Brer Rabbit, words seldom mean what they appear to mean. For the slave who takes his master's words at face value is a fatally disoriented man. He must learn instead to probe beneath the surface, assess the white man's motives, and adapt himself accordingly. In such a situation, mutual deceit becomes the norm. Masks proliferate and ambiguity prevails. The ever-changing guises of reality are reflected in the shifting façades of language. Irony thrives in such an atmosphere, as the ties that bind word and deed are dissolved.

It is in his fantasies of revenge that the black man's irony attains its maximum intensity. In a tale called "The Awful Fate of Mr. Wolf," Brer Rabbit kills off his hereditary enemy by scalding him to death. A sinister exchange takes place in the midst of Brer Wolf's agony. It is a scene that could have been imagined only by a race that has suffered from centuries of white hypocrisy. Revenge is sweet, and sweetest at its most ironic. Here the dislocation of word and deed reaches pathological proportions. And yet the dialogue that follows is no more cruelly cynical than the practice of enslaving blacks and calling it salvation.

> Den Brer Rabbit git de kittle en fill it full er water, en put it on de fier. "W'at you doin' now, Brer Rabbit?" "I'm fixin' fer ter make you a nice cup er tea, Brer Wolf." Den Brer Rabbit went ter de cubberd en git de gimlet, en commence fer ter bo' little holes in de chist-lid. "W'at you doin' now, Brer Rabbit?" "I'm a bo'in' little holes so you kin get bref, Brer Wolf. . . ." Den Brer Rabbit he got de kittle en commenced fer to po' de hot water on de chist-lid. . . . "W'at dat I feel, Brer Rabbit?" "You feels de fleas a bitin', Brer Wolf. . . ." "Dey er eatin' me up, Brer Rabbit," en dem wuz de las' words er Brer Wolf, kase de scaldin' water done de bizness. (66–68)

The most profound of the Brer Rabbit tales is the famous story of the Wonderful Tar-Baby. Brer Fox, hoping to trap Brer Rabbit, makes a figurine of sticky tar and places it in his victim's path. Brer Rabbit, attempting to exchange polite salutations with the stranger, is infuriated by his silence: "Ef you don't take off dat hat en tell me howdy, I'm gwineter bus' you wide open." But the Tar-Baby maintains his silence, so Brer Rabbit lams him with one fist. "Ef you don't lemme loose, I'll knock you agin," says Brer Rabbit, and the other fist is stuck fast. Whereupon he kicks and butts, only to find himself completely mired in the tar.

Hubris is the subject of this story. For once Brer Rabbit oversteps himself, taking on the white man's ways of arrogance and willfulness, and bullying the tarry representative of blackness. To bully is to be cruel and overbearing to others weaker than oneself, and for this psychological indulgence Brer Rabbit pays with one of his few abject defeats. On a deeper plane, the tale is concerned with the relationship of will and circumstance. To *force* circumstance, to browbeat or intimidate it, to want one's way no matter what, is a fatal attitude. For circumstance is sticky stuff that seems pliable enough, but leaves us, if we fight it, with a nasty problem of extrication.

The sequel to this tale, "How Mr. Rabbit Was Too Smart for Mr. Fox," delineates the proper relationship of will to circumstance. Brer Rabbit has been trapped, but he retrieves his error by *collaborating* with the force of circumstance, now embodied in the figure of Brer Fox. He manipulates his adversary by appealing to what Poe has called the imp of the perverse. As Brer Fox casts about for a means of killing his captive, Brer Rabbit counters each proposal by saying in effect: burn me, hang me, drown me, skin me, but whatever you do, don't fling me in that brier-patch. Which of course is the inevitable outcome, and Brer Rabbit skips off shouting triumphantly, "Bred en bawn in a brier-patch, Brer Fox—bred en bawn in a brier-patch!"

The brier-patch is an eloquent image of the uses of adversity. Lacking the defensive equipment of the porcupine, the rabbit borrows his defense from his environment; a hostile universe is thus converted to a sanctuary and a home. Such is the nature of antagonistic cooperation, as defined by Albert Murray in *The Hero and the Blues*. The nimble footwork, quick wit, and boundless invention of Brer Rabbit are called forth precisely by adversity. He is thus the forerunner of the blues hero who is equal to all emergencies and can extricate himself from any difficulty. This quality of improvisation in the face of danger, or as Hemingway would put it, grace under pressure, is in Murray's view the basis of the blues tradition.[13]

The Tar-Baby stories bring our discussion of the Brer Rabbit tales to a fitting close. For these are the supreme fictions of the folk imagination, as memorable for their esthetic form as for the wisdom they impart. When we consider that the artists who created these and similar animal fables were illiterate slaves, we can only stand in awe of their achievement. By this act of creativity they vindicated their humanity and established their claim upon the highest faculty of man: the moral imagination. In so doing they transformed their lives and overcame the limits of their low estate. They accomplished, in short, the crucial metamorphosis of a fate endured into a fate transcended.

In a poem called "O Black and Unknown Bards of Long Ago," James Weldon Johnson pays a moving tribute to the nameless authors of the Negro spirituals. Yet surely his sense of awe is no less appropriate to the anonymous creators of the animal tales:

> There is a wide, wide wonder in it all,
> That from degraded rest and servile toil
> The fiery spirit of the seer should call
> These simple children of the sun and soil.[14]

Johnson does in fact pay homage, if not to these black storytellers, at least to the folk hero that they made famous. In an early dialect poem, written in the manner of Paul Dunbar, he tells of a meeting in the forest where all the animals have gathered to decide "Who is de bigges' man." Judge Owl nominates Brer Rabbit, but this decision provokes so much jealousy that the animals fall to fighting among themselves. The outcome, as Johnson describes it, offers us a memorable image of the trickster-hero:

> Brer Rabbit he jes' stood aside an' urged 'em on to fight.
> Brer Lion he mos' tore Brer B'ar in two;
> W'en dey was all so tiahd dat dey couldn't catch der bref
> Brer Rabbit he jes' grabbed de prize an' flew.

Brer Wolf am mighty cunnin',
Brer Fox am mighty sly,
Brer Terrapin an' Possum—kinder small;
Brer Lion's mighty vicious,
Brer B'ar he's sorter 'spicious,
Brer Rabbit, you's de cutes' of 'em all.[15]

Notes

1. William Stanley Braithwaite, "The Negro in American Literature," in Alain Locke, ed., *The New Negro* (New York: Alfred and Charles Boni, 1925), p. 32.

2. See for example J. Mason Brewer, *American Negro Folklore* (Chicago: Quadrangle Books, 1968), and Richard M. Dorson, *American Negro Folktales* (New York: Fawcett, 1967).

3. Julia Collier Harris, *The Life and Letters of Joel Chandler Harris* (Boston: Houghton Mifflin, 1918), p. 162.

4. Dorson, *American Negro Folktales*, p. 17.

5. Letter from Harris to an unnamed Englishman, 9 June 1883. Quoted in Stella Brewer Brookes, *Joel Chandler Harris—Folklorist* (Athens: Univ. of Georgia Press, 1950), p. 26.

6. For a discussion of the Brer Rabbit tales which places them in this perspective, see Ellen Douglass Leyburn, *Satiric Allegory: Mirror of Man* (New Haven: Yale Univ. Press, 1956), pp. 57–70. Ed. note: Leyburn's analysis of Harris is reprinted in this collection, pp. 85–91

7. Bernard Wolfe, "Uncle Remus and the Malevolent Rabbit." *Commentary*, 8 (July 1949), 31–41. Ed. note: Wolfe's essay is reprinted in this collection, pp. 70–84

8. Jay B. Hubbell, *The South in American Literature* (Durham: Duke Univ. Press, 1954), p. 782.

9. Quoted in Hubbell, *The South in American Literature*, p. 793.

10. Harris, *Uncle Remus: His Songs and His Sayings* (New York: D. Appleton, 1880), p. xvii.

11. Harris, *Uncle Remus: His Songs and His Sayings* (New York: Schocken, 1965), p. 109. Subsequent references in the text refer to this edition.

12. William Farrison records just such an incident in *William Wells Brown* (Chicago: Univ. of Chicago Press, 1969), p. 33.

13. For a full elaboration of these ideas, see Albert Murray, *The Hero and the Blues* (Columbia: Univ. of Missouri Press, 1973), pp. 35–63.

14. James Weldon Johnson, *Fifty Years and Other Poems* (Boston: Cornhill, 1917), p. 7.

15. Johnson, "Brer Rabbit, You's de Cutes' of 'Em All," *Fifty Years*, p. 82.

"Uncle Remus and the Folklorists"

Kathleen Light*

No one was more surprised than Joel Chandler Harris himself to learn that the Negro animal fables he had written for the Atlanta *Constitution* had a "scientific" as well as a literary value. Yet within six months of the first weekly installment of the stories in the *Constitution* on November 16, 1879, John Wesley Powell of the Smithsonian Institution Bureau of Ethnology had written him concerning their ethnological importance. Powell's was but the first of a flood of such communications. As Harris later recalled, the collection of the stories under the title *Uncle Remus: His Songs and His Sayings*, published in December, 1880, "brought letters from learned philologists and folklore students from England to India. . . . from royal institutes and literary societies, from scholars and travelers."[1] Harris's biographers agree that he knew little if anything about the subject of folklore when he first began writing the Uncle Remus series,[2] and Harris himself in the introduction to *Uncle Remus* said that "ethnological considerations formed no part of the undertaking which has resulted in the publication of this volume."[3] It would have been surprising had Harris known much about the subject since it was at the time a relatively undeveloped field of study in America. The lore of Southern Negroes, moreover, was virtually unknown outside the South. Powell, who was a student of Indian folklore, had been completely unaware of the existence of the Negro animal tales until he saw them in the *Constitution*. As the *Journal of American Folklore* noted in its initial issue in 1888, it was Harris himself who first introduced Negro folktales to both the general public and the folklorists.[4]

If Harris knew little about folklore, he nevertheless betrayed a quick curiosity in the subject. When he announced the forthcoming publication of *Uncle Remus* in a *Constitution* article in April, 1880, he included a discussion of Powell's communication with him; and by the time he wrote his introduction to *Uncle Remus*, he had read enough in other folklore studies to formulate a short comparison of his Negro stories to South American Indian folklore. After the publication of *Uncle Remus*, Harris's

*Reprinted with the permission of the author and the publisher from *Southern Literary Journal*, 7 (Spring 1975), [88]–104.

interest in the subject appears to have grown rapidly. He became a subscriber to the *Folk-Lore Journal*, published in London, and added a number of folklore studies to his library.[5] Meanwhile, he continued to publish more Uncle Remus stories in the *Constitution* and national magazines, and when he collected these in 1883 in *Nights with Uncle Remus*, he provided a long introduction which reflected his increased interest in the subject of folklore. Harris could hardly have foreseen at this point that "ethnological considerations" would significantly influence his career as a writer. But it was such considerations which would prove a source of aggravation to him in *Nights with Uncle Remus* and would eventually lead him to the decision to retire Uncle Remus and write no more Negro folktales.

When Harris became concerned with the ethnological import of the tales, he found himself within a school of scientific thought which was in the process of constructing an elaborate argument which presumably explained the cultural inferiority of American Negroes. In the post-Civil War period, cultural anthropology, or ethnology, was influenced directly by Darwinian evolutionism. Ethnologists, as well as social evolutionists such as Herbert Spencer, believed that complex industrial societies were analogous to biologic organisms high on the scale of evolution while primitive societies were analogous to undifferentiated organisms at a rudimentary stage of biologic evolution. The most influential of the American ethnologists—Lewis Henry Morgan, Daniel G. Brinton, and John W. Powell, all of the Smithsonian Bureau of Ethnology—were convinced that each separate culture developed through well defined stages of primitivity, barbarism, and civilization, which, as Morgan stated it, were "connected with each other in a natural as well as necessary sequence of progress."[6] Although they understood the concept of cultural diffusion, they believed it to be a negligible force. Ethnologists generally denied that cultural borrowing was an important process in the evolution of a people, even where a cultural group was in close proximity to a more advanced society.[7] This concept of culture as "a cumulative social legacy" was indeed the central idea upon which the theories of the postwar anthropologists depended.[8] Adherence to such a theory inevitably led to a belief in raciocultural superiority. Since the logic of the ethnologists was based upon the axiom that the development of cultures followed a single, unitary pattern, they emphatically denied the notion of innate racial inferiority. But their devotion to a stage theory of cultural development resulted in the conclusion that certain peoples, American Negroes among them, had fallen behind the Caucasian race since their cultures had not yet developed to the final stage of industrial civilization.

It was not until the end of the nineteenth century that the theory of cultural evolution became widely popularized in a variety of educational, social, and legal theories which posited the separate status of Afro-Americans. Yet by the time Harris began writing, the theory was already so well developed among ethnologists that Powell could apply it to the Uncle Remus stories, finding in them a type of literature characteristic of a pre-civilized people. In a *Constitution* article of April 9, 1880, Harris related Powell's explanation that the animal fables, which were current also among American Indians, were to be considered a form of "zootheism, or animal-worship . . . being a characteristic mythology of that particular stage of culture which scientific anthropologists denominate as savagery." Harris then recounted Powell's evaluation of the significance of the tales within American culture: "Major Powell says that the legends which have appeared in *The Constitution* are doubtless in part a relic and in part a revival of the zootheism of savagery. They are, however, no longer a mythology proper, but a folklore. When a lower theism is superseded by a higher—as in the case of the negroes of this country, who accepted a theism of a higher grade which was enforced upon them—it is universally the case that relics of their original mythology remain, and such relics or revivals are properly denominated folk-lore."

The theory that American Negro folklore represented a lower, more primitive stage of culture might not have bothered Harris, had it not clashed with his original interpretation of the tales. In the same *Constitution* article in which he presented Powell's assessment of the stories, Harris wrote that for him the "unique" aspect of the stories lay not in their scientific implications but in the unusual role assigned the rabbit. "In the myth-legends of other races," he wrote, "the fox has figured as the embodiment of cunning and the wolf (or wehr-wolf) has represented the spirit of evil, but it remained for the imagination of the negro to invest the rabbit with the attributes of cunning and to make him the master of the situation under almost every conceivable circumstance." In the introduction to *Uncle Remus*, Harris, with a gentle thrust at scientific theories, elaborated upon this interpretation:

> The story of the Rabbit and the Fox, as told by the Southern negroes, is artistically dramatic in this: it progresses in an orderly way from a beginning to a well-defined conclusion, and is full of striking episodes that suggest the culmination. It seems to me to be to a certain extent allegorical, albeit such an interpretation may be unreasonable. At least it is a fable thoroughly characteristic of the negro; and it needs no scientific investigation to show why he selects as his hero the weakest and most harmless of all animals, and brings him out victorious in contests with the bear, the wolf, and the fox. It is not virtue that triumphs, but helplessness; it is not malice, but mischievousness.[9]

What Harris saw in the Brer Rabbit stories was a type of compensatory fantasy which portrayed the triumph of the black man over the white society that had enslaved him. The allegorical world Harris saw in his folktales was an upside down world which inverts the nature of things: power resides in "helplessness" and "mischievousness" rather than in "virtue" or "malice."

Where Harris originally considered the stories as the Negroes' response to a society which had rendered them inferior, the ethnological approach worked in an opposite direction: it claimed the stories themselves to be a proof of inferiority. Even when narrowly applied by ethnologists like Powell, the theory of cultural evolution forwarded the tales as "relics" of a primitive society—evidence that Afro-Americans had not yet achieved the advanced cultural stage attained by European-Americans. Harris's initial attitude toward Negro folklore clearly was not that of the ethnologists, but he proved to be susceptible to their way of thinking. The central problem with Harris was that although he genuinely respected the culture of Southern blacks, he himself was a white Southerner in good standing. He once admitted that as a writer he believed he had "two entities or personalities," for he seriously made a distinction between the man who wrote the editorials for the *Constitution* and the " 'other fellow' " who wrote the Uncle Remus stories.[10] The artistic result of this double consciousness was that there are always, as one critic has already pointed out, two levels to the Uncle Remus series: a "white" viewpoint and a "black" viewpoint.[11] For while Harris was careful to maintain the integrity and spirit of the black folktales in his fiction, he also, primarily through the character of Uncle Remus, managed to make them palatable to white readers. The balance Harris struck from his own ambivalence on race was a delicate one, and the dilemma presented by the theory of cultural evolution was that it forced him to try to resolve the racial ambiguities which were the essence of his writing.

The way in which the theory of cultural evolution exerted pressure on Harris is best seen in *Nights with Uncle Remus*, in which the thematic implications of a portion of the text contradict some of Harris's introductory comments. The introduction of *Nights* is indicative of Harris's growing interest in the subject of comparative folklore, for the ten-page introduction to the first volume is here extended to thirty-one pages. Most of the introduction Harris devotes to a comparison of his folktales with those in collections of Hottentot and Kaffir tales, Amazonian tortoise myths, and Creek animal legends. The primary impulse behind this discussion is simply his delight in discovering that recognizable counterparts to the Southern Negro tales exist in so many other places in the world. There is, however, a thread of argument running through these comments. Some folklorists, Powell among them, believed the Negroes had borrowed their stories from other peoples. Harris could not accept this explanation because for him the allegorical interpretation of the stories depended upon their being original with the Negroes. His desire to prove the African origins of his stories leads to a confused attempt to determine which versions of the stories are more authentic by deciding which more aptly depict the "peculiarities and characteristics" of the Negro race.[12] This approach in turn leads him to adopt the attitude of the ethnologist and to suggest at one point that the type of folklore told by a people will afford an index to their mental and cultural development.

Harris begins his remarks on folklore with a lengthy discussion of a recently published collection of Kaffir folktales, a collection he is suspicious of because the author admitted the stories had been revised by natives who not only told them but also wrote them down. Harris notes that the Kaffir tales substitute human characters for the victorious animal figures, and he sees in them "the story of the hare and other animals curiously tangled, and changed, and inverted" (p. xviii). By comparing the Kaffir tales with his own stories, he tries to adduce evidence of the existence of "a body of folk-lore among the Kaffirs precisely similar to that which exists among the negroes of the Southern states" (p. xvii). He concludes that in the Kaffir legends, "educated natives have 'cooked' the stories to suit themselves" (p. xvii) and that this body of folklore is "rather ahead of even the educated Southern negro" (p. xxiv). What Harris implies here is that the Kaffirs have evolved a more sophisticated body of folklore which reflects their relatively advanced cultural level. This evolutionary thesis, however, remains an implication only, for Harris always stops short of drawing any clear conclusions concerning the ethnological significance of the folktales he examines. In discussing the Kaffir stories, he admits that comparative evidence "may be worthless in this instance" (p. xvii). His typical remark after citing a variant to one of his stories is that the differences are "curious" or "interesting" and that they "offer a wide field for both speculation and investigation" (p. xxxii). The introduction to *Nights* reflects Harris's attraction to the methods of cultural anthropology and at the same time his reluctance to follow these methods to their logical conclusions.

The influence of ethnological considerations does not show itself in the text until approximately Chapter XXV when a new character, African Jack, is introduced.[13] As his name indicates, African Jack (also called Daddy Jack) is a native African, who at the age of twenty was brought to one of the Georgia sea islands and eventually sold to the brother of Uncle Remus's owner. The introduction of this character injects a flavor of primitivism into the book: Daddy Jack is known to be "a wizard, a conjurer, and a snake charmer" (p. 133), and he speaks the rhythmical Gullah dialect of the sea islands, which Harris describes in his introduction as "the negro dialect in its most primitive state . . . being merely a confused and untranslatable mixture of English and African words" (p. xxxiii). Daddy Jack is a fund of Negro superstitions and folklore, and he sometimes interrupts Uncle Remus's stories in order to give his own versions of the tales. This probing into comparative folklore reaches a climax in Chapters XXXIX–XLIII, in which five versions of the same story are recounted by Uncle Remus, Daddy Jack, and a third storyteller, Aunt

Tempy. The first story, told by Uncle Remus for the entertainment of the "little boy," who is his young master and primary audience in the series, is a model of the typical Brer Rabbit tale. Suffering from a particularly bad famine, Brer Fox and Brer Rabbit agree to sell their mothers in order to buy provisions. The fox sells his mother first, but the rabbit tricks him, steals the provisions, and never has to sell his mother.

As soon as the group is finished laughing "at a somewhat familiar climax," writes Harris, Daddy Jack "began to twist and fidget in his chair, and mumble to himself in a lingo which might have been understood on the Guinea coast." Finally, he exclaims impatiently, " 'Shuh-shuh! W'en you sta't fer tell-a dem tale, wey you no tell um lak dey stan'? 'E bery bad fer twis' dem tale 'roun' un 'roun'. Wey you no talk um stret?' " (pp. 236–37). Daddy Jack then gives his version, "Cutta Cord-la," a story which turns upon the use of a chant or holler. This chant motif prompts first Aunt Tempy, then Uncle Remus, and finally Daddy Jack to give three more variants. The series of stories which follows from Uncle Remus's first story represents roughly a movement backward in time. In his introduction, Harris identifies "Cutta Cord-la" as a story which "originated in San Domingo or Martinique" (p. xxxii). Aunt Tempy follows this sea island story with one she heard as a child in Virginia, and Daddy Jack's final story is obviously of African origin. This geographical movement toward an earlier black experience, along with Daddy Jack's opening comments criticizing Uncle Remus for twisting his story, may lead the reader to expect a concurrent movement toward more authentic and primitive stories whose modifications and variations will furnish insight into the cultural evolution of the Negro. Instead, the stories become increasingly complex, and the issue of cultural evolution is obscured rather than clarified. Through this sequence, Harris seems to be rejecting ethnological interpretations and reaffirming his belief that the stories are a conscious artistic representation of the black experience. For although the sequence of comparative stories reveals nothing about the cultural evolution of the Negro, it does open to the reader another dimension of the black mind, a dimension which is not usually admitted in the Uncle Remus books.

Daddy Jack's "Cutta Cord-la" makes a significant departure from the standard Brer Rabbit story. Brer Rabbit uses a song to identify himself to his grandmother, and she opens her door only at the sound of his voice. Brer Wolf overhears the words and succeeds in fooling the grandmother by imitating the rabbit's voice. Brer Rabbit, however, arrives in time to expose the imposter and save his grandmother by breaking the wolf's neck. This conclusion inverts the "familiar climax" Harris referred to at the beginning of the story, for trickery, instead of triumphing, here goes down to fatal defeat. Aunt Tempy then tells a story based upon a song trick, but it is Uncle Remus who elaborates upon the theme of justice suggested in Daddy Jack's tale. In Uncle Remus's "The Fire-Test," Brer Fox uses a song trick to gain entrance to Brer Rabbit's home and devour all his children. To discover the culprit, Brer Rabbit makes all the animals jump over a fire he builds in a pit. The fox, shaken by the knowledge of his guilt, falters in his jump and falls into the fire. This story is entirely unlike any other Uncle Remus has told previously either in *Nights* or *Uncle Remus*: Brer Rabbit becomes the victim instead of the prankster, while virtue is vindicated, trickery being punished by a type of justice uncharacteristic of the tales. The themes of guilt, justice, and retribution introduced by Uncle Remus undergo an interesting modulation in Daddy Jack's "The Cunning Snake." An African woman steals a nest of snake eggs, knowing she is in the wrong. The snake swears revenge, biding his time, however, until the woman has a child. By means of the now familiar song trick, the snake manages to deceive the child. He swallows her whole, but in making his escape he falls asleep along the road where the woman finds him and kills him. She then cuts the dead snake open and recovers her child, who subsequently revives.

To understand the meaning of the sequence, Daddy Jack's final story should be considered in the light of Harris's comments in the introduction to *Nights*. That "The Cunning Snake" bears some relationship to the Kaffir tales Harris had examined is apparent both because a human figure is substituted for the victorious animal and because the typical elements of the Brer Rabbit story are, as Harris had noted of the Kaffir tales, "curiously tangled, and changed, and inverted." The journey back to the African origins of the folktale thus concludes with a story which is neither a more authentic nor a more primitive version. According to Harris's implications in his introduction, Daddy Jack's final story is representative of a culture relatively high on the scale of cultural evolution, for it belongs to a body of literature he characterizes as "rather ahead of even the educated Southern Negro." But so much emphasis has been placed upon Daddy Jack as a primitive type that the reader can hardly accept him as a representative of a culture more advanced than that which has produced Uncle Remus or Aunt Tempy. Because of his peculiar speech and actions, Daddy Jack seems the most primitive of the storytellers, but by placing in his mouth what is presumably the most sophisticated story in the volume, Harris confounds the notion of cultural evolution. At the same time, it should be noted that this final story in no way appears to be "ahead of" the native American Negro. The themes of Uncle Remus's "The Fire-Test" are closer to "The Cunning Snake" than to the type of story he is in the habit of telling, indicating that he is quite capable of comprehending this particular type of story.

In this section of the book, then, Harris seems to be poking fun at the ethnological arguments behind his own introduction to the volume. And he gives point to his rejection of evolutionary theories by using the comparative folktale sequence to suggest that the Negro mind is not necessarily limited to any one frame of reference such as that portrayed in the standard Uncle Remus story. When Aunt Tempy is first reminded of a story from her childhood, Uncle Remus becomes very serious and warns her against " 'foolin' 'roun' 'mungs' dem ole times. De bes kinder bread gits sour' " (p. 242). Uncle Remus's objection is well made, for the storytelling session progressively takes on a more serious and embittered tone as the theme of justice becomes the central and explicit issue. What appears to happen is that as the storytellers recall other versions of Uncle Remus's first story, they move away from the allegory in which racial justice remains a submerged theme to another level of imaginative consciousness not bounded by the slave mentality. In effect, the final two stories of the series right the upside-down world of the Brer Rabbit tales, making a more direct statement on the themes of human rapacity, injustice, and retribution.

It is at this point that the racial ambiguities underlying the stories begin to dissolve, leaving Harris confused and troubled. For the process of discrediting evolutionary notions has led him to admit a level of black consciousness which threatens him as a white man. Harris's own discomfiture over the folktale sequence is reflected in the little boy in the chapter following "The Cunning Snake." Relieved at finding Uncle Remus alone in his cabin, the boy for the first time registers dissatisfaction with the stories he has been hearing. Not articulate enough to formulate a criticism of the metamorphosed themes and increasing seriousness of the stories, the boy nevertheless hits upon the crucial factors which motivate the sequence of variant tales. " 'I don't like these stories where somebody has to stand at the door and sing, do you?' " asks the child. " 'They don't sound funny to me.' " When the boy's objections lead to the snake in Daddy Jack's tale, Uncle Remus reminds him the snake cannot harm him because it is in Africa. The boy, however, provides a cogent reply to this argument: " 'Well, Daddy Jack, he came, and the snake might come too.' " (pp. 260–61). Uncle Remus's method of cajoling the boy out of his fears is to return him to the familiar story patterns of Brer Rabbit's trickery and triumph over the fox and wolf. The old man and the boy remain alone for awhile, during which time Uncle Remus tells nine Brer Rabbit stories, all of which adhere scrupulously to the original allegorical format. The other storytellers eventually return, but although they contribute several stories, there are no further excursions into comparative folklore, and there are no more stories which threaten the original allegory.

The comparative folklore sequence represents but a small portion of the stories and themes of *Nights with Uncle Remus*, but it reveals with some clarity Harris's own inner dilemma. Fascinated by ethnological theories, he nevertheless as an artist rejects them. Forced to confront racist interpretations of the folktales, he upsets the balancing of racial attitudes in the Uncle Remus series. The pressure was subtle, but it was enough to make Harris back away from the subject altogether. Nine years elapsed between the publication of *Nights* and the third volume of stories,

Uncle Remus and His Friends, and in the intervening years Harris's attitudes toward the study of folklore changed dramatically. The image of
himself Harris projects in the introduction to *Friends* is of a passive and
casual collector of folk stories. In his earlier introductions, Harris had explained his painstaking methods for collecting and verifying his folktales.
He now says that the present stories were "caught for me in the kitchen"
by his cook or brought to him by his children. "This work of verifying and
putting together," he adds laconically, "has been going on since 1884, but
not in any definite or systematic way."[14]

Typically, Harris does not discuss explicitly the theory of cultural
evolution in his introductory remarks. He does, however, make specific
reference to a *Popular Science Monthly* article, "Evolution in Folklore,"
which had applied an evolutionary reading to one of his stories. An
amateur folklorist, David D. Wells, had heard a variant of one of Harris's
stories from a South American slave who had been born in Africa. Wells
begins his article by postulating that "a careful study of the alterations
which take place in the typical legends of a people illuminates the history
of the race itself,"[15] and then proceeds to trace in the variations between
the African story and Harris's version the cultural evolution of the
American Negro. Wells notes that in Harris's story, unlike the original,
the characters sometimes question each other closely. Such questioning
procedures, says Wells, are typical of English rather than African
folktales. The discrepancy between the original and later versions
therefore shows proof of borrowing, for "this inquiry and thirst after information . . . is thoroughly English in spirit. The native African would
never have asked such questions, because he was by nature lazy and indif-
ferent. . . ."[16] More importantly, Wells contends, the original story
shows an understanding of cause and effect which is missing in the later
version. In the African story, a hunter is attacked by cows because he tries
to kill them; in Harris's story, a boy is attacked by a panther "for no
assignable reason whatsoever." Such a lapse is natural, concludes Wells,
for a people who, being enslaved, did not have to worry about providing
for themselves.[17]

Harris's impatience with this use of his story breaks through his
discussion of Wells's article, for he has his own history to give of the
folktale. The story he published was brought to him by his own child
who, he subsequently learned, had forgotten part of it. The full story as
he later heard it from a Georgia Negro "differs in no essential particular"
from Wells's version, and Harris concludes that the "variations are not
worth taking into account" (pp. v–vi). This incident leads to what is for
Harris a vehement repudiation of his earlier interest in comparative
folklore:

> But the folk-lore branch of the subject I gladly leave to those
> who think they know something about it. My own utter
> ignorance I confess without a pang. To know that you are ig-

norant is a valuable form of knowledge, and I am gradually
accumulating a vast store of it. In the light of this knowledge,
the enterprising inconsequence of the Introduction to "Nights
with Uncle Remus" is worth noting on account of its unconscious and harmless humor. I knew a good deal more about
comparative folk-lore then than I know now; and the whole
affair is carried off with remarkable gravity. Since that Introduction was written, I have gone far enough into the subject
(by the aid of those who are Fellows of This and Professors of
That, to say nothing of Doctors of the Other) to discover that
at the end of investigation and discussion Speculation stands
grinning. (pp. vi–vii)

Abandoning former racial considerations, Harris insists that his folktales
are valuable only "because of the unadulterated human nature that might
be found in them." As he wrote them he imagined children about him
laughing, and it seemed, writes Harris, "that these visions, vain though
they might be, were more promising than a hopeless journey through the
wilderness to discover at what place and at what hour the tribes of the
mountains and the citizens of the plains shook their hairy fists at each
other, and went jabbering their several ways" (pp. vii–viii). He then announces that this is the last of the Uncle Remus volumes, for he is consign-
ing the storyteller to a place among "the affable Ghosts that throng the
ample corridors of the Temple of Dreams" (pp. x–xi).

Harris stood by his decision to write no more Uncle Remus tales for
more than a decade, but popular demand for the stories finally led him to
revive the old man and his folktales in *Told by Uncle Remus*, published in
1905. Harris confided to a friend that he suspected the stories in this
volume were not "quite up to the old mark."[18] He might have appleid this
same judgment to *Uncle Remus and His Friends*, for the stories in the
later collection are perceptibly different from those of the first two
volumes. Having grown suspicious of his own materials and the spurious
interpretations that could be attached to them, Harris responded by strip-
ping the stories of all possible meaning. What he did in these later stories
was to emphasize the theme of trickery and mischievousness while at the
same time undercutting the theme of victory and triumph. The later
stories thus carry less allegorical force, being frequently nothing more
than settings for Brer Rabbit to display his precocity. The rabbit himself is
a much less commanding figure in these stories, and Uncle Remus frequently emphasizes his fallibility.[19] If it seems somewhat silly to discuss
the characterization of a rabbit, perhaps a more telling comment on these
later stories is that the Walt Disney movie, *Song of the South*, drew its
material almost exclusively from them rather than the stories of the first
two collections.[20]

The slant of these new stories was indicative of the direction Harris
was to take following his decision to retire Uncle Remus. In 1894, the year
after the appearance of *Friends*, Harris published the first of six books

designed specifically for children—the Sweetest Susan and Buster John series. No longer interested in the subject of folklore, he mixed stories of his own invention with English and Negro folktales without bothering to distinguish the origins of the various stories.[21] Even when he revived Uncle Remus, he did not return to his former interest in folklore. Harris never fully explained his abrupt abandonment of a serious perspective on Negro folklore, but the reasons may be traced both in his own personality and in the type of fiction he was trying to write. Not willing to cast himself as a champion of the Negro, he would not challenge openly the racist interpretations of the folklorists. For him the success of the Uncle Remus series depended upon his skill in submerging and disguising racial issues, but the theory of cultural evolution forced him to confront these very issues. Although earlier in this career, he had been confused by ethnological theories, there is enough evidence to conclude that he came to understand quite well how these theories degraded black folklore and thus undermined his own art. Harris never really forgot the folklorists: he satirized them in a sketch in 1898,[22] and in 1903 in the last of the Sweetest Susan series, he got his revenge on them by imprisoning one and forcing him to tell stories without expatiating on their scientific significance. The stories in *Wally Wanderoon and His Story-Telling Machine* are told by a professional storyteller who has been incarcerated in a box for the crime of giving scientific explanations of his stories. He identifies himself as an ethnologist when he explains his educational background: " 'It was one of the principles taught at the university where I graduated that a story amounts to nothing and worse than nothing, if it is not of scientific value. I would like to tell the story first, and then give you my idea of its relation to oral literature, and its special relation to the unity of the human race.' "[23] But Wally Wanderoon has the storyteller in his power, and by threatening him with dire physical reprisals, prevents him from pursuing his scientific speculations. " 'Why, just that kind of talk,' " Wally Wanderoon tells the storyteller, " 'has done more harm in this world than you can imagine.' "[24]

Notes

1. Quoted in Julia Collier Harris, *The Life and Letters of Joel Chandler Harris* (Boston and New York: Houghton Mifflin, 1918), p. 162.

2. *Life*, p. 161. See also Paul M. Cousins, *Joel Chandler Harris: A Biography* (Baton Rouge: Louisiana State Univ. Press, 1968), p. 111.

3. Joel Chandler Harris, *Uncle Remus: His Songs and His Sayings* (New York: D. Appleton, 1894), p. 4.

4. "On the Field and Work of a Journal of American Folk-Lore," *Journal of American Folk-Lore*, I (April-June, 1888), 5. The editors mention a recent "interesting collection" of Negro tales, an obvious reference to *Uncle Remus*.

5. *Life*, p. 154.

6. Lewis Henry Morgan, *Ancient Society, or Researches in the Lines of Human Progress from Savagery Through Barbarism to Civilization* (New York: Henry Holt, 1877), p. 3.

7. George W. Stocking, *Race, Culture, and Evolution* (New York: Free Press, 1968), p. 123.

8. Idus L. Murphree, "The Evolutionary Anthropologists: The Progress of Mankind, The Concepts of Progress and Culture in the Thought of John Lubbock, Edward B. Tylor, and Lewis H. Morgan," American Philosophical Society *Proceedings*, CV (June 27, 1961), 28.

9. *Uncle Remus*, p. 9.

10. Quoted in *Life*, pp. 384–85.

11. John Stafford, "Patterns of Meaning in *Nights with Uncle Remus*," *American Literature*, XVIII (May, 1946), 90.

12. Harris, *Nights with Uncle Remus* (Boston and New York: Houghton Mifflin, 1883), p. xxxi.

13. Chapters I–XVIII were published between May and August of 1881 in the *Constitution; The Critic*, I (February and April, 1881); and *Scribner's Monthly*, XXII (June, July, and August, 1881). That these stories were written within a year of the publication of *Uncle Remus* accounts for the fact that they, like the earlier stories, are not influenced by ethnological theories. Chapters XIX–XXVII were published during the summer months of 1883 in the *Constitution* and *The Century Magazine*, II (September, 1883). The remaining stories, including the comparative folklore sequence in Chapters XXXIX–XLIII, apparently were not published prior to *Nights* but were written specifically for the book.

14. Harris, *Uncle Remus and His Friends: Old Plantation Stories, Songs and Ballads with Sketches of Negro Character* (New York: Houghton, Mifflin, 1893), p. iv.

15. David D. Wells, "Evolution in Folklore," *Popular Science Monthly*, XLI (May, 1892), 45.

16. Wells, "Evolution in Folklore," p. 52.

17. Wells, "Evolution in Folklore," p. 53. Wells's argument is a flagrant misconstruction of the theory of cultural evolution. It is interesting to note how he manages to fault Negroes for both their African descent and their American experience.

18. Letters to James Whitcomb Riley, July 11, 1903, quoted in *Life*, p. 488.

19. *Uncle Remus and His Friends*, p. 54.

20. Cousins, *Harris*, p. 221.

21. Harris, *Little Mr. Thimblefinger and His Queer Country* (Boston and New York: Houghton, Mifflin, 1894), p. iii.

22. See Harris, "The Late Mr. Watkins of Georgia," *Tales of the Home Folks in Peace and War* (Boston and New York: Houghton, Mifflin, 1898).

23. Harris, *Wally Wanderoon and His Story-Telling Machine* (New York: McClure, Phillips, 1903), pp. 179–80.

24. *Wally Wanderoon*, p. 187.

"Uncle Remus and
the Ubiquitous Rabbit"

Louis D. Rubin, Jr.*

In late August of 1876, an epidemic of yellow fever struck the city of Savannah, Georgia. By the first of September, twenty-three persons had died, and physicians were advising all who could leave to do so at once. Among those departing was a twenty-seven-year-old newspaperman who feared for the health of his family and decided to seek safety in the higher elevation of Atlanta; it was not long before the editor of the Atlanta *Constitution*, Evan P. Howell, and his new associate editor Henry W. Grady arranged to have this man join the staff on a temporary basis. On November 21 the *Constitution* was able to announce that Joel Chandler Harris had accepted a permanent position.

Grady and Harris were old friends; each admired the other's work immensely. Thus it came about, as C. Vann Woodward points out, that during the 1880s there were at work across the desk from each other in the *Constitution* office the author of the Uncle Remus stories, which made of an animal-tale-telling plantation Negro a household symbol of the good old days, throughout the United States and overseas, and the ardent, exuberant promoter of a New South of commerce and industry that would supposedly break away from the outworn southern past and inaugurate a new era of progress and prosperity.

The alliance of Joel Chandler Harris and Henry Woodfin Grady was not as incongruous as it might seem. For both Harris and Grady were marketing the same product—reunion. The gentle old darky telling amusing tales of the days when the creatures could talk was one form of packaging; the image of a bustling, go-getting New South bent upon business and dedicated to the American way of thrift and enterprise was another. Both men were utterly sincere in their endeavors. There were depths to Harris' view of the Negro, which I suspect he secretly realized,

*This essay was originally published in *Southern Review*, NS 10 (October, 1974), 787–804. Reprinted by permission of the author and Louisiana State Univ. Press from *William Elliott Shoots a Bear: Essays on the Southern Literary Imagination*, by Louis D. Rubin, Jr. (Baton Rouge, La.: Louisiana State Univ. Press, Copyright © 1975), pp. 82–106. Professor Rubin is University Distinguished Professor at the University of North Carolina at Chapel Hill. His many books include *Thomas Wolfe: The Weather of His Youth* (1955), *The Curious Death of the Novel: Essays in American Literature* (1967), and *The Faraway Country: Writers of the Modern South* (1963).

that carried implications ultimately contradictory to the way that his stories were received during the years of their greatest popularity. Similarly, Grady's ideological approach to the good life contained contradictions that in the future would work directly against the promulgation of the racial and social assumptions that he was making. But in their time and place, what these two newspapermen accomplished was to help give the former slaveholding Confederate South a legitimate and accepted place in the American Union—a place in which southern racial and social attitudes would not serve to bar participation.

The impact of Harris' work, and the example he gave to subsequent southern writers, can be seen if we consider the following depiction of an old black retainer: "He was a large, broad-chested, powerfully made man, of a full glossy black, and a face whose truly African features were characterized by an expression of grave and steady good sense, united with much kindliness and benevolence. There was something about his whole air self-respecting and dignified, yet united with a confiding and humble self-sufficiency." And again, "Nothing could exceed the touching simplicity, the child-like earnestness of his prayer, enriched with its language of Scripture, which seemed so entirely to have wrought itself into his being as to have become a part of himself, and to drop from his lips unconsciously; in the language of a pious old negro, he 'prayed right up.' "

Now we may consider another such old black man: "The figure of the old man, as he stood smiling upon the crowd of Negroes, was picturesque in the extreme. He seemed to be taller than all the rest; and, notwithstanding his venerable appearance, he moved and spoke with all the vigor of youth. He had always exercised authority over his fellow-servants. He had been the captain of the cornpile, the stoutest at the log-rolling, the swiftest with the hoe, the neatest with the plough, and the plantation hands still looked upon him as their leader. . . . His voice was strong, and powerful, and sweet, and its range was as astonishing as its volume. More than this, the melody to which he tuned it, and which was caught up by a hundred voices almost as sweet and as powerful as his own, was charged with a mysterious and pathetic tenderness."

The second black man being portrayed is Uncle Remus; the first is Harriet Beecher Stowe's Uncle Tom. The similarity of the portraits is obvious, for the characterizations are very much alike. There are individual differences, to be sure: Uncle Remus is not so religious in his common utterance as Uncle Tom, and Uncle Tom is not given to reciting animal tales. But both uncles are "happy darkies": simple, gentle, unlettered but wise in human nature, tolerant of the foibles of mankind, kind to children, mellowed by time, unspoiled by the artificialities of too much civilization.

The enormous disparity between the reception of Mrs. Stowe's novel by the American reading public, and that public's response, less than thirty years afterward, to the Uncle Remus tales, did not lie, therefore, in the depictions of the black protagonists. Rather, it was the relationship of the black men to the resident whites that made the difference. Mrs. Stowe showed Uncle Tom as mocked, beaten, starved, his humanity denied, his virtue unrewarded. Harris showed Uncle Remus as honored, pampered, respected, his simplicity and gentleness cherished by his grateful and indulgent white patrons. Thus, if the northern reading public could feel that it was not Mrs. Stowe's version of black-white relationships, but Joel Chandler Harris', that typified life in the South, then the proper response was not to send armies southward to trample out the vintage where the grapes of wrath were stored, but to let the underlying amicability and mutual trust of black-white relationships down there exist free of the meddling of northern politicians and the blunders of misguided reformers. And this, all in all, was what the stories of Joel Chandler Harris and his imitators helped to accomplish. As Paul M. Gaston wrote in *The New South Creed*, "By convincing Northern readers that relations between the races were kindly and mutually beneficial, a principal obstacle in the way of sectional harmony was removed. The North had doubted this point, but on the authority of Harris and others it came to accept the Southern point of view." Such "acquiescence by the North in the Southern scheme of race relations permitted the South to deal with (or to fail to deal with) its race problems unmolested."[1]

Joel Chandler Harris was a complex, reticent man, who must secretly have pondered the contradictions and compromises in his own life, but if ever he revealed them to anyone, there is no record of it. The nearest he came to hinting of the agonies and doubts that especially in his earlier years must have plagued him was in some letters he wrote to a friend in Forsyth, Georgia, shortly after he left there to write editorial paragraphs for the Savannah *Morning News* in the early 1870s. To Mrs. Georgia Starke, he wrote letters full of loneliness and pain. He was in his early twenties, and no doubt the full implications of his illegitimate birth and lack of social position were sinking into his consciousness for the first time. "My history is a peculiarly sad and unfortunate one," he wrote to her, "—and those three years in Forsyth are the brightest of my life. They are a precious memorial of what would otherwise be as bleak and as desolate as winter." And again, "The truth is, I am morbidly sensitive. With some people the quality of sensitiveness adds to their refinement and is quite a charm. With me it is an affliction—a disease—that has cost me more mortification and grief than anything in the world—or everything put together. The least hint—a word—a gesture—is enough to put me in a frenzy almost. . . . You cannot conceive to what an extent this feeling goes with me. It is *worse* than *death* itself. It is horrible. My dearest friends have no idea how often they have crucified me."[2] Not too long after that Harris was married, and things improved for him, but to the end of his life the shyness and the melancholy remained. One senses it in the determined effort made in his later writings to have everything turn out happily, to gentle whatever was harsh or unpleasant, to insist, in spite of all, that people were basically good and kind, and everyone friendly and happy. In such assertions he goes too far, leaves out too much, makes too many disclaimers in the face of evidence to the contrary, for his idyllic portraits of simple life among the plain folk of middle Georgia to be accepted at face value.

He was an ambitious man. He was driven by the wish to succeed, to win renown as an author, and at the same time he was afraid of his ambition and constantly asserted his disinterest in fame and minimized his own abilities. He liked to pretend that he wrote without artifice or art and that he had done little more than transcribe the Negro folk tales that won him worldwide acclaim. Yet he once showed Ray Stannard Baker the drafts of sixteen introductory passages to a single story. He was tongue-tied and terribly embarrassed among strangers; never would he allow himself to speak in public. If he saw an unknown caller coming to his house he would sneak out the rear door. Yet among friends that he trusted, he was often the soul of mirth; when he came in for work at the *Constitution* office in the morning, if things appeared to be too serious, he would break into a little jig and shuffle in the center of the floor, so as to get everyone laughing. He wrote to his publisher on one occasion that his big mistake had been ever to allow his name to appear on his books: "There was no need for such a display and it has created for me a world of discomfort." Yet one of his last requests was that after his death the magazine that he was editing in his final years bear on it the legend "Founded by Joel Chandler Harris."

Just what manner of man Joel Chandler Harris was we shall never know, but one thing seems clear: he was certainly not the simple, gentle, easygoing soul pictured by his earlier biographers. Given the artistic sensitivity that made him into the writer he became, the very facts of his origins and early experience alone would render that unlikely. Harris was born in Eatonton, Georgia, on December 9, 1848. His mother's people were of pioneer Georgia stock. Apparently (for we actually know nothing definite about it) his mother fell in love with an Irish railway worker, and when her parents would not consent to their marriage, she ran away and lived with the man in Eatonton. Little is known about him; he seems to have departed shortly after his son's birth and was never afterward heard from. The mother retained her own family name, Harris, and gave it to the child. She was befriended by local citizens, reconciled with her mother, and earned her living as a seamstress in Eatonton. In later life Harris was always full of praise for the friendly, democratic society of the little town of Eatonton and repeatedly expressed his gratitude to the townsfolk for their kindness toward him and, by implication, their failure in any way to look down upon him when he was a boy or make him ashamed of his illegitimate origins. Yet it is obvious that, as he grew somewhat older, the clouded circumstance of his birth worried Harris very much. That it is not unrelated to his morbid shyness, his fear of new situations, his stammering and social unease, seems evident. Several of his novels, set in communities like Eatonton, involve orphaned, illegitimate children who later turn out to be the lost heirs of aristocratic families. Indeed, one has the suspicion that Harris was not always completely convinced that an itinerant Irish day laborer had been his real father at all.

There lived on Turnwold plantation, not far from Eatonton, a remarkable man named Joseph Addison Turner. He sometimes called at the Harris home with sewing work, and to judge from what happens in the novels, Harris would appear at times to have fantasized that Turner was his father. A planter, Turner had great literary ambitions. He published poetry and essays, started several magazines with the object of giving the South a literary outlet, and during the Civil War procured a Washington hand press and type and began issuing from his plantation a weekly literary paper, *The Countryman*, modeled on *The Spectator* and *The Tatler*.

Harris, who was a redheaded, freckled, homely lad, very small for his age, liked to hang around the Eatonton post office, reading the newspapers, and when in 1862 he found in the first issue of *The Countryman* an advertisement for "an active, intelligent white boy, 14 or 15 years of age to learn the printer's trade," he applied at once. Turner called for him, took him out to Turnwold, and Joel Harris began work as an apprentice printer. Quickly he learned to set type and was given the run of Turner's substantial library. Soon he began composing little items for *The Countryman*, some of which Turner was happy to print.

Harris described his days at Turnwold in a fictionalized autobiography, *On the Plantation* (1892), dedicated to Turner's memory. This book, which except for the Uncle Remus stories is by far his most readable work, shows young Joe Maxwell hunting, reading, working, and listening to plantation slaves tell stories. Between the boy and the blacks there was immediate rapport and trust. On one occasion the boy discovered a runaway slave from a nearby plantation and, instead of turning him in brought him food and looked out for him. After that the plantation slaves were assiduous in their attention to him. He also accompanied a search party using dogs to follow the scent of the fugitive, and while Harris will not exactly say so, it seems likely that Joe Maxwell went along with a view toward looking after the runaway slave's interests. At one point he observed a bateau drifting past along a stream, sitting low in the water, and surmised that it contained the runaway slave. Later another slave confirmed the suspicion.

Did this happen? Harris declined to identify what was fact and what was fiction in *On the Plantation*. What is interesting is the extent to which Joe Maxwell's situation is reminiscent of that in *Huckleberry Finn*. That child of uncertain parentage also befriended a runaway slave and helped throw hunters off his trail, and the incident with the bateau is not without its precedent in Mark Twain's novel. There are also numerous other similarities, both to *Huckleberry Finn* and *Tom Sawyer*. Harris was a great admirer of *Huckleberry Finn*, declaring in the *Critic* in 1885 that it was a genuinely great work of serious literature—a status that most critics were unwilling to accord the book at the time. But whether the episode with the runaway slave came from literature or life—my own feeling, based on the difference between the tone of the material and that of the other, clearly fictional episodes in the book, is that something like it must indeed have taken place—what is important about it is the relationship it sets up with the slaves. There was a sympathy, amounting to an identification of interests, that is unmistakable. As Jay B. Hubbell notes in *The South in American Literature*, "It is almost as though he were one of them. . . . His illegitimate birth seemed not to matter. It would have been different if he had been the son of a great slaveholder like Turner or perhaps if he had lived in Turner's house." This instinctive identification, so different from anything else in southern local-color fiction except for Clemens', was to be of absolute importance to the dynamics of the Uncle Remus stories Harris would later write and would remain valid in spite of Harris' conscious adherence to the official southern position on the subject.

While at Turnwold, too, as Hubbell points out, Harris first read *Uncle Tom's Cabin*, a book which he later said "made a more vivid impression on my mind than anything I have ever read since." Union troops came through Turnwold during Sherman's march to the sea, but did no damage except for some pillaging. It was in the wake of their departure that Harris witnessed an incident that he described in *On the Plantation* and elsewhere. He came upon an old Negro woman shivering and moaning. An old Negro man lay nearby, his shoulders covered with a ragged shawl:

> "Who is that lying there?" asked Joe.
> "It my ole man, suh."
> "What is the matter with him?"
> "He dead, suh! But, bless God, he died free!"

After postwar conditions ended publication of *The Countryman*, Harris worked as a printer on the Macon *Telegraph*. He also began reviewing books and writing poetry. Offered a job as private secretary to the publisher of a New Orleans literary magazine, he went there, but this did not work out well, so he returned home and was hired as assistant on a weekly, the Monroe *Advertiser*, setting type, printing the newspaper, and contributing humorous paragraphs. This led to a position, at the handsome salary of forty dollars a week, on the Savannah *Morning News*, edited by William Tappan Thompson, whose earlier *Major Jones' Courtship*, humorous sketches of middle Georgia life, had won him widespread notice.

It was while he was employed in Savannah that Harris met and in 1873 was married to Esther LaRose, the daughter of a French Canadian ship captain. In 1876 came the family flight to Atlanta to escape the yellow fever epidemic, and there Harris began the job on the *Constitution*. For that paper he wrote editorials and continued his comic paragraphing.

Harris' discovery of the Uncle Remus material came over the course of several years. The *Constitution* had been publishing some Negro dialect sketches by a member of its staff, Sam W. Small, in which one Old Si was used to make political comments and local observations. Upon Evan P. Howell's purchase of the paper in 1876, Small left the staff. Looking around for someone to continue the feature, Howell asked Harris to try his hand at it. Harris wrote two sketches, one of them involving a Negro character named Uncle Remus, who related a story about another Negro's ill-fated attempt to ride a recalcitrant mule. These were well received, and Harris tried some more, some of them also involving Uncle Remus. These earliest sketches, which were later included in Harris' first book, were not animal tales, but conventional anecdotes of the minstrel variety, poking fun at the vagaries of uneducated blacks, along with political sermons to promote the *Constitution's* policies. What chiefly distinguished them from numerous such pieces by other journalists was their richness of idiom and their attention to the nuances of dialect. Gradually Harris began evolving the characterization of Uncle Remus, and though at this stage he was made to exhibit many of the attributes of the comic darky stereotype, Remus was coming to possess a dignity and a pride that transcended his merely comic role.

Later that year Sam Small rejoined the *Constitution*, and Harris gave up his Negro sketches and began writing essays for the Sunday edition. He could not, however, stay away from Remus. After some months Harris reintroduced Remus as the hero of a story describing how during the war the old Negro had been left in charge of the plantation and had spied a Federal sharpshooter in a tree, taking aim at a Confederate on horseback whom the slave recognized as his own master, whereupon he had raised his own rifle and killed the sharpshooter. In many ways the story was a conventional local-color yarn, designed to exhibit the slave's fidelity to his white owner. When Harris published his first Uncle Remus book several years afterward, he revised the tale so that the Yankee sharpshooter, instead of being killed, was merely wounded and was subsequently nursed back to health by his intended victim's family and ultimately wed to the daughter.

Such a plot, of course, could as well have been produced by a thoroughgoing plantation apologist such as Thomas Nelson Page. There is, however, one difference. When, in the book version, the northern woman to whom he is telling the story asks Remus, "Do you mean to say that you shot the Union soldier, when you knew he was fighting for your freedom?" Harris has Remus reply, "Co'se I know all about dat, en it sorter made cole chills run up my back; but w'en I see dat man take aim, en Mars Jeems gwine home ter Ole Miss en Miss Sally, I des disremembered all 'bout freedom en lammed aloose." Page would never have included this; he would not have had his Negro feel any such debt to a Yankee, or allowed any hint of conflicting loyalties. The difference here is not vital, so far as the overall meaning of the story itself is concerned, but it is indicative of a quality in Harris that Page did not possess: that of being able to recognize the existence of a difference between the interests of the slave and those of his white owner. Harris was not always consistent in this perception; in a later volume such as *The Chronicles of Aunt Minervy Ann* it is singularly absent. But it is precisely this awareness, however consciously played down in much of the non-Remus fiction, that made the Uncle Remus animal stories possible.

In the December issue for 1877, *Lippincott's Magazine* published an article, "Folklore of the Southern Negroes," by William Owens. Harris commented on it in the *Constitution* for November 21, 1877, and remarked on the author's lack of expertise in translating dialect. But the article made Harris realize that literary value existed in the animal stories and myths that he had once heard from slaves in Eatonton and at Turnwold. So he moved Uncle Remus from Atlanta back to "Putmon County," where he had been a slave for "Mars Jeems," and set him to telling the six-year-old white boy of the plantation a story of how Mr. Rabbit outwitted Mr. Fox. The account appeared in the *Constitution* for July 20, 1879. He waited four months before publishing a second animal story, which appeared on September 17. Mr. Rabbit and Mr. Fox now became Brer Rabbit and Brer Fox, and the story was about how Brer Fox fooled Brer Rabbit by constructing a tar baby. Harris had found his subject. More than that, he had found a way to tell what he knew in print.

The format of the Uncle Remus animal stories, developed at the start and maintained with little change through eight books, has the little white boy—in later volumes, the first little boy's son—visiting Uncle Remus in his cabin on the plantation and listening, with occasional comments, while Remus tells about the days when the creatures could talk.

Clearly it is not the folktale subject matter as such that provides the chief appeal of the Uncle Remus stories, though when he began publishing them Harris discovered to his surprise that he was indeed contributing to the literature of folklore and that the same stories of rabbit, fox, wolf, terrapin, raccoon, and opossum that plantation Negroes in Georgia had told to him were known to ethnologists the world over, with their counterparts existing among the Indians of North and South America, the bushmen of Australia, and the Moro tribesmen of the Philippines. The appeal lies in the way that they are told and in the dynamics of the relationship between Uncle Remus, the successive little white boys who listen, and the animal protagonists of the tales themselves, notably

Brer Rabbit. The animal legends were necessary to Harris for the basis of his stories; when he exhausted his stock of recollections he advertised for more, and his readers supplied him with new materials. But Mark Twain was quite right when he told Harris that "in reality the stories are only alligator pears—one merely eats them for the sake of the salad dressing." The importance of the stories is that, because of their content and the associations they had for Harris, they enabled him to tap wellsprings of creativity hitherto unknown and fully available to him in no other form. When he tried to do it through other guises, it was never the same. In the Uncle Remus stories Harris was indeed able to *see* the world as a black man did, and also to sense *why* the black man looked at it in that fashion.

The important thing to remember about the Uncle Remus stories is that not merely the old Negro telling the stories, but the animal protagonists themselves, are southern rural blacks. What they do is inseparable from the idiom used to describe their actions. It is Brer Rabbit, and occasionally Brer Terrapin, whose antics provide the plot of the stories. The various tricks that Brer Rabbit plays on the fox, the wolf, the bear, the cow, and sometimes even Mr. Man himself, all exhibit his cunning and his resourcefulness, and it is this that Uncle Remus most admires as he relates them. Sometimes Brer Rabbit acts in order to procure food, sometimes to protect himself from being eaten, sometimes to avoid work while enjoying its benefits. At times his chief motivation is that of gaining revenge for attempted attacks on himself or his family. His dignity is also very important to him; he is quick to avenge any insult or slight. Sometimes, too, he will go to work on his fellow creatures merely in order to keep them mindful of his identity. Occasionally he is prompted by sheer mischievousness; in company with Brer Terrapin he will suddenly decide to have some fun with the others.

Harris knew very well that the rabbit was a Negro. In the preface to the second published volume, *Nights with Uncle Remus*, he declared of the black man's preference for the rabbit as hero of his folklore that "it needs no scientific investigation to show why he selects as his hero the weakest and most harmless of all animals, and brings him out victorious in contests with the bear, the wolf, and the fox. It is not *virtue* that triumphs, but *helplessness*; it is not *malice*, but *mischievousness*." Several critics have pointed out, however, that strictly speaking, this last is not true of the Uncle Remus stories, for usually Brer Rabbit is more than merely mischievous: he can be quite malicious at times, and he is very much set on maintaining his prestige and reputation. Often his triumphs are based on the instinct for sheer survival rather than on any taste for prank-playing. But it is something of a mistake to allegorize these stories, as some have done, merely as showing the Negro rabbit using his helplessness and his apparently insignificant status as weapons against the white power structure in the guise of the fox, bear, and wolf. The matter is a trifle more complex than that. What the rabbit exemplifies is the capacity to survive and flourish in a world in which society can be and often is predatory. The rabbit confronts life; the realism with which his situation is depicted, as Louise Dauner shows, "precludes any sentimentality. . . . Both life and death must be fatalistically accepted."[3] The power is in the hands of the strong; the weak cannot trust to any supposed belief in benevolence or fair play, for the real rules are those of power. That this had profound implications for the situation of the black man in rural southern society is obvious; yet what makes the stories work so well is not any such direct political and social allegory, but the realism with which Harris can view the life he is depicting.

It is not that Harris was, consciously or unconsciously, trying to allegorize the plight of the black man; these are not parables of protest, and their success comes because they are not thus shaped. If they are moral, they are so as all great art is moral: through depicting the actualities of the human situation and by implication contrasting them with what we hold to be ideal. Through his instinctive identification with the black man, Harris was able to depict society as it confronted the underdog (or under-rabbit, perhaps). Writing about animals, he could describe humans, and with a realism that was not subject to verification by the rules of poetic justice. A slave—or a sharecropper—must accept things as he finds them, not as he might like for them to be. "De creeturs dunno nothin' 'tall 'bot dat dat's good en dat dat ain't good," Uncle Remus tells the little white boy. "Dey dunno right fum wrong. Dey see what dey want, en dey git it if dey kin, by hook er by crook. Dey don't ax who it b'longs ter, ner wharbouts it come fum. Dey dunno de diffunce 'twix what's dern en what ain't dern." In telling about the animals, Harris did not have to shape the morality and motivations of his characters in accordance with what the ideality of his time and place decreed ought to be; he could view their actions and responses in terms of what truly *was*. Uncle Remus could accept harsh actualities in a way that a white narrator might not have been able to do, because the experience that was Remus'—the experience of the plantation slave, as Harris had been privileged to perceive it—was all too elemental and devoid of merely sentimental gestures. "In dem days," Remus tells the little boy on another occasion, "de creeturs bleedzd ter look out fer deyse'f, mo' speshually dem w'at ain't got hawn en huff. Brer Rabbit ain't got no hawn en huff, en he bleedzd ter be his own lawyer." Harris knew this, but it was only when writing of Negro life in the guise of the animals that he could, as a writer, tell what he knew.

Writing about black experience in the form of animal stories, therefore, served to liberate Joel Chandler Harris' imagination. It provided him with a technique whereby a writer who had once been a shy, stammering, redheaded, illegitimate youth and faced social realities in a way that was direct and unprotected, could draw upon what he knew and create stories that depicted reality as few other writers of his time and place were able to do. He could make use of his humor, his awareness of the savageness and the remorseless nature of human circumstance, his sense of fatality, without the inhibitions of the genteel literary tradition, social respectability, or southern racial imperatives.

The Uncle Remus animal stories are not tragic; they are comic. But the comedy is decidedly not that of foolish, childlike darkies, the standard fare of local color. It is not comedy sweetened by sentiment. When, for example, in the story entitled "Why Mr. Possum Has No Hair on His Tail," the rabbit and possum decide to raid the bear's persimmon orchard, and the rabbit decides to have some fun and informs the bear that Brer Possum is up in his persimmon trees, it is not Brer Rabbit who gets punished, either for his collaboration in theft or his betrayal of his accomplice. The possum is the one who suffers; he is shaken down from the tree, flees, and just as he escapes through the fence the bear grabs his tail in his jaws and rakes if forever clean of fur. The rabbit enjoys the spectacle thoroughly. The aggression, the pleasure taken in the possum's discomfiture, the cleverness of the rabbit, are amusing, but only because the characters are animals; one cannot imagine Harris or any other such writer suggesting a smiliar outcome to a story involving people. Yet the characters *are* people—black people. Thus was Harris enabled, however obliquely, to deal with reality, whether white or black.

As for the narrator, Uncle Remus, he enjoys the whole account. *He*, of course, wouldn't do such things; for he is the kindly, noble local-color retainer. But he tells the little white boy about a world in which such things do happen, and then, when the little white boy occasionally becomes disturbed by the indifference of the creatures to conventional ethics, Uncle Remus reminds him that rabbits, foxes, bears, possums, terrapins, and the like cannot be judged by human standards. As Louise Dauner says, "In Uncle Remus we have the symbol of the wisdom of Things-As-They-Are, a realistic acceptance and humorous transmission of the strenuous conditions and paradoxes of life. In Brer Rabbit we have the inescapable irony of the Irrational, coupled with man's own terribly humorous struggle for survival." Truly, the implications of the Uncle Remus stories are ferocious—as ferocious as those of the Mother Goose poems.

Only in the animal stories can Harris offer such an unsentimental version of reality. Those Uncle Remus stories which are not centered on animal fables achieve no such directness, nor did they enjoy any such popularity as the animal tales. In those Atlanta sketches, Uncle Remus is all but indistinguishable from a hundred other literary plantation uncles.

Harris wrote a large quantity of fiction. Several of the early stories, notably that entitled "Free Joe and the Rest of the World," are among the better local-color fiction. Harris does, in that story, come closer to imagining the black man's situation than does most local-color fiction. The story describes a freed Negro during slavery times and tells of how, because he has no economic value to the white community, he is separated from his wife, who is still a slave, and left to starve. Some critics—Darwin Turner, for one—have read the story as an example of white racism, declaring that it exemplifies Harris' habit of thinking of Negroes who are not protected by white men as pathetic creatures. There is truth to this. Turner criticizes the depiction of Mom Bi, in "Mom Bi: Her Friends and Enemies," as so selflessly devoted to her white family that she resents less her aristocratic master's selling her daughter than his sending his son off to fight side by side with low-caste whites in the Confederate army, where he is killed.[4] Such devotion, Turner remarks, is rather farfetched. Harris' insistence in print that white southern fear of the black man is without rational basis is explained by Turner as being due to his view of blacks as harmless, comical children: "One does not hate or fear a child or a pet, even when he misbehaves."

Again, there is justice to what Turner says. But the difficulty with such criticism is that it is ahistorical and thus cannot recognize and acknowledge what was quite clear to Harris' own contemporaries: that, viewed not by the standards of the 1960s and 1970s but in the historical context of white-black relationships in the South and of the depiction of blacks in fiction, Harris' black characters represent an important advance in the literary representation of the black man's humanity. Harris was not writing his stories at a time when that humanity was generally acknowledged, whether in the South or the North. He was showing black characters as suffering because mistreated, misjudged, misunderstood—during an era when the very depiction of the fact that, for example, a Free Joe could be deprived of all human dignity and joy by cruel or thoughtless whites merely because he was black constituted something of a rebuke to contemporary attitudes. In stressing the loyalty of his blacks to the whites, he was advancing the hypothesis that a people capable of such loyalty were worthy of help and trust and fair treatment, and such was decidedly not what a great many southerners were interested in giving them at the time, or willing to concede that they merited. It is quite true that portraiture along such lines, no matter how well intended, is ultimately demeaning; but that was not the issue in the years of the 1880s when Harris was writing those stories. The issue was much more stark and elemental. It was whether, as a recipient of the policies and attitudes of the white majority, the black man was worthy of the treatment accorded to a human being. In story after story, Harris said he was, and that was a great deal more than many of his fellow southerners were prepared to admit, if the political and social developments of the late nineteenth century are any indication. If the attitudes of today seem far removed from those of the 1880s and 1890s, it might be proper to suggest that writers such as Joel Chandler Harris had something to do with that.

A large portion of Harris' writings, from the early novel *The Romance of Rockville* onward, is focused not upon the black but the plain folk. He considered the area of middle Georgia where he grew up the most democratic region in the country; and in many of his stories, as well as his two later novels, *Sister Jane* (1896) and *Gabriel Tolliver* (1902), he sought to recreate that democratic village environment in fiction. This was in line with Harris' own origins and his views; as one of a relatively few important southern writers after 1865 who did not come from the gentry, he did not envision everyday southern experience as primarily an affair of plantations, but of small towns and villages. Uncle Remus, it is true, lives on a plantation; but the stories he tells are of the days when the creatures could talk, of the rural farming community, and have little to do with plantation life. Even the autobiographical *On the Plantation* is the account of a youth employed on a plantation, associating not with the planter and his family so much as with the slaves, the Irish journeyman printer, nearby middle-class whites, and villagers. In a story, "Ananias," Harris dealt rather sarcastically with one Colonel Flewellyn, who is clearly modeled on Joseph Addison Turner, emphasizing his impractical-ity and foolishness. In *Sister Jane* the local squire turns out to be the seducer of a farm girl. Indeed, it might be said that in the long run Joel Chandler Harris worked importantly to undercut the plantation literary tradition. He not only shifted the center of attention from the lordly master and lovely lady to the black slave, but he made the plain folk of the village the focus of his non-Negro stories, thereby opening the way for much realistic southern fiction of a later day.

Yet it must be said that except perhaps for one or two stories such as "Free Joe and the Rest of the World," the only work of Harris that has importantly survived its day are the animal stories. To some extent this may be ascribed to the format of the Uncle Remus stories; Harris was able to handle such episodes of 1,500 to 2,500 words with a formal expertness that he was not able to bring to longer, more complicated stories, and when he sought to work at the novel length he was out of his depth. In this respect his journalistic limitations stayed with him always; once he exceeded the length of the newspaper format he got into trouble. Yet this by itself will not suffice as an explanation; for when he tried the same thing later on, with his Billy Sanders sketches, with the spokesman-protagonist a sage, humorous middle Georgia white farmer, the results are not impressive.

The real difficulty would seem to be that except when he was writing about life as experienced by southern Negroes in the guise of rabbits, ter-rapins, and other animal creatures, he became too much the sentimen-talist and all too unwilling or unable to look at life without making everything come out right. There *had* to be happy endings: village life had to be shown as sweet, tolerant, without prejudice; slaves had to be treated with kindness; seducers had to have hearts of gold; blacks during the Reconstruction and afterward had to be loyal to the white folks. Only in the tales told by Uncle Remus do people steal, lie, and triumph even so; only in them do people live by their wits and enjoy it; only in them are deception and trickiness portrayed as virtues and economic necessities as more binding than moral imperatives. Harris never read any of the animal tales to his own children. "I was just thinking," the little boy remarks to Uncle Remus after an episode in which Brer Rabbit cleverly steals Brer Fox's provender, "that when Brother Rabbit got the chickens from Brother Fox, he was really stealing them." To which Remus replies, "Dey ain't no two ways 'bout dat. But what wuz Brer Fox doin' when *he* got um? Pullets an' puddle ducks don't grow on trees, an' it's been a mighty long time sence dey been runnin' wil'. No, honey! Dey's a heap er idees dat you got ter shake off if you gwine ter put de creeters 'longside de folks; you'll hatter shake um, an' shuck um. . . . Folks got der laws, an' de creeturs got der'n, an' it bleeze ter be dat away." Life in the world of Uncle Remus is no picnic; as he remarks upon another occasion, "ef deze yer tales wuz des fun, fun, fun, en giggle, giggle, giggle, I let you know I'd a-done drapt um long ago. Yasser, w'en it come down ter gigglin' you kin des count ole Remus out."

Was Harris fully aware of what he was doing in those stories? Such remarks as that just quoted seem to leap out of the page with startling clarity. What are they doing there at all? We know that Harris was quite aware that he was writing about black people. It seems inevitable that, having heard the stories under the circumstances that he did, he would have known that they were not, in their symbolic action, without relevance to the daily lives of the blacks. Yet before we go too far in crediting Harris with any secret racial subversiveness—and for a modern reader the temptation is all too real—we must remember that very little in his nonanimal stories involving black people in the South will validate any such theorizing, while there is considerable evidence to show that Harris was of his time and place and that, however benevolent his attitude, he did not transcend his circumstance. Furthermore, whatever it may have been that Harris intended, and whether consciously or unconsciously, his audience surely did not read the stories as subversive. In their time the stories seemed only to confirm the stereotype of the contented darky. They told readers that the black man was happy. They seemed to glorify life on the old plantation.

He was a curious man—not at all the simple sage of Snap-Bean Farm that he is made out to be, but a very private and complex person. It is as if there were two Joel Chandler Harrises—the journalist, citizen of Georgia, and man of letters who wrote pleasant, optimistic, moral tales in which right triumphed and the plain folk were good and kind; and the fiercely creative artist, his uncompromising realism masked to the world and to the other Harris as well by the animal-tales format, one who saw life devoid of sentiment and unclouded by wishful thinking.

He himself sensed this. Here is what he once wrote to his two daughters:

You know all of us have two entities, or personalities. That is the reason you see and hear persons "talking to themselves."

They are talking to the "other fellow." I have often asked my "other fellow" where he gets all his information, and how he can remember, in the nick of time, things that I have forgotten long ago; but he never satisfies my curiosity. He is simply a spectator of my folly until I seize a pen, and then he comes forward and takes charge. . . . Now, I'll admit that I write the editorials for the paper. The "other fellow" has nothing to do with them, and, so far as I am able to get his views on the subject, he regards them with scorn and contempt; though there are rare occasions when he helps me out on a Sunday editorial. He is a creature hard to understand, but, so far as I can understand him, he's a very sour, surly fellow until I give him an opportunity to guide my pen in subjects congenial to him; whereas, I am, as you know, jolly, good-natured, and entirely harmless.

Now, my "other fellow," I am convinced, would do some damage if I didn't give him an opportunity to work off his energy in the way he delights. I say to him, "Now, here's an editor who says he will pay well for a short story. He wants it at once." Then I forget all about the matter, and go on writing editorials and taking Celery Compound and presently my "other fellow" says sourly: "What about that story?" Then when night comes, I take up my pen, surrender unconditionally to my "other fellow," and out comes the story, and if it is a good story I am as much surprised as the people who read it. Now, my dear gals will think I am writing nonsense; but I am telling them the truth as near as I can get at the facts—for the "other fellow" is secretive. Well! so much for that. You can take a long breath now and rest yourselves.[5]

In his later years, Harris grew increasingly out of sympathy with the booming, bustling, progressive spirit that continued to exemplify Atlanta commercial and civic life, the heritage of his friend Grady. He did not like the new ways and did not share in the latter-day enshrinement, as he saw it, of the almighty dollar. There was too much materialism in the air; more and more he looked back at the village life of his childhood as having embodied a simplicity and a spiritual cleanliness that he thought was disappearing now from Georgia and the South. He never repudiated or even criticized what his friend Grady had meant for the South, and yet he must have realized that it was Grady's program that was more than a little responsible for the emphasis on money-making that was building huge skyscrapers along Peachtree Street and mansions in Druid Hills, even while the slums grew more dilapidated along Rusty Row and Decatur Street. "We hear a good deal about Progress," we find him writing in 1907; "it is held over the head of the conservative in the semblance of a big stick, but there is nothing crueler or more sinister, for progress is nothing more than the multiplication of the machinery and methods by which certain classes and people increase their material gains.

The necessity of trade and barter has always existed . . . but modern business is the result of a partnership between greed and gain, and it consists in nothing but an abnormal cleverness in assembling and dispersing pieces of paper that stand for nothing, and in massing the details of large and unnecessary transactions." It was a long way from Henry W. Grady that he had traveled, toward the end.

On July 3, 1908, at the age of fifty-nine, Joel Chandler Harris died of uremic poisoning, the result of cirrhosis of the liver. Two weeks before his death he sent for a Catholic priest, Father O. N. Jackson, and asked to be baptized in his wife's faith. "I have put off this important matter too long," he told the priest, "but procrastination has been the bugbear of my life; and I feel that the Lord will make allowance for this weakness, for I have believed the teachings of the Catholic Church for many years." Father Jackson reported that when he asked whether fear of criticism by others had helped cause Harris' delay in joining the Church, he was told, "No, I should say shyness had more to do with it."

Notes

1. Paul M. Gaston, *The New South Creed: A Study in Southern Mythmaking* (New York: Alfred A. Knopf, 1970), pp. 181–82.

2. Harris to Mrs. Georgia Starke, 9 September 1870 and 18 December 1870, quoted in Julia Collier Harris, *The Life and Letters of Joel Chandler Harris* (Boston: Houghton Mifflin, 1918), pp. 78, 83–84.

3. Louise Dauner, "Myth and Humor in the Uncle Remus Fables," *American Literature*, 20 (May 1948), 135.

4. Darwin T. Turner, "Daddy Joel Harris and His Old-Time Darkies," *Southern Literary Journal*, 1 (Autumn 1968), 36. Ed. Note: Darwin Turner's essay is reprinted in this collection, pp. 113–129

5. Harris to Lillian and Mildred Harris, 10 March 1898, quoted in *Life and Letters*, pp. 385–86.

"Underlying Despair in the Fiction of Joel Chandler Harris"

Michael Flusche*

When the Uncle Remus stories began appearing in the early 1880's in newspapers, magazines, and, finally, books, readers around the country were curious about the author who created the kindly old man with the endless string of tales. But Joel Chandler Harris was not much given to talking about himself. He fled reporters and visitors, hated to give autographs, and tried to maintain a quiet, sedate life as an editorial writer for the Atlanta *Constitution*. When a gang of children gathered at George Washington Cable's house in New Orleans to meet Harris, they were disappointed to find that Uncle Remus was not black, but had red hair and a freckled face. Worse, they learned that the shy and stuttering storyteller was frightened even of them and could not begin to tell them a story.

Even in the brief autobiography Harris finally agreed to write for *Lippincott's Magazine*, he dismissed his career as that of an "accidental author" and quickly passed over the most significant aspects of his life. Of his early days he said simply, "I was born in the little village of Eatonton, Putnam County, Georgia, December 9, 1848, in the humblest sort of circumstances." Except for the interest in writing which grew from hearing his mother read *The Vicar of Wakefield*, he mentioned nothing more about the first twelve years of his life; certainly he scarcely hinted at the sources of the profound insecurity that plagued him the rest of his days and drove him to write compulsively from the time he was fourteen years of age. Nor did he mention the fears and suspicions he still harbored concerning society, for he tried desperately to disguise his melancholic pessimism.[1]

In this brief autobiography and in his fiction, as he tried to come to

*Reprinted with the permission of the author and the publisher from *Mississippi Quarterly*, 29 (Winter 1975–76), [91]–103. Michael Flusche is Associate Professor of History and Associate Dean of the College of Arts and Sciences at Syracuse University. He has published articles and reviews in the *New York Historical Society Quarterly*, *Journal of American Studies*, *Virginia Magazine of History and Biography*, *Southern Humanities Review*, *America*, *North Carolina Historical Review*, and other journals.

grips with the unpleasant aspects of life, Harris tended to idealize his own past beyond recognition. His pessimism dominated his imagination even though his genteel conception of the role of literature led him to write optimistic and uplifting tales. The result was that in almost all his works, while the overt message is cheerful and light, just beneath the surface is a world in which every man is an island with few bonds to the other members of society.

I

Perhaps the most significant legacy of Harris's childhood was his lingering sense of inadequacy. His father, who was said to be an Irish laborer, disappeared before Harris was born. His mother, who never married, was a destitute seamstress sharing her one-room shack with her son and, for a time, her mother. The cabin itself was a gift of a prominent citizen of Eatonton. As an illegitimate lad dependent on others' charity, Joel was no doubt troubled by his position near the bottom of society. His fears bubbled to the surface in a mock oration he wrote in his copybook: "Which is most respectable," he asked, "poor folks or niggers?"[2]

Very early Harris developed one of the traits that stayed with him for life; even as a boy he consistently put a pleasant face on things. As he was growing up and staging the "Gully Minstrels" with his friends, one of his ambitions was to become a clown, for he loved to make others laugh. But even in the rough-and-tumble backwoods, his extraordinary hunger for rough pranks earned him the reputation of the hellion of the neighborhood. The laugh of the practical joker, however, could scarcely disguise the hostility he felt towards his playmates. He gave one of his friends a blistering ring around his neck by pretending to cut his throat with a hot pancake flipper. Another he tricked into jumping into a pig pen crawling with large fleas. He knocked onto the head of a third a large hornets' nest alive with its inhabitants.[3] All his rough pranks, however, never won him self-confidence; he remained exceedingly shy and never got over his prohibitive stammer.

When he left home at age thirteen to become a printer's apprentice, he received his first experience in journalism at the plantation of Joseph Addison Turner.[4] After the collapse of the Confederacy and the end of Harris's idyllic employment, he followed his early training and began pushing himself upward through the ranks of the Georgia press. All the while, however, he suffered intensely from his sense of inadequacy and loneliness. When he joined the Macon *Telegraph*, the rest of the staff teased the young newcomer for his flaming red hair, his awkwardness and stammer, and his naive innocence. At his initiation into the typesetters' union, he was so frightened that he could not repeat the oath and had to be excused from the ceremony. Still, his ambition urged him on, and he moved to New Orleans for a while, then back to Georgia. In 1870 he received the flattering offer to become an associate editor of the Savannah *Morning News*,[5] where he established his name as one of the leading humorists and editorial writers in the state.

Although Harris was encouraged by his success, old fears and suspicions lingered on. In a series of letters to Mrs. Georgia Starke, a young matron in Forsyth, Georgia, he poured out his anguish to the only close friend he had. Torn between ambition and self-doubt, he dreamed of moving to New York to pursue his career, but he feared such high ambition would come to nothing because of the "bitter destiny" that shaped his life. On his twenty-second birthday, he reflected on the years that had passed. "My history," he confided to Mrs. Starke, "is a peculiarly sad and unfortunate one." Because he was incapable of dealing with others and because even the most trivial misunderstandings tortured him immensely, his self-contempt swelled as he longed for the ultimate peace: "I have wished a thousand times that I was dead and buried and out of sight . . . what a coarse ungainly boor I am—how poor, small and insignificant." He longed to be alone at the same time he desperately needed others. "I do not love my friends," he wrote, "because they love me—(I could never be sure of *that*, you know)—but because I must love someone."

For the time, Harris determined to put aside his fears and suspicions for the sake of his career. He knew that his morbid sensitivity and fear of strangers approached at times the pathological, for the "slightest rebuff" tortured him "beyond expression." His peculiar tendencies seemed to him so abnormal that he was sure they lacked "only *vehemence* to become downright insanity." But the "main point," he concluded, "is success and advancement." Friends could be an obstacle to his success, so he resolved that forming friendships at this time was "not to be thought of." Rather than listen to their biased judgment, he would trust "entirely to merit for success."[6]

Not even his future wife, Esther, could easily gain his confidence; about a year before their marriage, Harris could not bring himself to see his sweetheart off as she left on a trip. The next day he wrote her the explanation: "I wanted to tell you good-bye, but I knew I would have to hide my real feelings and say something commonplace. I despise and detest those false forms of society that compel people to suppress their thoughts." Then, after telling her how "blank and desolate" his life would be without her and how patiently he would "watch and wait and long" for her return, he succumbed to the fear that haunted him constantly: "I daresay you are laughing at me as you read."[7] But Esther did gain his trust, and once they were married, she tried to shelter him from everything that disturbed his peace.[8]

Within a few years Harris had moved to Atlanta and had become an associate editor of the Atlanta *Constitution*. After a while, however, the strain of the work so told on him that he had to flee the city to spend days in the country by himself. He often would complete his assignments in the quiet of his study rather than face the confusion and personal contacts in the office. For twenty-four uncomfortable years, he contributed almost daily to the editorial page. But even as he wrote for the voice of the New South and industrial development, for Harris the good life was represented not by hustling downtown Atlanta but by the seclusion of "Snap Bean Farm," his home beyond the end of the street car lines.[9]

II

Because Harris felt so isolated from those around him, he longed for a harmonious and homogeneous society where the poorest illegitimate lad could be the equal of the planter's son. Indeed, as Harris looked back from middle age, he felt that the Middle Georgia he had known as a boy was such a place. "The same families had been living there for generations," he wrote, without mentioning the vast numbers who had been pushed off the land, "and they intermarried until everybody was everybody else's cousin. Those who were no kin at all called one another cousin in public . . . everybody was comfortably well off, so that there was no necessity for drawing social distinctions . . . the humblest held their heads as high as the richest."[10]

In the process of romanticizing the past, Harris transformed his memories of a colorful and exciting childhood into bland and stylized narratives. As a boy, for instance, he had helped train a neighbor's fox hounds by scampering across the countryside dragging a fox pelt and then climbing a tree to wait for the hounds to find him. When he wrote of fox hunting later, he became the master of ceremonies and the urbane escort for a fair young lady visiting the plantation for the first time. Although Harris, the illegitimate and impoverished youth, did not fit at all into the Old South as he later described it, from the perspective of the post-Civil War South, the old order took on an obsessive appeal. The "old plantation days" lived in his dreams with a charm and warmth they had certainly lacked when he lived through them.

The Uncle Remus animal tales, upon which Harris's fame rested, are a particularly clear example of his tendency to cloak a pessimistic view of life beneath a lighthearted grin. The tales, at least the first two volumes containing over one hundred stories, were based on authentic folklore Harris had heard as a boy from the slaves. As the slaves had told them, the stories reflected a humorous recognition that beneath all the graceful amenities the world was a hostile place. Every man was a possible enemy in spite of his smiles and grins, and only the fool was unwary. But in Harris's version, the humor that was always present became predominant, for the author heightened the appearance of cordiality among the animals and softened their hostility. The philosophic old Uncle Remus who told the stories to the little boy in a plantation setting muted the real meaning of the stories. Harris was so successful in giving, as he desired, "a genuine flavor of the old plantation," that readers such as Mark Twain felt that Uncle Remus was more interesting than the stories themselves.[11]

In addition to the Uncle Remus stories, Harris wrote over twenty volumes of fiction employing characters and themes drawn straight from the plantation tradition. Under gentle masters, slavery became the school of civilization for a race that otherwise would have remained barbarous and shiftless. A number of marriages between Union soldiers and Southern belles celebrated and strengthened national unity by showing once again that "one may be a Yankee and a Southerner too, simply by being a large-hearted, whole-souled American."[12] Early in his career, Harris distinguished his stories from those of Thomas Nelson Page by introducing characters from the whole range of Southern society. Poor whites, either mountain folk or sandhillers, and middle-class citizens, lawyers and shopkeepers, were central in about half of the stories in the first two volumes he published. But by the end of the century Harris had abandoned his efforts to depict poor whites and turned to sentimental domestic fiction and children's stories. In these, the sky was seldom darkened by a social problem.[13]

In the 1890's, after Harris passed his fiftieth year, he began the first of three books that were largely autobiographical. In these, his pessimism struggled with his desire to produce a suitably sunny account of his experiences. The result in the first story, *On the Plantation*,[14] was an idealization of his life as it could have been, a mixture of fact and fancy. Although Harris had previously related that he had "been without sympathy" a good portion of his life, in the story the young boy became everyone's favorite. The life that he had formerly described as "bleak and desolate as winter" became an endless summer of adventure. But all the cheery welcomes the boy in the story received from runaway slaves or plantation workmen could not hide his rootlessness. The only mention of the young boy's mother was her parting kiss as he left home to become a printer's apprentice. For the rest of the story he remained a smiling but lonely figure wandering from adventure to adventure.[15] There were no permanent bonds to hold the little social atom anywhere.

Strong encouragement from Walter Hines Page led Harris to publish in 1896 his first real novel, *Sister Jane*.[16] The book developed the image of the outsider, the frightened observer of life around him, this time as a grown man. Set in a small Georgia town a decade before the Civil War, the novel dealt with the events between the disappearance of a neighborhood boy and his reappearance five years later. Harris wrote the novel to embody a number of characters who, he said, "were capering about" in his mind. At the same time, he wanted to wash away "the bad taste of some pessimistic books"[17] he had read but did not name.

In the absence of strong nuclear families or any common purpose, the only bond that united the characters was superficial geniality. Much of the dialogue and incidental activity was intended to establish that the characters were indeed friends. The emphasis on cordiality resembled the animals' ritual of etiquette in the Uncle Remus stories. The reality beneath the surface was the opposite of appearances. The manners of the animals hid their hostility, while the cordiality of the characters in *Sister Jane* disguised their isolation. The facade of the small town and its elaborate social niceties hid the wasteland of human relationships that was always in the background of Harris's mind.

The characters who were capering about in his mind were pathetic figures. William Wornum, the narrator, was a middle-aged lawyer incapable of mastering the daily trifling matters of the household. Frightened and ineffective, he fled to his study at the approach of the young woman next door, who had been the object of his infatuation for years. When a friend of Harris's remarked that William Wornum resembled the author, Harris responded, "That's just the trouble, I'm afraid some one will find out who he is and ruin me."[18] Wornum lives with his sister, Jane, a man-hating harridan who dominates the household; she has raised her brother from his infancy and continues to dominate his life. The family next door is singular indeed: the husband has fathered the illegitimate son of a poor girl in the neighborhood, and when his wife, who has been almost a complete recluse, learns of this, she suddenly tries to elope with an old suitor, a drunkard. The beautiful daughter is unexplainably in love with William Wornum, who is perhaps two decades older than she; and the son is kidnapped and lost for five years. More than two dozen other characters drift in and out of the story, strange individuals who seem to have no purpose in life, no family, no bond to the society in which they live—and frequently no connection to the main story line. In an incredible conclusion, families are united, all wrongs forgiven, and lovers joined in happiness.

Harris may have felt that this novel helped counteract the flavor of the pessimistic books that disturbed him; but most of his readers were disappointed. The novel was rambling and dull, smacking heavily of saccharine. "It is a pity," the reviewer for the New York *Tribune* remarked in a scathing notice, "that Mr. Harris should have published it."[19]

When Harris retired from the Atlanta *Constitution* in 1900, the first project he took up was a novel he had been thinking about for years. When it was finished, he wrote to a friend that the book, *Gabriel Tolliver*,[20] was "not precisely autobiographical," but "more than reminisicent for I have put myself into it in a most unreserved way. . . . It is mine; it is *me* . . . I mean by this that I surrendered myself wholly to the story and its characters."[21] Perhaps for this reason, this story, more than any other, expresses Harris's sense of personal isolation.

The setting for the story, as was usual for Harris, was a small town in Middle Georgia during the Civil War and Reconstruction. Although the novel is subtitled *A Story of Reconstruction*, it was not a problem novel such as Albion Tourgée had written. Several chapters describe the attempts of the Union League to organize black voters; but the tenuous unifying strand that runs through the book is the romance of Gabriel Tolliver and his childhood sweetheart, Nan Dorrington.

The reviewer for the New York *Times* commented that Harris had indeed "accomplished quite a feat . . . for he has written 448 pages . . . about nothing. From start to finish Gabriel Tolliver's life is very uninteresting." The story, continued the reviewer, "plods along through its numberless chapters of tranquility leading the reader yawningly after it."[22] In fact, the novel presents three romances, a night ride by the Knights of the White Camelia, the murder of a carpetbagger, and the daring escape of Gabriel Tolliver from the Union Army.

More significantly, Harris was unable to present a straightforward narrative because he had no conception of an organic society that could provide a genuine bond between people. A seemingly endless stream of characters enters the story, mostly to engage in ponderous conversation about trivia. The narrator can only define how the characters relate to each other by describing their slightest interior or exterior reaction. The result is a labored attempt to depict a society closely knit by friendship and personal concern.

All the tortured overwriting could not, however, disguise the bizarre society consisting mostly of orphans, widows, spinsters, and bachelors. Married couples are rare; the few that do exist never appear together or are scarcely recognizable because of the confusing names. Relations between parents and children are uniformly tragic. The mothers of three characters die in childbirth; two more are left invalids. Margaret Bridalbin relates that she has "not such a father as I would have selected."[23] Silas Tomlin and Paul, his son by his second wife, cannot talk to each other, for they have nothing in common. Silas's first marriage has ended in disaster, for when his wife bore him a child, she "was seized with such a horror of the father than the bare sight of him could cause her to scream, and she constantly implored her people to send him away."[24]

The romances in the novel likewise have a strange air about them. Pulaski Tomlin becomes engaged to the daughter of a woman to whom he has once been engaged, but who broke the engagement in order to marry another man. She later divorces her husband, and before her death appoints Pulaski legal guardian of her daughter. Silas Tomlin, Pulaski's older brother, has himself been twice a widower when he becomes engaged to Rita (or Ritta; the spelling varies) Claiborne, a widowed mother of a daughter. Even after weeks of visiting Rita in her parlor every evening, Silas still believes she is his first wife whom he last saw in a state of hysteria more than twenty years before. When she informs him that she is not his first wife, but her twin sister, the following conversation takes place:

"Then you have never been married to me," Silas suggested, still frowning.

"I thank you kindly, sir, I never have been."

"Well, you never denied it," he said.

"You never gave me an opportunity," she retorted.[25]

A census taker's report on the communities that Harris pictured in his other late fiction would reveal a similarly stricken population. In two-thirds of the marriages represented in the stories, one of the spouses has already died; in one-third of the marriages in which both partners are alive, one is maimed or crippled. Of those who wed in the stories, in almost one-third of the instances one of the partners is handicapped in some way. More than two out of three children have lost one parent or both. Often, if a person is physically intact, he is feeble-minded or thought to be insane.[26]

If a family is alive and well, it is probably peripheral to the main line of the story, as in "How Whalebone Caused a Wedding," which is really about a foxhunt.[27] If the family relations are central to the plot, usually the father is displaced as the seat of authority in the household by another, his son-in-law, for example. Or, more tragically, the parents disown their children.

In all these cases, Harris matter-of-factly presents his readers with sad and grotesque details which usually have no functional connection with the plot; instead, they are obstacles to its flow, for most of the stories are cheery romances with happy conclusions. Harris seems fervently to have hoped that smiles and good wishes could bind society together.

The isolation of the individual, always present in Harris's fiction, was occasionally explicitly described. One of his favorite stories and one that Theodore Roosevelt particularly liked was "Free Joe and the Rest of the World," a pathetic tale of a free Negro in Georgia in the 1850's. Joe is a "black atom, drifting hither and thither without an owner, blown about by all the winds of circumstance."[28] He becomes the ultimate symbol of rootlessness for Harris, whose name he shares, as he waits months, at the base of a poplar tree in the swamp for the return of his wife and small dog. Finally, alone and unknown, he dies.

III

In spite of Harris's ever-cheerful appearance, life for him was essentially somber, "even for the most fortunate of those who drink deeply from its chalice." Harris's first literary efforts, done when he was a printer's apprentice on the Turner plantation, were imitations of gloomy romantic poems. In these, according to Harris's biographer Cousins, "In the excess of the romantic qualities of melancholy, despair, hopeless love, and terror . . . he outdid those whose works he was imitating." Later in life he continued to think in terms of "troubles which inhabit the world by right of discovery and possession," "this miserable world," and "bitter destiny." He concluded, as he wrote his son, that "life has very little to offer outside the contentment of home." Almost at the end of his life, his mind was still "full of deep and dark suspicions."[29] Although Harris was essentially pessimistic about life, to his friends he did not appear to be bitter. His acquaintances thought of him as a "diamond in the rough"[30] and the public considered his fiction warmly humorous. In his writings and in his life, however, the joy was forced; it did not flow naturally nor did it hide completely the underlying despair. The South, Old and New, that he pictured in his fiction seemed on the surface congenial and pleasant; in reality it was filled with isolated and alienated individuals. If Harris's characters were universally affable, it was to cover the deep-seated hostility and suspicion which he suspected all men shared. If Harris pictured society as unified and homogeneous, it was to cloak the breaches he sensed. Harris's fiction, in short, was a fantasy world in which all conflicts and difficulties were made right.

Notes

1. Joel Chandler Harris, "An Accidental Author," *Lippincott's Magazine*, NS 11 (April 1886), 417–20. The fullest recent biography of Harris is Paul M. Cousins, *Joel Chandler Harris: A Biography* (Baton Rouge: Louisiana State University Press, 1968).

2. Copybook, Joel Chandler Harris Memorial Collection, Emory University.

3. For accounts of Harris's early days, see Cousins, pp. 24–33; Julia Collier Harris, *The Life and Letters of Joel Chandler Harris* (Boston: Houghton Mifflin Company, 1918), pp. 10–22; and Robert Lemuel Wiggins, *The Life of Joel Chandler Harris from Obscurity in Boyhood to Fame in Early Manhood* (Nashville: Publishing House Methodist Episcopal Church, South, 1918), pp. 9–20.

4. On Turner, see Cousins, Chapters 3 and 4, and Wiggins, pp. 20–52.

5. The editor of the paper was William Tappan Thompson, author of the humorous *Georgia Sketches* and *Major Jones's Courtship*, one of the last of the Southwestern humorists.

6. Harris to Mrs. Starke, 20 June 1870; 9 December 1870; 18 December 1870; 4 June 1872; 23 December 1901, Joel Chandler Harris Collection, Duke University.

7. Harris to Esther LaRose, "Journal to Essie," 2 June 1872, reprinted in *Life and Letters*, p. 118.

8. Perhaps the fact that Esther was eighteen years old and Harris thirty when they were married enabled her to win his confidence. Romances between young girls and older men figured in several of his stories.

9. See Raymond B. Nixon, *Henry W. Grady: Spokesman of the New South* (New York: Alfred A. Knopf, 1943). On Harris's editorial contributions, see pp. 64, 128–129, 155, 166, 202. To R. W. Gilder, Harris complained that he was suffering "with fatty degeneration of the mind." Harris to Gilder, 22 July and 12 October 1886, typescript, Harris Collection, Emory. Harris apparently became a victim of alcoholism and attended a Keeley Institute for a cure. The Keeley treatment, which was opposed by the medical profession because of Keeley's commercialism, employed techniques of suggestion and injections of double choride of gold.

10. Joel Chandler Harris, *Tales of the Home Folks in Peace and War* (Boston: Houghton, Mifflin and Company, 1898), p. 377; *On the Plantation* (New York: D. Appleton and Company, 1892), p. 233.

11. Joel Chandler Harris, *The Complete Tales of Uncle Remus*, comp. Richard Chase (Boston: Houghton Mifflin Company, 1955), p. xxi. Twain wrote to Harris: "You can argue *yourself* into the delusion that the principle of life is in the stories themselves and not in their setting. . . . In reality the stories are only alligator pears—one merely eats them for the sake of the salad-dressing." Twain to Harris, 10 August [1881], in Emory *Reprints*, Series VII, No. 3, p. 10. For a suggestive analysis of the Uncle Remus tales, see Bernard Wolfe, "Uncle Remus and the Malevolent Rabbit," *Commentary*, 8 (July 1949), 31–41. Ed. note: Wolfe's essay is reprinted in this collection, pp.

12. Joel Chandler Harris, *Free Joe and Other Georgian Sketches* (New York: Charles Scribner's Sons, 1898), p. 98. Of the five stories in this volume, three developed the theme of reconciliation of North and South: "Little Compton," "Aunt Fountain's Prisoner," and "Azalia."

13. Houghton, Mifflin and Company brought out a series of Harris's most notable children's stories: *Little Mister Thimblefinger and His Queer Country: What the Children Saw and Heard There* (1894); *Mr. Rabbit at Home: A Sequel to Little Mr. Thimblefinger and His Queer Country* (1895); *The Story of Aaron (So Named), The Son of Ben Ali* (1896); *Aaron in the Wildwoods* (1897). From 1907 until his death the next year, Harris was editor of *Uncle Remus's Magazine*, a family magazine begun by his son. A number of Uncle Remus tales and *The Bishop, the Boogerman and the Right of Way* (later published as *The Bishop and the Boogerman* [New York: Doubleday, Page, and Company, 1909]) first appeared in this magazine.

14. New York: D. Appleton and Company, 1892.

15. *Ibid.*, p. 233. Harris to Mrs. Georgia Starke, 9 December 1870, Harris Collection, Duke, reprinted in *Life and Letters*, pp. 76–81.

16. *Sister Jane, Her Friends and Acquaintances* (Boston: Houghton, Mifflin and Co., 1896).

17. In Harris's private notes, quoted in *Life and Letters*, p. 341.

18. Harris to John H. Garnsey, n.d., quoted in Julia Harris, *Life and Letters*, p. 344; also Harris to Garnsey, 14 February 1897, in *Life and Letters*, p. 345.

19. 20 December 1896. The New York *Times* also condemned the book, but in gentler terms, remarking that "In his own sphere, Mr. Harris is perfect, incomparable; but the domestic novel is of another world than his" (26 December 1896).

20. New York: McClure, Phillips and Company, 1902.

21. Quoted in *Life and Letters*, pp. 454–55.

22. New York *Times*, 22 November 1902.

23. *Gabriel Tolliver* (New York: McClure, Phillips and Company, 1902), p. 383.

24. *Ibid.*, p. 106.

25. *Ibid.*, pp. 405–406.

26. I analyzed thirty-three short stories from six collections: *Mingo, Free Joe, Balaam, Tales of the Home Folks, The Chronicles of Aunt Minervy Ann, The Making of a Statesman*. I did not consider several of the stories in these collections because they contained characters already introduced or gave no indication of the character's family connections.

27. *Tales of the Home Folks* (Boston and New York: Houghton Mifflin Co., 1898), pp. 1–33.

28. *Free Joe*, p. 1.

29. Joel Chandler Harris, "The Old Letter Box," *Uncle Remus's Magazine*, 1, No. 2

(July 1907), 8–11; Cousins, pp. 22, 66. Harris to Julian LaRose Harris, 1 September 1890, in *Life and Letters*, p. 272; also, p. 477.

30. Charles W. Hubner to Paul Hamilton Hayne, 6 October 1883, Hayne Collection, Duke.

"Joel Chandler Harris:
An 'Accidental' Folklorist"

Florence E. Baer*

"In reality the stories are only alligator pears—one eats them merely for the sake of the dressing." Thus Mark Twain wrote to Joel Chandler Harris in 1881, on the publication of *Uncle Remus: His Songs and His Sayings*. Twain intended only praise, but when the letter was published in Julia Collier Harris's biography in 1918, Elsie Clews Parsons, an eminent and influential folklorist, picked up the metaphor and added with some asperity, ". . . now and then one hears of somebody who fancies alligator pears without dressing."[1] Had Twain only commented as he did of Fenimore Cooper that his "gift in the way of invention was not a rich endowment," he would have been closer to the mark, and the nineteenth-century view that Harris had made a real contribution to American folklore may well have carried over into the twentieth century without any important detractions.

Instead, in his otherwise extremely valuable introduction to *American Negro Folktales*, Richard Dorson pursues Parson's tack of disparaging the folkloristic value of the Uncle Remus tales with assertions that "Harris himself had not sought to reproduce literally the narratives he heard," and "plot outlines sufficed for his literary purposes." He goes on to dismiss the "excessive dialect . . . as a literary device to emphasize the quaintness of regional characters."[2]

Among Harris's published work and material in the Joel Chandler Harris Memorial Collection at Emory University in Atlanta, there is ample evidence with which to counter the above judgments and to set the record straight.[3]

Harris's immediate incentive to begin compiling American Negro "myths and legends" was an article on "Folk-Lore of the Southern Negroes," by William Owens (*Lippincott's Magazine*, December 1877). As an editor for the Atlanta *Constitution*, Harris read and reviewed the article and found it "remarkable for what it omits rather than for what it

*Florence E. Baer teaches English and folklore at San Joaquin Delta College, Stockton, California. She is the author of *Sources and Analogues of the Uncle Remus Tales* (1980) and has indexed the twenty-six volumes of *Ainsworth's Magazine* for *The Wellesley Index of Victorian Periodicals*, vol. 3 (1979). Her essay was written specifically for this volume and is published here for the first time.

contains."[4] What it contains is a smattering of "superstitions," Owens's belief that most American Negro folklore originated in Africa, and brief retellings of ten Negro stories—in formal English except for dialogue. Harris saw two defects: Owens did not seem to understand the dialect he did use, and the stories were not told as Harris remembered them. As with many nineteenth-century collectors, Harris regarded the tales and the special language of tale-telling as survivals, rapidly disappearing relics in a changed world, and he wanted a record preserved. He had good reason to believe the record would not be authentic unless he saw to it himself; there were already in existence what he called "literary" treatments and the "intolerable misrepresentations of the minstrel stage."[5] His first resource was his own memory, and he began to write down stories and fragments of stories he had heard as a boy in Putnam County, Georgia.

Joel Chandler Harris was born in the small town of Eatonton to Miss Mary Harris. The only family he knew as a child was his mother and his maternal grandmother; an unmarried mother was too great a scandal for the rest of the family, who at first disowned her. While as far as is known the townspeople were more charitable, Joe Harris's position was as anomalous as that of the other rarity in a southern town during the 1850's—the freed black man. It is perhaps revealing that among his Negro characters, "The most pathetic of all is Free Joe, who, protected by no master, becomes the slave of all white men."[6] But Joe Harris found a master. At the age of thirteen he answered an advertisement in a local paper, *The Countryman*. "Wanted: An active, intelligent white boy, 14 or 15 years of age, to learn the printer's trade." The notice was placed by the owner/publisher of the paper, Joseph Addison Turner, a cotton and corn planter with literary aspirations.

Harris got the job and spent the war years at Turnwold, working on the only paper ever to have originated on a plantation. Turner provided him with a place to live, a trade, a chance to write, and—as it turned out—something to write about. It was Turner's conviction that the songs of the plantation Negroes should be preserved and in the dialect in which they were sung.[7] If the songs, why not the stories? Harris remembered, some twenty years later, "it was on this and neighboring plantations that I became familiar with the curious myths and animal stories that form the basis of the volumes credited to Uncle Remus."[8]

Not only the animal stories but the physical setting and human characters of the frame story were supplied by his life at Turnwold. In the evenings after work, Harris and the Turner boys frequently visited the slaves' cabins to hear tales. Again, twenty years later, Harris wrote to Joe Syd Turner:

> Did it never occur to you that *you* might be the *little boy* in 'Uncle Remus'? I suppose you have forgotten the comical tricks you played on old George Terrell, and the way you wheedled him out of a part of his ginger-cakes and cider.[9]

The character of Uncle Remus seems to owe a good deal to "old George . . . then in his late seventies, as he mended shoes in his cabin, made baskets, and did other jobs."[10] However, Uncle Remus is actually a composite of several of the plantation slaves: he leads the singing as did Big Sam, and he tells tales as did Aunt Chrissy. As for the name, as far as is known there was no Remus on the plantation. After the war Harris worked for the *Monroe Advertiser* in Forsyth, Georgia, where the town gardener was called Uncle Remus. A colleague later recalled that the name had appealed to Harris.[11]

It is characteristic of his modest demeanor that a fully realized, adult Harris-figure does not appear in the tales. Instead, he once wrote, "There is nothing here but an old negro man, a little boy, and a dull reporter. . . ."[12] Such a sense of apartness may have been psychologically significant, but, given his other attributes of memory, intelligence, a good ear, and the ability to reproduce accurately what he heard, it provided ideal conditions for collecting songs, sayings, and tales. His life experiences well qualified him for the undertaking he had set himself: to supply an authentic record of plantation lore.

Soon after he decided to collect folktales, Harris recognized that memory alone was not going to be enough for the complete accuracy he required. In order to verify a tale he would need to get an oral version, preferably more than one, told to him by Negroes who had lived on the plantations before the war. With this in view, in December 1879, he placed an advertisement in the Darien (Georgia) *Timber Gazette:*

> We would be glad if any of our readers who may chance to remember any of the Negro fables and legends so popular on plantations would send us brief outlines of the main incidents and characters. . . . The purpose is to preserve these . . . myths in permanent form.[13]

He used material thus obtained not as the basis for a literary treatment, but to jog his own memory and to elicit oral versions from Atlanta blacks who knew some of the old fables. Examination of the few handwritten tales still in the Memorial Collection makes it clear that although he asked for "outlines," that is not necessarily what he got. While not always precise about spelling and punctuation, the writers provided complete stories, sometimes a good deal longer than the eventual oral version that became the published tale. The "outlines" still in the Collection contain, on the whole, incidents which Harris did not publish; he held them in hope of hearing oral versions to verify their authenticity. And the ones he used? He was after all a newspaperman. Once a tale was set in type, all notes and handwritten copy went on the floor to be swept out at the end of the day.[14]

The charge of altering (a practice Harris called "cooking") a folktale for any reason whatsoever was as offensive to Harris as to any modern folklorist. George M. Theal proudly announced that in preparing Kaffir folktales for publication, he saw to it that the tales had "all undergone a thorough revision by a circle of natives. They were not only told by natives, but were copied down by natives." Harris was not impressed. He wrote, "the educated Negroes have 'cooked' the stories to suit themselves."[15]

For his own first volume of tales, Harris selected one version of each that he considered "most characteristic." In *Nights with Uncle Remus* (1883), as he became more of a folklorist, he sometimes included variants. Actually, from the standpoint of modern collecting methods, Harris's chief fault is that he rarely named informants, mentioning only three by name and including identifying data on one other. While he has also been faulted for using the generalized frame setting of Uncle Remus and the little boy rather than detailing the specific occasion on which he heard a particular tale, the fact is that the plantation setting is one he vividly recalled, and it enabled him to include a good deal of information about tale-telling occasions and tale-telling as performance. To glean the details therein contained is of more value to the folklorist than "to retire the framework either to a footnote or to complete oblivion."[16]

The collecting method Harris advocated and practiced is now called that of participant observer in an induced natural context.[17] His account of a story-telling session at a railway station near Atlanta in 1882 illustrates his belief that to verify a tale you must get an oral version, and to get tales you must tell tales.[18] It was night, and a group of Negroes who had been working on the railroad were laughing and joking with one another. He sat down next to one of the liveliest talkers, and when someone in the crowd mentioned "Ole Molly Har'," he used that cue to tell the Tar Baby story in a low tone. The exclamations of the worker attracted other members of the group who gathered around. Without waiting for a pause, Harris then told the story of Brer Rabbit and the Mosquitoes; and before he had finished that one, various blacks were vying for a turn to tell tales. That night he collected many new tales as well as others he remembered and half-remembered. With his trained memory and thorough knowledge of the story-telling dialect, he had little problem waiting until he got home to write down what he had heard. The anonymity of the darkness also made for ideal story-telling conditions. Based on his own successful experiences, he advised others:

> The only way to get at these stories is for the person seeking them to obtain a footing by telling one or two on his own hook—beginning, for instance, with the Tar Baby.[19]

There is no question that from the time Harris first knew there was such a thing as "folklore" (his introduction to the term was probably the title of Owens's article), he viewed himself as a serious collector and enthusiastically learned what he could about the scientific investigation of the subject. He subscribed to the British *Folk-Lore Journal*, was a charter member of the American Folklore Society, and read available collections of tales as well as theoretical articles. While he had little use for the theoreticians, he occasionally took time for some raillery:

> . . . if Brer Fox runs Brer Rabbit into a hollow tree, we have the going down and the rising of the sun typified. And, really, the sun-myth does nobody any harm; if it is quackery, it is quackery of a very mild kind. In the meantime, let us be thankful that a genuine interest has been developed in American folk-lore.[20]

While, to his many correspondents from the academic communities of Europe and the United States he disclaimed any knowledge of comparative folklore, he was busy acquiring it. He titled his first book "Uncle Remus's Folk-Lore"; the publisher changed the name to *Uncle Remus: His Songs and His Sayings* to appeal more broadly to the Christmas book-buying public. Harris made it clear in the introduction that regardless of the publisher's intention, his purpose was serious—to preserve the legends and the dialect of the old plantation. He devoted the rest of the introduction to a discussion of the intriguing resemblance of specific tales to those of North and South American Indians and to his belief in the common African origin of the tales.

In addition to the Uncle Remus tales, the book contained maxims and proverbs, plantation songs, and Atlanta sketches, and the whole collection was hailed by Thomas F. Crane of Cornell University as "a valuable contribution to comparative folk-lore."[21] Crane went on: "The true value of the book, however, is in the thirty-four inimitable 'Legends of the Old Plantation'. . . ." He praised Harris extravagantly for "representation of the dialect better than anything that has been given" and called him "a master in the difficult art of collecting popular tales." Crane selected a few of the tales for comment and tended toward a view that many of them originated in Europe although he believed that tales with parallels in Brazil were, "beyond a doubt," brought initially from Africa. In his discussion of South American parallels with the plantation tales, Crane did not clearly indicate that much of his information had already been covered by Harris in the Introduction to the volume. Harris had in fact stated:

> . . . if ethnologists should discover that they [the tales] did not originate with the African, the proof to that effect should be accompanied with a good deal of persuasive eloquence.

This first volume was reviewed by one other folklorist, Robert L.J. Vance, in 1888 (Vance made no mention of Harris's *Nights with Uncle Remus*, a collection of seventy tales, published in 1883). But Vance's article focused more on Charles Colcock Jones's *Negro Myths from the*

Georgia Coast, and he favored European *märchen* as the source of both Harris's and Jones's collections.[22]

In the meantime Harris had become a thorough-going comparativist. The Introduction to *Nights with Uncle Remus* is a thirty-two page footnoted treatise on the folkloristic value of the tales. In addition to the previously mentioned description of a taletelling session at the railroad station and his criticism of "cooking," Harris emphasized the necessity—and the difficulty—of obtaining oral versions of tales. He included comparative notes on African collections, pointing out close parallels in Uncle Remus, and mentioned variants he had obtained from correspondents, but had not used. He argued with Bleek's opinion that "The White Man and the Snake" (Aarne-Thompson Tale Type 155) was of European origin, supporting his position with cognate tales from Brazilian Indians and southern American Negroes. He presented the naturalist Charles Hartt's conclusion that Brazilian animal stories were of African origin, and devoted four pages to the subject of North American Indian/southern Negro borrowings. On the basis of his own close examination of a collection of Creek Indian tales, Harris had the temerity to disagree with Major John Wesley Powell of the Smithsonian Institution's Bureau of Ethnology about who borrowed from whom. Harris was convinced the Indians had adopted Negro tales, rather than vice-versa. In addition, repeating that "the dialect is a part of the legends themselves," he provided a brief glossary of Gullah terms to facilitate reading the Daddy Jack stories. In conclusion, he assured his readers that he was merely the "editor and compiler . . . responsible only for the setting" but that the setting was fictitious only in the sense that pre-war plantation life no longer existed. The assurance was almost identical to that in a letter he had written but not sent to Lawrence Gomme, Secretary of the British Folk-Lore Society.

Harris's introduction was the first truly comprehensive survey of the probable origins and dissemination of Afro-American folktales documented with comparative texts from African, South American, and North American Indian sources. Additionally, it contained criteria and a methodology for collecting and recording oral texts more rigid than any that had been previously formulated. Surely this was not written primarily for the benefit of the general public nor for children. The collection itself, furthermore, with its explanatory notes and inclusion of variants seems intended for serious consideration by the learned community of professional folklorists.

Yet within a decade Harris had repudiated "the folk-lore branch of the subject" and "the enterprising inconsequence of the Introduction . . . worth noting on account of its unconscious and harmless humor." Reference to the professional folklorists had now become quite sardonic:

> Since that Introduction was written, I have gone far enough into the subject (by the aid of those who are Fellows of This

and Professors of That, to say nothing of Doctors of the Other)
to discover that at the end of investigation and discussion
Speculation stands grinning.[23]

By 1892 he had dropped his memberships in both the British and
American Folk-Lore Societies. It is tempting to speculate about what
happened, but the most likely answer is that *nothing* had happened.[24] In
addition to Vance's 1888 article, Adolph Gerber's "Uncle Remus Traced
to the Old World" appeared in the *Journal of American Folklore* in 1893
and Colonel Ellis's "Some West African Prototypes of the Uncle Remus
Stories" in *Popular Science Monthly*, 1895. All drew upon the Uncle
Remus stories for their own comparisons, and Gerber used the African
sources Harris had cited; but none of them mentioned Harris's pioneering
introduction. Except for a footnote in Mooney's *Myths of the Cherokees*
(1900), no American folklorist or ethnologist acknowledged that the
introduction had been written not to mention that it qualified Harris as
one of their circle.[25] Collector, yes; folklorist, no. Harris himself never
again expressed anything but opposition to the scientific study of
folktales. Near the end of his career he presented the folklorist as a
storyteller in a machine, mechanically uttering his credo:

> It was one of the principles taught in the university where I
> graduated that a story amounts to nothing and less than
> nothing, if it is not of scientific value. I would like to tell the
> story first, and then give you my idea of its relation to oral
> literature, and its special relation to the unity of the human
> race.[26]

To Harris, on the other hand, all that was important by this time was the
story itself and how it was told.

For *Uncle Remus and His Friends* (1892), Harris had modified his
former rigid requirement that he must personally hear an oral version of a
tale to verify it. Instead, his children acted as collectors, "discovering a
new story . . . or verifying one already in hand."[27] He would provide the
child with a word or phrase—for instance, "a little boy and his
dogs"—and have the child relay this cue to the storyteller. Two of the
Negroes from whom stories were thus obtained, the fifteen-year-old John
Holder and a thirteen-year-old girl, were skilled taletellers and said so.
The Harris child carefully wrote out the particular tale with all remarks
the teller had made incidental to it. This written version, with minor
changes, became the story as told by Uncle Remus. The fact that Harris
had first heard folk tales as a young boy may be what prompted him to use
the children; but whatever the reason, he was anticipating a procedure
not advocated until the twentieth century.[28] In the matter of collecting,
Harris was still a folklorist in spite of himself.

Before publication of *Told by Uncle Remus* (1905), Harris had
become more and more of a recluse, subject to long bouts of ill-health.

The oral tradition in Atlanta is that "Mistah Harris drank," but there are only slight hints of that in published biographies. In view of his physical problems, whatever they were, it is not surprising that he had little heart for "the new Remus stuff" which "isn't up to the old mark." This he confided in a letter to his friend, James Whitcomb Riley. He went on:

> I had in my notebook a number of unverified outlines of stories, which I had thrown aside. But someone sent me a copy of Heli Chatelaine's [sic] book on Angola, and in that I have verified every outline that I had practically thrown away.[29]

The letter implies that there were a large number of tales involved when in fact only three of the stories told by Uncle Remus in *Told by Uncle Remus* have analogues in *Folk-Tales of Angola*: "How Wiley Wolf Rode in the Bag," "Brother Deer and King Sun's Daughter," and "Why Mr. Dog is Tame." More significant, there was a time when "verify" to Harris meant to hear an oral version. Using a printed reference would have been as unthinkable as "cooking." However, reading Chatelain's collection must have reconfirmed Harris's once-held belief that the tales, at least some of them, originated in Africa. In the interim he apparently had lost confidence (thanks to the Fellows, Professors, and Doctors?) in his own ability to determine origin. Harris's early conviction that Africa was the chief source of the folktales he collected has been supported by my own research, which shows that more than two-thirds of the total canon of Uncle Remus tales have close analogues in African traditional oral literature.[30]

Although Harris died in 1908, the last of the tales were not published until 1948. Now, with 184 tales in his official canon, we can recognize Harris's contribution to the study of American folklore. His is the first serious attempt to record the folktales, songs, and sayings of southern American Negroes in the precise language and style in which they existed.

The most immediate result of Harris's collecting was the encouragement and direction he provided others. His wish that W.O. Tuggle publish the Creek Indian tales the latter had collected was finally realized by John Swanton, who included the Tuggle Collection in *Myths and Tales of the Southeastern Indians*.[31] Charles Colcock Jones's *Negro Myths from the Georgia Coast*, so highly acclaimed by folklorists, were collected at Harris's instigation.[32] His indirect influence can be only estimated, but collectors from Jamaica to Africa acknowledged, publicly and privately, the effect of Harris's work in arousing their own interest in folktales.[33] This part of his contribution is justly acknowledged by Richard Dorson: "the Uncle Remus books did tap folklore and inspire methodical field collections."[34]

But more important for current folklore scholarship, Harris's insistence on exact literal reproduction enables us to compare not only plot episodes and character relationships, but also narrative devices with

European and African tales and with more recent performances of African and Afro-American taletelling. Such comparisons are no longer motivated by ethnocentric concerns with origin; instead, given knowledge of what came from where, what has been retained, what discarded, and what replaced, the folklorist can arrive at an understanding of both changing and unchanging values, hopes, and concerns of the people who tell and listen to the tales.

Among the most interesting African retentions in Uncle Remus that have not been previously commented on are a number of stylistic devices. For example, African and Afro-American taletellers include with a narrated action the distinctive sound of that action.[35] Robert S. Rattray translated as literally as possible his collection of *Akan-Ashanti Folktales*.[36] Such lines as "They cut the sticks, and threw them against the Silk-cotton tree, pim! pen! pim! pen! (was the sound they made)" occur constantly. In Uncle Remus, "Eve'y time he'd fetch a whoop, he'd rattle de cups and slap de platters tergedder—*rickety, rackety, slambang!*" and "eve'y motion he made, de leafs dey'd go *swishy-swushy, splushy-splishy.*" Knocks on the door vary from "blip! blip!" to "blam! blam!" depending on how loud they are. "Blip!" is also the sound of Brer Fox's being hit whether by Brer Terrapin or by a walking cane. When the Akan describe a character's movement, "The Leopard ran, yiridi! yiridi! (was the sound of his feet), and the Duyker, too, began to run, prada! prada! prada! prada!" Brer Rabbit runs, "lippity-clippity, clippity-lippity."

Also notable is the use of repetition to express and intensify a continuous action. For instance, "He roll, he did en de leafs dey stick; Brer Rabbit roll, en de leafs dey stick, en he keep on rollin' en de leafs keep on stickin'." In an African tale, "The water stirred in that pool, the water rolled, it rolled, it rolled!" and "The *nabulele* came, it came. . . ."[37] Other striking similarities include integration of songs and chants, elements of disguise among which is name-changing, and titles and salutations of respect among the animal characters. The dressing on the alligator pears is, to an important degree, not Joel Chandler Harris's but his informants—and they used an old traditional recipe. Harris's record will be increasingly appreciated as folktale studies continue to focus on performance style and on text in context.

Notes

1. "Joel Chandler Harris and Negro Folklore," *Dial*, 17 May 1919, p. 493.

2. *American Negro Folktales* (Greenwich: Fawcett, 1967), p. 14.

3. For other evaluations of the folkloristic value of Harris's collections, see: Arthur Huff Fauset, "American Negro Folk Literature," in *The New Negro: An Interpretation*, ed. Alain Locke (New York: Albert and Charles Boni, 1927), repr. in *Black Expression*, ed. Addison Gayle, Jr. (New York: Weybright and Talley, 1969), pp. 14–19; Stella Brewer Brookes, *Joel Chandler Harris—Folklorist* (Athens: University of Georgia Press, 1950); David A. Walton, "Joel Chandler Harris as Folklorist: A Reassessment," *Keystone Folklore Quarterly*, 11

(Spring 1966), 21–26; Michael Flusche, "Joel Chandler Harris and the Folklore of Slavery," *Journal of American Studies*, 9 (December 1975), 347–63. For an overview of Harris and the folklorists, see R. Bruce Bickley, Jr., *Joel Chandler Harris* (Boston: Twayne, 1978), pp. 66–68; and for an extensive listing of references to Harris and folklore, see also Bickley's *Joel Chandler Harris: A Reference Guide* (Boston: G.K. Hall, 1978).

4. Review in Atlanta *Constitution*, 21 November 1877, quoted in Robert L. Wiggins, *The Life of Joel Chandler Harris: From Obscurity in Boyhood to Fame in Early Manhood* (Nashville: Publishing House Methodist Episcopal Church, South, 1918), p. 132.

5. "Introduction," *Uncle Remus: His Songs and His Sayings* (New York: D. Appleton, 1880), repr. in *The Complete Tales of Uncle Remus*, ed. Richard Chase (Boston: Houghton Mifflin, 1955), p. xxi.

6. Darwin T. Turner, "Daddy Joel Harris and His Old-Time Darkies," *Southern Literary Journal*, 1 (Autumn 1968), p. 38. Ed. note: Darwin Turner's essay is reprinted in this collection, pp.

7. Paul Cousins, *Joel Chandler Harris* (Baton Rouge: Louisiana State University Press, 1968), pp. 54, 131.

8. "An Accidental Author," *Lippincott's Magazine* NS 11 (April 1886), 417–20, rept. in *The Negro and His Folklore in Nineteeth Century Periodicals*, ed. Bruce Jackson (Austin: University of Texas Press, 1967), p. 245.

9. Julia Collier Harris, *Life and Letters of Joel Chandler Harris* (Boston: Houghton Mifflin, 1918), pp. 159–60.

10. Cousins, p. 45.

11. *Life and Letters*, p. 146.

12. "Introduction," *Uncle Remus and His Friends* (Boston: Houghton Mifflin, 1892), p. x.

13. Wiggins, p. 149.

14. Dr. Thomas H. English, Emory University, Atlanta, Georgia, personal interviews, 22–23 December 1976. I wish here to express my appreciation to Dr. English for making available the folklore materials in the Joel Chandler Harris Memorial Collection as well as providing a great deal of valuable information on Harris's interests and methods of working.

15. "Introduction," *Nights with Uncle Remus* (1883, repr. New York: Century, 1911), p. xvii.

16. Walton, p. 23.

17. Kenneth S. Goldstein, *A Guide for Field Workers in Folklore* (Hatboro: Folklore Associates, 1964), pp. 78, 87ff.

18. "Introduction," *Nights with Uncle Remus*, pp. xv–xvii.

19. Letter to R.W. Grubbs of Darien, Georgia, 3 February 1883, quoted in *Life and Letters*, p. 193.

20. "Indian and Negro Myths," [Letter to the Editor], *The Critic*, 9 September 1882, p. 239.

21. "Plantation Folk-Lore," *Popular Science Monthly*, 18, (1881), 824–33.

22. [Robert] L[ee]. J. Vance, "Plantation Folk-Lore," *Open Court*, 2 (1888), 1029–32, 1074–76, 1092–95.

23. "Introduction," *Uncle Remus and His Friends*, p. vii.

24. See Kathleen Light, "Uncle Remus and the Folklorists," *Southern Literary Journal*, 7 (Spring 1975), 88–104, for another possible explanation of Harris's change of attitude toward "the folk-lore branch of the subject." Some of our interpretations of the data and resulting conclusions are at variance, but the likelihood is that Harris's disenchantment with the science of folklore had a number of determinants. Ed. note: Light's essay is reprinted in this collection, pp.

25. James Mooney, *Myths of the Cherokees*, Nineteenth Annual Report of the Bureau of American Ethnology, Part 1 (Washington: Smithsonian Institution, 1900), p. 234, n. 1.

26. *Wally Walderoon and His Story-Telling Machine* (New York: McClure Phillips, 1903), p. 180.

27. "Introduction," pp. iv–v.

28. Goldstein, pp. 150–51.

29. *Life and Letters*, p. 488.

30. Florence E. Baer, *Sources and Analogues of the Uncle Remus Tales* (Helsinki, Finland: Academia Scientiarum Fennica, 1980).

31. Bureau of American Ethnology Bulletin 88 (Washington: Smithsonian Institution, 1929).

32. (Boston: Houghton Mifflin, 1888).

33. (Miss) Florence M. Cronise, Letter to Joel Chandler Harris, 13 February 1901; Alice Carter Cook, Letter to Joel Chandler Harris, 15 March 1895; Charles C. Jones, Jr., Letter to Joel Chandler Harris Esq., 23 March 1882. All are letters in the Joel Chandler Harris Memorial Collection.

34. *American Negro Folktales*, p. 14.

35. For a discussion of this device, which he refers to as "ideophones," see Philip A. Noss, "Description in Gbaya Literary Art," *African Folklore*, ed. Richard M. Dorson (Garden City: Anchor, 1972), pp. 73–101.

36. (London: Oxford University Press, 1930).

37. *African Folklore*, pp. 541–42.

"Joel Chandler Harris and the Genteeling of Native American Humor"

Louis J. Budd*

One of the most sweeping passages in the fiction of Joel Chandler Harris begins: "Almost without exception, since money became a power, the real politicians in all ages have been and are the leading financiers. . . . Your true historian will be the man who is fortunate enough to gain access to the records of the most powerful financial institutions of the various nations of the earth." Like an early muckraker he goes on:

> The great political leaders of the world who have not been dominated by the financiers may be numbered on the fingers of your hands. . . . This is true, not because politicians are corrupt (though many of them fall in that category), but because the financial interests of the world are more powerful . . . than all the superficial issues of politics. Thus it is that parties, political contests, wars, and all great movements of mankind are so manipulated by the master minds of finance that neither the beneficiaries nor the victims have any notion of the real issues that have been contended for, or the results that have been brought about.

Without hedging, Harris as the patent narrator rounds off that "these manipulations do not constitute, they are the origin of history, and it is only occasionally that they may be said to become obvious."

How this analysis strikes anybody depends somewhat on his politics. It can be called a quasi-Marxist manifesto, or an after-shock of Populism, or a sedately paranoiac theory of history. In any case it attacks consensus thinking in 1900, the year it appeared first in the *Saturday Evening Post* and then in Harris's next collection of stories, *On the Wing of Occasions*.[1]

The story itself, "The Whims of Captain McCarthy," is surely as

*Louis J. Budd is Professor (and formerly Chairman, 1973–79) in the Department of English at Duke University. He has published numerous articles, and *Mark Twain: Social Philosopher* (1962), *Robert Herrick* (1971), and *A Listing of and Selection from Newspaper and Magazine Interviews with Samuel L. Clemens* (1977); he has also edited (with others) *Toward a New American Literary History* (1980). Professor Budd is also Managing Editor of *American Literature*. His essay was written specifically for this volume and is published here for the first time.

superficial as any that he wrote. It has the head of the Confederate spy ring in New York City outwit completely the two Federal agents sent to arrest him. Having kidnapped them instead, he sets them free after persuading them to quit the secret service. As a further strain on credulity one of them is a double agent, that is, a traitor to the Confederacy who himself assumes he will be shot. The smiling readers of "The Whims of Captain McCarthy" must have skimmed past its mini-editorial, lulled by their general impression of Harris.

Like the New England worthies, he had already become a "schoolroom" author fit for edifying the young. A Southern educator had recently capped an essay with gratitude for the "fresh and beautiful stories, the delightful humor, the genial, manly philosophy, and the wise and witty sayings in which his writings abound."[2] A Northerner had likewise enshrined him in a set of esays meant for the secondary schools. More sophisticated yet similar praise kept mounting up during his later years. Undoubtedly it all pleased rather than surprised him. The prospectus he sent out in 1906 for *Uncle Remus's Magazine* promised that "as much care will be given to the editing of its advertising pages as to the rest . . . so that, from beginning to end, it may enter the homes of its friends clean, sweet and wholesome." His own writing for the magazine honored this standard both in his fiction and in his essays, one of which advised:

> Wherever, or whenever, you find in a book the apt and happy portrayal of *human nature*, its contests with its own emotions and temptations, its striving toward the highest ideals, its passions, its platitudes, its meanness, its native longing for what is true and wholesome, its struggles with circumstances, its surrenders and its victories, and, above all its *humor*, there you will find the passport and credentials that will commend it to readers yet unborn.[3]

Near the end of his career a responsible one-sentence judgment ran: "Joel Chandler Harris, with a tender sympathy and gracious humor, interprets the essentially human touch in the negro, in the Georgia Cracker, and in the aristocratic planter."[4]

Such a view of Harris may seem right to somebody who remembers reading or hearing the "best" of Uncle Remus, though those tales, in their full range, can be as troublesome thematically as they are masterful in technique. Critics have shown this so richly that we have mostly come to forget about the two largest bodies of Harris's other work, his serious journalism and his non-Remus fiction. Except for insisting on the solidity of the former, I will also pass over it even though Harris as late as 1896 described himself to Ambrose Bierce as primarily a writer of "political editorials"[5] and though several times he had Uncle Remus address topical affairs in Atlanta. I will center upon the fiction now usually typified by "Free Joe," which carries more weight than it deserves as it migrates from one anthology to the next. Not that the public is overlooking lost treasures. No amount of professorial support can raise Harris back to even the status of William Dean Howells, much less Henry James. Collectively his short stories and novels can do no better than to exemplify some of the major problems besetting an American writer in the last quarter of the nineteenth century.

Several reasons make Harris especially appropriate as the focus for these problems. First of all his fiction won high praise in the 1880s, joining with the Uncle Remus tales to hoist him from the sixty-second ranking in a poll that the *Critic* ran among its audience in 1884. In 1890, after death had already taken nine of the "Forty Immortals" whom the pollsters hoped would become an American Academy on the French model, Harris was among the replacements elected by the survivors.[6] Nor was this rise in standing merely a fluke; we are still too quick to underrate the taste of genteelist readers and their mentors. As for Harris's taste, his commentary on the classics of Western literature is graceful, urbane, and perceptive. More important, his Uncle Remus tales prove that he had genius, which does flicker up in his fiction. Any amateur Freudian can also see he had massive tensions that sought relief through humor. If he now impressed us as greater than Mark Twain, we could explain why it should be so. The critical biography by R. Bruce Bickley, Jr., ends:

> Harris found at least some therapeutic value in his writing and in his participation in public life, but his well-cultivated sense of humor was probably his greatest psychological asset. He lived by it, it informed some of his best writing, and he died by it. His humorous sensibility . . . gave Harris's contradictory and anxiety-filled life the only wholeness he would ever know.[7]

By itself neurosis will hardly produce a major humorist. Like Mark Twain he had the more positive luck of starting out early in journalism. By 1876 he had reached the Atlanta *Constitution*, for which he wrote editorials almost daily during the next twenty-four years; by 1881 Walter Hines Page believed him responsible for making it the most influential newspaper in the South. In other words he had acquired a keen, disciplined grasp on current events. Furthermore, he had the benefit of a regional heritage that, added to his gifts, could have carried him to the heights that leaders of cultural opinion once claimed for him.

Already buffeted by reality in childhood Harris broke into the newspaper world at the age of thirteen. Many reporters witness so much that deviates from Sunday school myths that they become incorrigible cynics. At least overtly Harris did not react that way; yet no detailed proof is needed that he got to the inside of the social and political structure embodied in an imperfect humankind. While his horse-sense sage Billy Sanders takes seriously the issues of the day, he can be genially quizzical or irreverent about the persons who act them out. Harris had learned to see far around and beneath official rhetoric. One of his better short stories explained that a vigorous man had avoided the Confederate draft because his family "had a good deal of political influence. If you think that war shuts out politics and politicians you are very much mistaken. On the contrary, it widens their field of operations and thus sharpens their wits." Harris's sketch of Henry W. Grady broke its elegiac tone to remark that "we have had so many" political and financial "rings" that they blurred in his memory. There is a naive notion that he muddled through on the *Constitution* while his mind, brooding in the realms of art, ignored the details of one of the more corrupt periods in our public life. From his Savannah years (1870–76) at the very latest, when he also became the local correspondent of the New York *Sun*, he fully understood that the newspapers took a vigilant interest in county, state, and national politics. But he stuck to journalism as his livelihood, whisked up its ladder, and dreamed of graduating from Savannah to " 'that shining Sodom called New York'."[8]

More particularly, Harris had a thorough schooling in the trade of newspaper humor and, in fact, quickly rose to the head of his class in Georgia. The drive for mass circulation drew on lighter material to leaven the political reports and pages of ads. In 1873 a responsible history of journalism noted that every daily or weekly had "one or more" humorists attached to it. When still a printer's devil on the *Countryman* Harris handed in both essays in the *Spectator* vein and sentimental or tragic lyrics; inevitably he also tried his skill with comic paragraphs, along with one-liners and puns, and it was his humor that got the attention, helping to lead him to a string of better jobs.[9] In 1870 the Savannah *News* assigned him to meet the "unrelenting daily demand" for twenty-five to fifty paragraphs that "consisted of humorous comments on personalities and events."[10] William Dean Howells had carried the same chore for the Columbus *Ohio State Journal* ten years earlier. Concurrently, Mark Twain was hoping to jack up the Buffalo *Express* with a column headed "People and Things." Harris's "State Affairs" was soon considered the best of its kind. As early as 1873 the Atlanta *Constitution*, in a sketch of "Jinks Conundrum Harris" whose "very suggestion . . . sets our paper to capering with laughter," granted him kinship with Rabelais, Falstaff, and Mark Twain and reprinted some "distinguished specimens" of his paragraphs.[11] Obviously this side of Harris whetted the desire of the *Constitution* to land him; his first contribution was a column of paragraphs entitled "Roundabout in Georgia." By then the psychologically insecure, observant, yet ambitious Harris had surely learned beyond forgetting that the public hungered for humor.

The luckiest feature of his apprenticeship was that it took place in the heartland of the native humor of the Old Southwest. Though he insisted late in life that he had "never been, and probably never will be able to relish and digest any form of humor" such as *Don Quixote* that "has for its basis the ridicule of the afflictions of mankind,"[12] he had evidently been quick to relish the earlier humorists of his region. When he went to work for the Savannah *News* he knew that William Tappan Thompson, still active, would be his editor. For the *Constitution* in 1879 he wrote a pair of editorials, "Georgia Crackers: Types and Shadows" and "The Puritan and the Cracker," that proved the acuteness of his reading in the provincial humorists of the North as well as the South.[13] An essay of his in 1905 would declare that the "vernacular" is the "natural vehicle of the most persistent and most popular variety" of American humor. Of course he had long honored this precept. The yarns of Billy Sanders, his last major spokesman, almost stagger under the weight of dialect. Among many other characters his Aunt Minervy Ann best exemplifies the rambling vernacular narrator first common to native humor, while "Blue Dave" (in *Mingo and Other Sketches in Black and White*) achieves a tour de force through two country preachers whose down-home conversation frames the serious tale. Most important of all for the matrix of many of his short stories, he learned from A. B. Longstreet, Thompson, and others to perceive in his Middle Georgia the incongruous mixing of classes, and the clashing of standards in mores or behavior. As a corollary he was sensitized, even before the outcome of the Civil War, to history as cultural and social and not only political change.

Once alerted to the richness of his background in both native humor and hurly-burly journalism, we can easily draw serious themes from his fiction. All in all he showed far more of the dark side of antebellum and Reconstruction days than Thomas Nelson Page or other contemporaries now dismissed as romancers. In 1884, when first in full swing with his short stories, he declared:

> The American character is seen and known at its best in the rural regions; but it is a fatal weakness of American literature that our novelists and story-writers can perceive only the comic side of what they are pleased to term "provincial" life; for it is always a fatal weakness to see what is not to be seen. It is a remarkable fact that the most characteristic American story that has ever been written should approach rural life on the tragic side. This is "The Story of a Country Town," by E. W. Howe.[14]

Harris's warm friendship with James Whitcomb Riley would blossom only later.

Given encouragement we pay more thought to slaves who, with no apologies to Free Joe, hit their bullying overseers and therefore must run away, perhaps to join up with others who have still better cause for flight. Anticipating a vein of the irony in *Adventures of Huckleberry Finn* one such runaway moves an eight-year-old to decide, "When I get a man I'm going to save up money and buy Blue Dave. I thought at first I wanted a pony, but I wouldn't have a pony now." More gingerly, Harris could work in the fact of miscegenation, with lace-doily heroics in "The Case of

Mary Ellen" but with a grim tone in "Where's Duncan?" Beside that story about a farmer who is butchered by the mother for selling off his mulatto son, the forgiveness toward the cases of white adultery and bastardy in *Sister Jane* (1896) seems innocuous.

Still, his fiction did not associate blacks with all of the worst physical or emotional violence. Even though his persona in "A Bold Deserter" proclaims that antebellum Middle Georgia was the "most democratic region in the world,"[15] tensions vibrate between economic classes of whites, reaching their extreme in the often-cited tirade by Feratia Bivins in "Mingo." In other stories Confederate officials fail in their duties toward the families of conscripts, who desert while protesting that they pay the commoner's price of lacking friends in high places. Harris had yet greater sympathy for the hill folk who, refusing to soldier for the "Restercrats' " right to own slaves, shoot conscripting officers as well as the revenuers trying to knock over their whiskey stills. As for postbellum society, he could show all levels sullenly coping with a poverty that goaded some lower-class whites into persecuting the freedmen. Cautiously, indeed, he would even get around to the Klan riding against those who dared to meddle in politics.

Weighing such details and adding a biographical argument, Michael Flusche can conclude that for Harris life was "essentially somber," that the "isolated and alienated individuals" in his fiction betray an "underlying despair" rooted in "deep-seated hostility and suspicion."[16] However, Flusche grants that readers—preceded by the editors catering to them and the critics confirming what they had liked—"considered his fiction warmly humorous." Nor were they unwittingly absorbing that tragic view he had saluted in Edgar Watson Howe. Presumably he would have liked to ground at least some of his stories in serious themes treated unswervingly. But the gentle dreamer imagined by devotees of the Remus stories respected the laws of the literary marketplace enforced by subscribers to magazines and by buyers of books. William Peterfield Trent showed his usual soundness when he grouped Harris with those who "have either made their humor an excuse for writing stories or have infused it into everything they have written."[17]

Humor can bite to the bone, as Mark Twain learned better and better to prove either by using it to project his pessimism about the damned human race or his rages at the flaws in society. These latter, topical themes Harris did touch upon, but only with an enveloping tone of good will while keeping any attacks on human nature superficial or muffled in comedy. "Mingo," in which a lowerclass woman—whose son married a girl over the snobbish objections of her family—refuses gloatingly to let the mother even see her dead daughter's child, is often cited as one of Harris's harshest stories. Still, Harper & Brothers found it suitable for a glossy Christmas folio, and to the Southern educator already quoted the old family retainer's "gratitude and watchful and protective love" for the dainty granddaughter softened the hauteur and spite into a "smiling comedy" displaying again the "humor and sympathy" that were Harris's "chief qualities."[18]

The central problem of his fiction makes a triangle along which critics must pace: from his seriousness (even, to Flusche, somberness) of mind to his grounding in public affairs and a rambunctious school of humor to the actual *oeuvre*. Eschewing tragic depth or even indelible evil, his fiction formed a composite picture of a kindly, redeemable mankind. When Richard Watson Gilder of *Century Magazine* accepted "At Teague Poteet's"—which, Bickley remarks, raises but "fails to explore at any length the problem of violence in the South"—he observed that it leaves a "very agreeable human feeling."[19] To find the constituents of this effect it is better to search for the reader's responses than the author's intentions. For humor that succeeds, the answers should coincide though its workings in the creator's psyche are more intricate and condensed. Answers must be speculative from either approach since humor bolts through subconscious circuits at which reason can only guess. Likewise, Harris's audience cannot be cross-sectioned reliably, though the patrons of the magazines that continued to buy his stories—*Scribner's*, *Century*, *Harper's Monthly*, and the *Saturday Evening Post*—were more likely to be middle-class, schooled rather than self-educated, female, urban more than rural, older white Anglo-Saxon Protestants living in the Northeast or Midwest. Furthermore, their reactions to any single story must have differed. Indeed the single reader evidently had a range of feelings about it which could be and were contradictory at the level of rational explication.

An obvious ambivalence concerned the crackers and the semi-literate loungers, who bore much more of the humor than the local elite. His readers must have felt happy that they had moved to the cities and the benefits of genteelist culture. Yet a modernized version of the cracker-barrel sage still had appeal (*David Harum* would start its many reprintings in 1898), and Harris fathered a line of highly colloquial but wise spokesmen culminating in Billy Sanders. The use of dialect encapsulated the matter. A poor-white aroused laughter of relief at being better educated, but Billy Sanders and black Minervy Ann made their shrewdest points in their most striking localisms. A similar ambivalence played around Harris's towns and the lagging South in which they drowsed. Obviously, readers smiled gratefully for living in more progressive areas. Yet his fiction often seemed to aim at genre painting in which a simpler, older way of life charmed readers who might have recently migrated from some Shady Dale.

Until as late as the 1890s any distinctly Southern story ran some risk of being confronted with the "bloody shirt," but Harris kept his nostalgia disciplined. His fiction, just like the covert political thrust of his Remus tales or the last three chapters of his history of Georgia (1896), took care to avoid insulting the Union side while inviting sympathy both for a once-stable past and a prostrated society that would solve its problems in a way best for both races if left alone. As his editorials for the *Constitution* stated, this way nevertheless accepted Northern patterns of industry and finance. From the start his fiction sided with the forward-looking veteran, the entrepreneur who put solvency above family pride. The only real question is whether Harris's caution rose from the need to keep his tone light or from daily reminders that Johnny Rebs were swearing never to get reconstructed. After 1900 his fiction could be blatantly New South, as in the love plot of *The Bishop and The Boogerman* (1909), or in both the love plot and overt commentary in the uncollected "Miss Little Sally" (*Uncle Remus's Magazine*, December 1907).

While neither pole is acceptable today, the most glaring ambivalence in Harris's readers concerned his black characters, who kept close to the stereotypes favored by a white society moving toward the "separate but equal" decision of 1896. The background blacks, the bit players, often supply the broadest edge of the humor with their ignorance or their over-reaching with vocabulary (did any black actually say "surgeon er de armies" for "sergeant at arms"?). Harris's most distinctive tactic was to make just about every black quick to deride his race and sometimes himself as a member of it. These gibes confirmed the all-too-familiar clichés about the black as shiftless, easy to scare, slow witted, and ever thirsty for a "dram."[20] High-pitched Minervy Ann was the most tenacious at this self-belittlement. Hardly one of her tales lacks some such aside as that "niggers" cannot resist "totin' off what ain't der'n" or that "de niggers what been growin' up sence freedom is des tryin' der han' fer ter see how no 'count dey kin be." For Harris's audience this pole was prob-ably balanced by his many blacks who show utmost dedication to their owner. Their stealing and begging to get food for ole Marsa and Mistus seem credible beside Mom Bi, who is angrier at her "family" for sending the white son off to the Confederate army and death than for selling away her daughter. Minervy Ann is more clearly comical when she is allowed to help her former master by shoving one white man into a briar patch and felling another with a rock, or when she feeds her white folks by taking away most of the salary her husband gets as a legislator under Black Reconstruction. I, a white, confess that I find myself smiling. Is it at the absurdity of people acting too nobly for their own welfare? Is it relief at believing that the hostility of the downtrodden is merely imagined by sour radicals? Is it gratitude for irrepressible human goodness? A simpler comic reversal comes through the blacks who bully their masters into acting more wisely for their own happiness, such as by reconciling with a daughter who eloped. Once more Minervy Ann is the leading figure for both her impudence and loyalty.

By now it should be evident that the crises raised in a Harris story merely lead to mastery over the contrariness or evil left in a few of our fellow men. The good guys (more often women) triumph so briskly through such infallibly laid plans that Bickley notes "slapstick" in some of

Minervy Ann's schemes, which are no more subtle or believable than the Our Gang comedies from the infancy of Hollywood. Probably the public took many of Harris's stories on such a level. Today anybody who reads all of them soon gets a Bergsonian effect of repetitive pattern, that is, of fairly identical characters fretting through essentially the same problems to a climax which, by implication, brings a happy stasis for the rest of their lives.

Likewise the virtually required plot or subplot of courtship must have even then struck some readers as more of a hollow pattern than an interaction of "real" lovers. Especially intriguing is the fact that humor was so often woven into the courtship.[21] Partly, Harris was trying to enliven clichés, but love had such professed sanctity that it would not be surprising if humor on the subject had been taboo. The humor probably went to keep the love motif from getting too passionate and, more positively, to shift emphasis toward the importance of family ties and the resulting social stability for which humanity had refined the sexual impulse or God had implanted it. Even the formulaic repetition, which the Harris narrator himself could intimate had its Bergsonian kind of comedy, added to the denaturing effect, helped to distance the anarchic drive of instinct. In turn the focus on courtship served to distance or "escape" major social conflicts, kept at best on a second or third rung of importunity before disappearing during the joy of betrothal. Helped by other sources of humor such as dialect, the love plot in "Trouble on Lost Mountain" (*Free Joe and Other Georgian Sketches*) or "A Conscript's Christmas" (*Balaam and His Master*) smiles away the acts of violence, which by the 1880s got much play in the Northern press as a barbaric-chivalric habit holding the South back from the civil order needed for a business society. Whatever the troubling subthemes, the course of Harris's true lovers smoothly overran them, with any misunderstandings working out for the best and accidents or coincidences proving benign.

His fictional world turned on a yet more basic effect. Quite typically the hero of "Little Compton" (*Free Joe and Other Georgian Sketches*) has eyes that "glistened with good-humor and sociability," and Billy Sanders (in *Gabriel Tolliver*) "went around scattering cheerfulness and good-humor as carelessly as the children scatter the flowers they have gathered in the fields." Harris's benevolent humankind shares a delight in joking that draws the line only at cruelty; any grumpy traits lie "all on the surface," merely making yet more delightful the tender soul below. Like many popular authors Harris never tired of building a climax on the discovery of noble virtue beneath modest exteriors. His finely ironic mind did not drive at cosmic incongruities or the gap between appearances and reality on earth, did not disturb anyone's sense of an underlying moral order. Rather it delayed confirming that order only long enough to accentuate the positive, to chide any doubts that might have arisen.

His ironic mind did set limits on his willingness to oblige popular taste. Those familiar with the worst in his era must be grateful that he practically never used religious bromides, inventing no deathbed conversions though he would undergo one himself. Just when his late work seemed locked into stereotypes he could stay dry-eyed about a seduction in "The Cause of the Difficulty" (*Tales of the Home Folks in Peace and War*). But the genteel readers' demand for humor in their fiction was so insistent that William Dean Howells, Henry James, and even Stephen Crane played along. By the time Theodore Dreiser discarded the urbane and amused narrator, Harris had few years left, and he could not resent a reviewer of *Gabriel Tolliver* (1902) who was "held, not by a desire to know how the problem of reconstruction was solved in Georgia, or how the story ends, but by an anxiety to miss no stray bit of humor or character sketching."[22] Actually readers wanted plot too, or Harris might have written other loose-jointed books like *On the Plantation: A Story of a Georgia Boy's Adventures During the War* (1892), a minor classic of tone holding together a gamut of episodes. The distortions caused by the iron maiden of plot can be seen by comparing the early "Mingo," which constructs an impasse and should leave a gritty aftertaste, with "The Baby's Christmas" (in *Tales of the Home Folks in Peace and War*). In the latter story another of the black mammies shockingly uppity when they are doing good reunites the leader of Atlanta high society with her toddling granddaughter, whose plebeian father is needy, crippled, and unjustly under arrest.

We have no right to expect reckless integrity from Harris, who never made pompous claims, who was modest to the point of timidity. Vibrantly alert to the touchiness about race, he accepted the lesson in the "social ostracism" suffered by George Washington Cable for *The Grandissimes*:

> It would probably be an exaggeration to say that there would have been no social safety for a native writer who set himself down to draw an impartial picture of Southern civilization, its lights and its shadows; but every thoughtful person . . . is perfectly aware of the limitations by which our writers have been surrounded—limitations, let us hasten to add, that fitted perfectly the inclinations and ambitions of the writers themselves.[23]

When drawing heroines for whom young and old "worship the very ground" they tread, he was likewise aware that mariolatry raged strongest in the South. An ex-colonel in "Miss Irene" states that "no Southern gentleman (I don't care who he is) can afford to do anything calculated to worry a young woman." Since megalomania was foreign to Harris, his newspaper work easily convinced him he could not reverse mass attitudes. Besides, starting in the 1880s, eminent persons kept praising him as an agent of high causes, particularly that of national unity. In 1905 President Theodore Roosevelt, making it clear that he meant the non-Remus fiction which "exalts the South in the mind of every man who reads it, and yet has not a flavor of bitterness toward any other part of the Union," declared that Georgia had "never done more" for the country than when it produced Harris.[24] Success had also brought a comfortable income, which naturally reinforced the feeling that his life and his world were well run. His essay "Humor in America" (1905) ended with a salute to our lively enterprise in business and our recent emergence on the stage of foreign affairs.

Though the native humorists might encourage an heir to resist soft respectability, they could also incline him toward the school of local color. Its vogue, unfortunately, depended on superficial sketching of characters lumbering through a plot dedicated to quaintness and sentimentality. The gusto for sharply provincial types, who might be clayeaters or bullies or monumental liars or swindlers, was slowly dulled to discovery of hearts of gold beneath linsey-woolsey. Supposedly this softening of raw contours and rowdy laughter brought a transcendence of mere sectionalism, a stride toward "universal" types and themes.[25] But to court the universal meant in practice to "ignore the dominant social and political forces of the national life," while to package the "odd and freakish" in genteel comedy was to misrepresent the home folks after all and thus court oblivion when popular taste changed.[26]

Editors of the well-paying magazines were the formal cause directing Harris toward ideality and humor fit for the parlor. Though our taste dissents, Richard Watson Gilder was quick to decide that the heroine of "At Teague Poteet's" was "not sentimentalized nor lifted out of her plane." When Robert Underwood Johnson, his assistant at the *Century* office, edited the story he agreed it was "keen in insight of the female characters"; however, he warned that it was less rollicking than the admirers of Uncle Remus would expect. After some resistance Harris made the changes wanted.[27] More often editors had to cope with his diffidence, but their praise can be as revealing as their demurrers. In 1886 Gilder informed Harris that his stories were "vital, humorous, pathetic, tragic, and full of character."[28] When a top magazine backed up such inclusive praise with money, going along was hard to resist. It was just as hard to resist a proven wizard of the marketplace like S.S. McClure:

> Do you remember that splendid story I published entitled "The Comedy of War"? Did not that Irishman, O'Halloran, have any other adventures? It seems to me he is too good to waste on one short story. Cannot you give me four or five short stories like [it]? . . . If you could have the same character in the heart of the stories, or as a central figure, it would make a capital book, and we could publish it, giving you a good royalty.[29]

The platform McClure wanted to build upon was spindly, and O'Halloran would wallow in laughable coincidences just once again.

However, Harris did turn more to stories of battle, which no one today acclaims as his metier, and to unflappable Captain McCarthy.

Critics and reviewers taught Harris no sounder perspectives. Dazzled by the Remus books they insisted his picture of blacks, "next in vitality to Nature's," reached to the heart of race relations in the South.[30] More generally the accolade of "realistic" recurred again and again.[31] The puff for *Gabriel Tolliver* in the Atlanta *Constitution* promised a "real, photographic, and psychologic" study; however, it also promised "romance, humor, pathos." In other words the literary consensus held that in the highest realism a fidelity to experience would combine with trust in the ideal to support man's aspiring side. A reviewer of the *Free Joe* volume in the *Nation* (46 [1 March 1888], 183) found that "fortunately for those who like a pleasant tale, the author stands apart from the crusade to divorce the true and the beautiful." The bridging quality between the real and the ideal was most often a pathos that critics today are likely to call sentimentality. Pathos in Harris was acclaimed still more regularly than realism for winning through to the "untutored spirit" of humankind.[32] Of course humor stood high in any litany of praise. Thus, *Tales of the Home Folks in Peace and War* showed Harris "at his best," combining "reality" with "cheerfulness" or "mingling sadness and mirth" or simply infusing his genial personality into each episode.[33] The realism, affirmation, pathos, and humor blended into an *oeuvre* that the spokesmen for culture approved as indelibly ours. Without jealousy Grace King proposed that Harris stood along with Mark Twain at the head of our quintessential authors: "Not only have they contributed to the literature of the world new, original, and characteristic elements of American genius, but we may say absolutely that what they wrote could not have been produced on any but American soil; and that they are Americans in every sense of the word."[34]

Solemn praise can burden the sense of responsibility, and up until his death Harris showed flashes of cold honesty. A very lightweight novel, for example, allows a black a protest which runs in part: "You white folks don't keer much what you do—I've done took notice of that; but when it comes to a plain nigger, why, he's got to walk as thin as a batter cake; he's got to step like he's afeard of stickin' a needle in his foot."[35] Still, each generation finds less to attrack it as the profundity once claimed for Harris appears to depend on transient values, presented in their alleged rather than their actual efficacy. As the dean of Southern historians concludes, Harris did not attain an incisive vision of his society, believing to the end in "neighborly love" as the "talisman against all evil."[36] The Southern Renaissance would not invoke Harris.

Nevertheless, admirers of William Faulkner should remember that Harris brought the black and the poor white a long step toward literary visibility. Also, since Faulkner read the Southern humorists with especial zest, scholars can spot echoes of Harris. If nothing else he helped to reinvigorate the vocation of authorship in the postbellum South. In other words he is an ancestor, a main link in the received tradition. His flawed achievement warns critics and editors to do better by the creative minds of our own time.

Notes

1. (New York: Doubleday, Page), pp. 249–50.

2. William Malone Baskervill, *Southern Writers: Biographical and Critical Studies* (Nashville: M.E. Church, South, 1897), p. 88.

3. Quoted in Julia Collier Harris, *The Life and Letters of Joel Chandler Harris* (Boston: Houghton, Mifflin, 1918), pp. 526 and 570.

4. Henry M. Snyder, "The Reconstruction of Southern Literary Thought," *South Atlantic Quarterly*, 1 (April 1902), 150.

5. Julia Collier Harris, ed., *Joel Chandler Harris: Editor and Essayist* (Chapel Hill: Univ. of North Carolina Press, 1931), p. [2].

6. *Critic*, N.S. 1 (12 April 1884), 169, and 14 (19 July 1890), 33. The first two Remus books had been published by 1883 and the next complete one would not come until 1892; meanwhile appeared three volumes of short stories, many of which ran first in the "family" magazines.

7. *Joel Chandler Harris* (Boston: Twayne, 1978), p. 148.

8. Jay B. Hubbell, *The South in American Literature 1607–1900* (Durham: Duke Univ. Press, 1954), p. 787; *Harris: Editor and Essayist*, pp. 13–14.

9. Paul M. Cousins, *Joel Chandler Harris: A Biography* (Baton Rouge: Louisiana State Univ. Press, 1968), pp. 62–63. Even much later, James L. Ford, "A Century of American Humor," *Munsey's Magazine*, 25 (July 1901), 489, would list Harris among the school of humorists, such as the "Danbury *News* Man," identified with a particular newspaper.

10. Cousins, pp. 80–85; Robert L. Wiggins, *The Life of Joel Chandler Harris* (Nashville: M.E. Church, South, 1918), pp. 102–103.

11. 23 April 1873, p. [3]. *Life and Letters*, p. 98, prints some other tributes—"Harris is the wit of the press," for example—which are "typical of the many" during his Savannah years.

12. Reprinted in *Harris: Editor and Essayist*, p. 374. Biographical legend has it, incidentally, that adolescent Joe Harris played practical jokes worthy of Sut Lovingood.

13. Reprinted in Wiggins, pp. 181–83. Merrill M. Skaggs, *The Folk of Southern Fiction* (Athens: Univ. of Georgia Press, 1972), who begins with discussing the legacy of Old Southwest humor, analyzes well (pp. 190–98) the continuing use of the frame in Southern local color fiction.

14. "The American Type," *Current*, 2 (13 December 1884), 373.

15. P. 186 in *Tales of the Home Folks in Peace and War* (Boston: Houghton, Mifflin, 1898). Almost the exact words appear in an uncollected story about Halcyondale—"Miss Irene," *Scribner's Magazine*, 27 (February 1900), 216. Skaggs recurringly discusses Harris's attitudes toward both the gentry and the plebeians.

16. "Underlying Despair in the Fiction of Joel Chandler Harris," *Mississippi Quarterly*, 29 (Winter 1975), [91]–103. In fairness it must be granted that Flusche also suggests Harris's fiction was a "fantasy world in which all conflicts and difficulties were made right." Ed. note: Flusche's essay is reprinted in this collection, pp.

17. "A Retrospect of American Humor," *Century*, 63 (November 1901), 47.

18. Baskervill, pp. 72, 81. Skaggs, pp. 210–17, analyzes the ingrained techniques for comedy in local color fiction.

19. Bickley, p. 112; Gilder is quoted in *Life and Letters*, p. 202.

20. See especially "Aunt Fountain's Prisoner," in *Free Joe and Other Georgian Sketches* (New York: Charles Scribner's Sons, 1887); "Ananias," in *Balaam and His Master and Other Sketches and Stories* (Boston: Houghton, Mifflin, 1891); "A Run of Luck" and "The Comedy of War" in *Tales of the Home Folks in Peace and War;* "Flingin' Jim and His Fool-Killer" and "Miss Puss's Parasol" in *The Making of a Statesman and Other Stories* (New York: McClure, Phillips, 1902).

21. Bert Hitchcock, *Richard Malcolm Johnston* (Boston: Twayne, 1978), p. 74, notes of Johnston's later work that "almost all of the courtship tales" have a "redeeming humor."

22. Quoted in *Life and Letters*, p. 458.

23. Editorial in Atlanta *Constitution*, 20 February 1881—quoted in *Harris: Editor and Essayist*, p. 46. Referring again to Cable he made the same point in *Uncle Remus's Magazine* as late as 1907.

24. Quoted in Walter Blair and Hamlin Hill, *American Humor from Poor Richard to Doonesbury* (New York: Oxford Univ. Press, 1978), p. 272. Wade H. Hall, *The Smiling Phoenix: Southern Humor from 1865 to 1914* (Gainesville: Univ. of Florida Press, 1965), p. 7, calls Harris the "great humorist-conciliator of the postwar period."

25. See, only typically, Baskervill's essay; the review of *Sister Jane* in Nashville (Tenn.) *Daily American*, 31 January 1897, p. 13; Edwin Mims, "The Passing of Two Great Americans," *South Atlantic Quarterly*, 7 (October 1908), 327.

26. Benjamin T. Spencer, *The Quest for Nationality: An American Literary Campaign* (Syracuse: Syracuse Univ. Press, 1957), pp. 261–63.

27. *Life and Letters*, p. 202; Cousins, pp. 138–39. Hall, p. 19, observes that after the Civil War the "dominant trend was toward a mild, refined humor."

28. Quoted in Herbert F. Smith, "Joel Chandler Harris's Contributions to *Scribner's Monthly* and *Century Magazine* 1880–1887," *Georgia Historical Quarterly*, 47 (June 1963), 174.

29. Quoted in *Life and Letters*, p. 398. The story had been printed in the June 1893 number of *McClure's*.

30. For the *Balaam and His Master* volume only, see *Nation*, 53 (6 August 1891), 107; New York *Times*, 7 June 1891, p. 19; Brander Matthews, "On Certain Recent Short Stories," *Cosmopolitan*, 11 (September 1891), 639.

31. Kate Upson Clark, "Realism and Romanticism," *Independent*, 52 (26 July 1900), 1793; "Editor's Literary Record," *Harper's Monthly*, 69 (September 1884), 640–41; *Atlantic Monthly*, 68 (November 1891), 711; review of *Sister Jane* in New Orleans *Daily Picayune*, 17 January 1896, p. 11. Hitchcock, pp. 66, 73, and passim, cites similar praise of the "best sort of realism" and "satisfying realism."

32. Review of the *Mingo* volume in *Nation*, 39 (7 August 1884), 115–16; almost at random see reviews of the *Free Joe* volume in New York *Times*, 15 January 1888, p. 14, and *Overland Monthly*, 2nd Ser. 11 (April 1888), 435 = 36, and the review of *Tales of the Home Folks* in Boston *Daily Advertiser*, 12 April 1898, p. 8.

33. *Outlook*, 58 (30 April 1898), 1078; New York *Bookman*, 7 (June 1898), 353; *Nation*, 66 (26 May 1898), 407.

34. "The Most American Books/A Southern View," *Outlook*, 72 (6 December 1902), 787.

35. *The Bishop and the Boogerman* (New York: Doubleday, Page, 1909), pp. 118–19.

36. C. Vann Woodward, *Origins of the New South: 1877-1913* (Baton Rouge: Louisiana State Univ. Press, 1951), pp. 168–69.

" 'In Stead of a "Gift of Gab" ': Some New Perspectives on Joel Chandler Harris Biography"

Joseph M. Griska, Jr.*

I

"Honestly speaking, I have tried to keep Joel Chandler Harris as much out of my works as possible," Harris wrote on 18 March 1895 in a letter to William Malone Baskervill.[1] That in part is why the reader must depend heavily on Harris's letters to help limn his complex personality; more importantly, his letters often reflect more accurately than personal accounts left by his contemporaries the honest way in which he viewed his life and his writings. For Harris was such a diffident and reticent man in the presence of his friends and acquaintances that their observations typically fall short of giving the emotional content and personal philosophy of his frankest letters. "My letters are exact transcripts of my thoughts. They stand me in stead of a 'gift of gab,' which, most unfortunately, I do not possess," Harris confided to Mrs. Georgia Starke in a letter of 18 December 1870.[2] But nowhere did Harris express his ideas on the psychological authority of letter-writing as well as he did in a letter to his son, Evelyn, dated 5 April 1900:

> We usually say more in a letter than we do in conversation, the reason being that, in a letter, we feel that we are shielded from the indifference or enthusiasm which our remarks may meet with or arouse. We commit our thoughts, as it were, to the winds. Whereas, in conversation, we are constantly watching or noting the effect of what we are saying, and, when the rela-

*Joseph M. Griska, Jr., is Associate Professor of English at Shaw University, Raleigh, North Carolina. He has published articles and reviews in *American Literature*, *Literature and Psychology*, *Papers on Language & Literature*, *South Atlantic Quarterly*, and other journals and is currently preparing an edition of Harris letters begun under an Andrew W. Mellon Research Fellowship at Duke University. Professor Griska is also an Advisory Editor for *Literature and Psychology* and a member of the Executive Committee of the National Association for Psychoanalytic Criticism. His essay was written specifically for this volume and is published here for the first time.

tions are intimate, we shrink from being taken too seriously on the one hand, and, on the other, not seriously enough.—But people no longer write letters. Lacking the leisure, and, for the most part, the ability, they dictate dispatches, and scribble messages. When you are in the humor, you should take a peep at some of the letters written by people who lived long ago, especially the letters of women. There is a charm about them impossible to describe, the charm of unconsciousness, and the sweetness of real sincerity. But, in these days, we have not the artlessness nor the freedom of our forbears. We know too much about ourselves. Constraint covers us like a curtain. Not being very sure of our own feelings, we are in a fog about the feelings of others. And it is really too bad that it should be so. I fear I am pretty nearly the only one now living who is willing to put his thoughts freely on paper even when writing to his own children. This is the result, as you may say, of pure accident. I am really as remote from the activities of the world, and from the commotions that take place on the stage of events as any of the ancients were. It is the accident of temperament, for I am very sure that the temperament has been moulded by circumstances and surroundings. All that goes on has a profound significance for me, but I seem to be out of the way, a sort of dreary spectator, who must sometimes close his eyes on the perpetual struggle that is going on.[3]

Of course Harris could not claim that he never affected a pose in his letters, for his subject matter and his audience—including his family—would inevitably produce shifts in the style and rhetoric of his letter-writing. While he may have wished to avoid covering himself with "the curtain of constraint" and "art," occasionally he slipped behind the curtain. For the most part, however, his letters are revealing—a mirror of his thought and personality.

Accordingly, the central problem of Harris biography is the fact that all studies were and continue to be based on an incomplete collection of the author's letters.[4] These studies are greatly confined, limited to materials which were first in the possession of Esther LaRose Harris, Harris's wife, and their children, and which later were presented as gifts to the Emory University Library, establishing the Joel Chandler Harris Memorial Collection. These studies do not include many letters which have come to rest in over thirty major libraries across the United States or the later letters from Harris to his family which were donated by heirs to the Emory Library. Also, the Emory Library staff has in recent years collected some additional letters not available to the writers of these early studies.

Analyzing the more than 700 previously unpublished Harris letters and restoring the passages omitted from letters that have appeared clarify some of the ambiguities that previous scholars have noted in Harris's personality and add new facts about his life and career. More specifically, a psychoanalytic study of his letters and of some recurring patterns and themes in his published literary work strengthens a series of contentions that have been made, with greater or lesser conviction, over the years: Harris's abandonment and imagined rejection by his father, which he probably began to understand by his ninth or tenth year, contributed markedly to a profound depression, brooding nature, and inferiority complex, the symptoms of which were more intensely manifested in Harris's early manhood yet never completely left him at any point in his life; there were other probable causes for the formation of his depression; and in spite of his stance that Uncle Remus and his other successes were literary accidents, Harris hoped for—indeed actively sought—recognition, financial rewards, and fame from his "literary work." And by striving to achieve these rewards from his creative writing, he coped with his depression and sustained himself throughout his often difficult life.

II

Harris never knew his father, who abandoned him and his mother shortly after his birth. The unpublished letters afford additional support for the view offered by some critics that "the search for the father" was more than an empty Freudian cliché for the insecure Harris. Scattered throughout his published writings, furthermore, are hints that Harris's sense of rejection by his father at least reinforced his innate shyness, inferiority complex, and feelings of identification with a persecuted and rejected race. "Accursed," a poem published in his mid-teens while Harris worked on the *Countryman*, features an abandoned mother and child and the eventual suicide of the guilty father; "Mr. Wall's Story," from Chapter V of the autobiographical *On the Plantation* (1892), is the fanciful account of how a young boy is enabled to destroy his witch stepmother so that he may be happily reunited with his father[5]; "Free Joe" (1884), probably Harris's most accomplished story of separation, and *Sister Jane* (1896), a rambling novel narrated by a clearly identifiable Harris persona that has illegitimate birth as its central theme, are two of several other works of fiction that reveal Harris's continuing preoccupation with dislocation or rejection. And of course, among other enduring characters, Harris created one of the most intriguing father-figures in American letters—Uncle Remus.[6] Although several scholars have explored the psychological complexities of Harris's writings, an especially suggestive commentary on veiled self-portraiture and masked anxieties in Harris is Michael Flusche's "Underlying Despair in the Fiction of Joel Chandler Harris." While not arguing that the absence of a father was a major cause for Harris's life-long depression, Flusche has thoroughly surveyed the broken or marred family groups that are so prevalent in Harris's works.[7]

Modern psychology defines depression as a mood disorder in which tension and anxiety are expressed in the form of dejection. It is a reaction to loss or threatened loss, to failure, discouragement, or disillusionment. Significantly, the depressed person usually never totally withdraws from effective interaction with his environment; he maintains a close hold on object relationships.[8] Modern psychology points out, too, that separation anxiety or anxiety over the loss of love falls into the category of depression and that the expressions of worthlessness, inferiority, and inadequacy in depression are exceptionally clear examples of the adult repetition of early childhood feelings, when a parent seemed absent or chronically unloving and the child seemed to himself unlovable.[9] Indeed, the predisposition for the depression may be acquired in early childhood by such a loss or traumatic experience.[10] Also, it is well documented in case histories that angry outbursts, sulking, gloomy daydreams, and suicidal fantasies are nearly always a part of the depressive picture.[11]

Harris's awareness of the loss of his father is the first experience on record that a psychologist might term traumatic, and the evidence is that throughout his life Harris continued to dwell, consciously or unconsciously, on the implications of his illegitimacy. As late as 1900, in fact, Harris told an interviewer that during his early years in Eatonton he had been "too young to know something of the difficulties of life or the troubles that inhabit the world by right of discovery and possession," implying that with maturation had come a fuller sense of his own special kind of deprivation.[12]

While in his early twenties and working on the Monroe *Advertiser* for James P. Harrison, Harris became acquainted with Mrs. Georgia Starke, of Milledgeville, Georgia, Harrison's sister, and a friendship ensued between the two that would last throughout Harris's lifetime. Harris was terribly self-conscious then and "morbidly sensitive," as he confided to Mrs. Starke in a letter of 18 December 1870 on receiving what he felt was a shun from Miss Nora, Harrison's younger sister:

> With some people the quality of sensitiveness adds to their refinement. . . . With me it is an affliction—a disease. . . . The least hint—a word—a gesture—is enough to put me in a frenzy almost. The least coolness on the part of a friend—the slightest rebuff tortures me beyond expression, and I wished a thousand times that I was dead and buried and out of sight. . . . My dearest friends have no idea how often they have crucified me. . . . I can no more control it [the feeling] than I can call into life the "dry bones" or bid the moon to stand still "over the valley of Ajalon." (LL, pp. 83–84)

And even when little Nora Belle, Mrs. Starke's daughter, had failed to recognize him on one occasion, Harris told Mrs. Starke in the same letter, he withdrew into himself for months and never "allowed my love for her to show itself to any great degree after that" (LL, p. 84). This severe reaction to rejection could have been related unconsciously to an earlier imagined rejection by his father—a rejection which during his life he could never fully understand or accept but would continue to relive, as it were.

Indeed, Harris's "sensitivity" did slip into stages of pathological "melancholy" and suicidal fantasy when he felt rejected. These periods of brooding were more than just "shyness" because of his embarrassment over his red hair, gawky appearance, and stuttering—on which Harris biographers have frequently commented. Rather, the stuttering was symptomatically the result of a conflict more profound—a conversion reaction where Harris, perhaps feeling unworthy to hold a father's love and feeling guilty over driving a father away, transformed his feelings into his own physical and psychological punishment.[13]

Likewise, his phobic shyness, including his habitual refusals to speak before an audience, had the same effect of projecting his own fears of inadequacy onto an external object—or onto a gathering of people—and preventing him from risking rejection by letting slip his feelings of unworthiness. Between 1880 and 1886 Harris had the opportunity, more than once, to give up newspaper work and to go on tours to read his works to audiences. In the spring of 1882 Joseph Hopkins Twichell, as Clemens's messenger, had called on Harris to propose a joint tour of public readings. Harris then wrote to Clemens on 6 April 1882, expressing his gratefulness, saying that "if successfully carried out," the tour would enable him "to drop this grinding newspaper business and write some books" (LL, p. 171). Yet even a meeting with Clemens in New Orleans could not convince Harris to make the lecture tour. When Clemens, Harris, James R. Osgood, and George Washington Cable gathered in New Orleans in April 1882, to discuss the proposed tour, Clemens was not only disappointed in Harris's declining the proposition, which would have been an ideal blending of business and pleasure, but he was also surprised at Harris's timidity in refusing to read his dialect tales before a group of children at Cable's house: "Mr. Cable and I read from books of ours to show him [Harris] what an easy trick it was; but his immortal shyness was proof against even this sagacious strategy; so we had to read about Brer Rabbit ourselves."[14] In April 1885 Harris turned down another offer, this time for a joint tour with Thomas Nelson Page, which was extended by the noted American lecture agent, J. B. Pond. Pond telegraphed a second offer of $10,000 if Harris would consent to read his work with Clemens and Riley (LL, p. 214). Later, in a letter to William Malone Baskervill of 14 July 1887, Harris confided that he would not stand upon a public stage for $100,000,000 (SL, p. xlvi).

Not only did Harris refuse to give public readings, but he did not wish to leave home or to have any attention drawn to him in public. Totally embarrassed, he ran from a dinner of writers, artists, and publishers held at the New York Tile Club in June 1882, after he had been asked repeatedly to make a speech. While still in the city, he was invited to what he thought was to be a business conference with Appleton's. When he learned from a friend that the occasion was in fact to be a banquet held in his honor, the thought of meeting another group of celebrities resulted in his immediate departure for Atlanta. When he was in Boston in September 1883, researching in the Harvard College Library's folklore collection in preparation for writing his introduction to *Nights with Uncle Remus* (1883), he excused himself from keeping an engagement with William Dean Howells. He later apologized in a letter to Howells that a boil on his neck, brought on by "certain untimely dissipations with Mr. Anthony and Mr. Osgood," had led to a severe headache and that this "would enhance my natural stupidity to such an extent as to throw a deep gloom over our entire community—so to speak" (SL, pp. 126–27). Harris's reasons for declining the conference with the famous editor were partly physiological, but they owed a great deal to Harris's habitual shyness in the presence of celebrities.

III

The most common precipitating factors of depression are losses of love or emotional support, personal and economic failure, and the threat of new responsibilities.[15] Before Harris had reacted so strongly to the shun from Miss Nora in December 1870, he had informed James Harrison that he was leaving the *Advertiser* to work on the Savannah *Morning News* as associate editor, at the invitation of the owner J. H. Estill. Harris's motivation for leaving the paper was economic in nature—the substantial offer of forty dollars per week and the opportunity to further his career on one of Georgia's more influential newspapers. Nevertheless, Harris did not make this move without ambivalent feelings, stemming from a fear that he might betray Harrison's trust after the owner had, in a sense, taken him into his own family (LL, p. 78).

Losses of emotional support and the threat of new personal and professional responsibilities, such as Harris was about to face on the *News*, were not at all foreign to the young man. Indeed, during the previous five-year period, Harris had held four different jobs. His first job was given to him in 1862 by Joseph Addison Turner, the editor of the *Countryman*, who was described by Harris years later as a man of "varied accomplishments" who keenly observed Harris's personal growth: "he took an abiding interest in my welfare, gave me good advice, directed my reading and gave me the benefit of his wisdom and experience at every turn and on all occasions."[16] Undoubtedly, Turner gave Harris the guidance and direction of a father during those four years Harris lived with him on Turnwold Plantation. Writing to his eldest son, Julian, on 20 May 1896, praising him for his encouraging letters to his younger brother, Evelyn, Harris recalled that "That's the way Turner (in Putnam long

ago) . . . braced me, and it does a world of good" (SL, p. xxxiii). Before
he left Turner in 1866, he had been trapping rabbits and selling their skins
for about twenty cents each to make extra money, but at the end of the
war he sadly discovered that the money, which was Confederate cur-
rency, "went instantly and permanently out of circulation when Lee surrendered at Appomattox court house."[17] Thus the Civil War, which
ruined Turner, temporarily dealt Harris a double economic blow. He
literally had to start all over again, without a penny to show for his years
at Turnwold.

After a few months he found work as a typesetter for the Macon
Telegraph, and in 1866–1867 he was private secretary to the editor of the
Crescent Monthly in New Orleans. Beginning in the summer of 1867 he
worked on the *Advertiser* for Harrison, setting type, running the press,
keeping the books, and sweeping the floor, all done under the impressive
title of "editor" and for a salary of fifteen dollars a month. It is not surprising, then, that Harris would break his Monroe ties for a job on the
News at the remarkable salary of forty dollars per week.[18] However, the
threat of losing friends who, by Harris's own admission, were like family
to him, coupled with the pressures of new job responsibilities, apparently
reintroduced the symptoms of depression.

It is clear from Harris's letter to Mrs. Starke of 18 December 1870
that he was at first lonely in Savannah and longed for his old friends in
Forsyth. But he soon came to know well and work closely with the chief
editor, William Tappan Thompson, author of *Major Jones's Courtship*
(1843). Thompson, during those six years Harris was employed on the
News, assuredly encouraged Harris to write. During those years, too,
Harris developed a regional reputation as a composer of humorous paragraphs. Had it not been for Thompson and Mrs. Starke, who encouraged
him to continue writing and to stay in the South and not go to New York,
as he had once considered doing, Harris might never have developed into
the author he became.

Meeting Captain Pierre LaRose and his wife, Esther Dupont, both of
whom boarded with Harris at Savannah's Florida House in 1870, eventually led to Harris's marriage to the couple's seventeen-year-old daughter, Mary Esther, recently graduated from a convent school near Mon-
treal. Their courtship was alternately effusive and strained. Harris apparently tried to express his feelings openly, while Essie at times kept hers
in reserve—which periodically caused Harris to doubt the strength of
their love. Yet whenever the two were separated for any length of time, as
when Esther returned for a visit to Canada, Harris was miserable.

Harris continued to articulate his love for Essie in letters from June
1872 through April 1873, as well as in a journal which he kept for her.
When sometimes she did not reciprocate as intensely as Harris wanted, he
again felt the pain of rejection. As late as 26 June 1872, Harris wrote Essie
that if he had been aware of her feelings, she "would never have been

troubled with my impertinent attentions," the overall result of her letter being that he had "entirely recovered" his "melancholy" (SL, p. 43). On 12 January 1873, only four months before their marriage, he wrote Essie that she had "never done me full justice in the matter of my feelings toward you. . . . your actions, as well as your words, have, on more than one occasion, betrayed something nearly akin to distrust." Harris went on to request of Essie that she place more of her faith in him "without which there can be no real love" (SL, p. 46). The matter of doubts was finally resolved when the couple was married in Savannah on Sunday night, 20 April 1873.

During the anxious and uncertain periods of his courtship, it is not surprising that Harris turned again to Georgia Starke for "bracing." In a letter to her on 4 June 1872, Harris brooded with romantic melancholy over his Byronic fate to be "different" from others and an outsider:

> Do you really think it is a merit to be different from other people—to have different thoughts and ideas about everything? I have a suspicion sometimes that it is the result of some abnormal quality of the mind—a peculiarity, in fact, that lacks only *vehemence* to become downright insanity. I have been convinced for many years that the difference between lunacy and extreme sensitiveness is not very clear. Like the colors of the prism, they blend so readily that it is difficult to point out precisely where the one begins and where the other leaves off. I have often thought that my ideas were in some degree distorted and tinged with a coloring of romance fatal to any practical ambition. But if it be so, so be it.(LL, p. 87)

But he also admitted that his idiosyncrasies and self-styled sorrow had their satisfactions:

> You may be sure that I shall cling to my idiosyncrasies; they are a part of me and I am a part of them. They are infinitely soothing, and I would not be without them for the world. Why, sometimes—do you know?—I give myself up to the sweet indolence of thinking for hours at a time, and at such times, I am supremely and ineffably happy—happy, whether my thoughts are tinged with regret or flushed with hope. Not the least of my pleasures is the pleasure of melancholy. Sorrow is sometimes sweet—*always* sweet, when it brings back to us, through the unexplorable caverns of the nights that have fled, some dear dead face—the touch of some vanished hand—the tone of some silent voice. Those who have not groped through the mystery of pain, who have not been wrapped about with the amber fogs of sorrow—have not experienced the grandest developments of this life, and from my soul I pity them. (LL, pp. 87–88)

Near the end of his confessional Harris implied that Georgia provided the kind of bracing that he had still not found in Essie: "Upon my word, I wish that every lonely soul had some dear friend like you. I think the world would be infinitely better" (LL, p. 89).

Published and unpublished correspondence reveals few details of Harris's personal life from 1873 to 1880. On 21 June 1874 Harris's first child, Julian, was born, and on 21 August 1875, fourteen months later, a second son, Lucien. One year later, in August 1876, an epidemic of yellow fever broke out in Savannah, and Harris turned in his resignation to Thompson, moving his family to the Kimball House, Atlanta, and the safety of higher ground. Henry Woodfin Grady, with whom Harris had earlier become friendly when Grady was employed on the Rome, Georgia, *Commercial*, had been working for the Atlanta *Herald*, which had recently ceased publication. Grady had just accepted an editorial position from Evan P. Howell, who had bought controlling interest in the Atlanta *Constitution*. Soon after Grady's appointment, Grady carried Howell's offer to Harris of twenty-five dollars a week as an editorial paragrapher. Since the disaster in Savannah had temporarily closed the *News* and prevented Thompson from reemploying Harris at his former salary of forty dollars a week, Harris began his duties on the *Constitution* during the day, working a few hours a night as a telegraph editor for an extra five dollars per week.

Sometime after his employment on the Atlanta *Constitution*, Harris moved his family to a five-room home on Whitehall Street. On 8 December 1876 a third son was born, named Evan Howell after the editor-in-chief of the *Constitution*. The Howells were neighbors of the Harrises, and the two families became close. Harris would later remember that it was Howell who especially "braced" him during those early years in Atlanta.

In 1877 Harris's mother came to live with the family in the Whitehall Street home. Harris had taken to drinking frequently with other local newspapermen, and it was Mary Harris who influenced him to stop altogether, for the sake of his family and because the quality of his work was suffering. She also helped Esther run the Harris home on Harris's meager salary.

From 1877 to 1885 Harris struggled with personal difficulties. His work on the *Constitution* often interfered with his literary output; in addition, illness and financial worries drained him both physically and psychologically. However, Harris would overcome these handicaps by drawing strength from the large family circle. Also, he managed to find time to collect folklore, correspond with friends and publishers, and produce his first three books.

In May 1878 Harris contracted measles and passed it on to all three of his children. As a result, his youngest son Evan died, and Harris had to mourn alone that summer, since the rest of the family had gone to stay with the grandparents in Canada. Julia Collier Harris summarizes a letter written by Harris during that period which "tells of his sad nightly homecomings, and how in his dreams he hears the empty cradle rocking" (LL, p. 138). Harris's grief gradually subsided after Evelyn, the fourth son, was born on 18 September of the same year. On 29 December 1879, Mary Esther, Harris's first daughter, was born. Harris soon after purchased a six-room home on a five-and-a-quarter-acre tract in the West End, occupying it at the end of the summer 1881.

It is interesting that in 1880, when Uncle Remus had already achieved notoriety in the newspaper, Harris, perhaps discontented in his relationship with some of the staff of the *Constitution*—but more probably because he was seeking a better financial arrangement with the paper—sought to join the staff of the Washington *Post*; his application was made in a letter to its owner Stilson Hutchins, of 2 April 1880 (SL, pp. 54–55). That Harris was certainly interested in the position can be seen in his personally covering the 1880 Democratic National Convention in Cincinnati and arranging to meet Hutchins there to discuss the proposition, as indicated in another letter to Hutchins of 28 June 1880. He made it clear to Hutchins that he wished to earn "a reasonable salary on the Post" and that "he would not accept a position where the meagerness of the salary . . . would compel me to do outside work" (SL, pp. 61, 63). In the same letter, however, he mentioned his "morbid views in regard to permanence" as "one reason why I hate to break my Atlanta connections" (SL, p. 62). Harris had quickly left Cincinnati on 23 June 1880, however, without meeting Hutchins. One could speculate that the *Constitution* agreed to raise Harris's salary since Harris remained with that newspaper until his retirement in 1900. Harris probably showed Howell both his letters to Hutchins and Hutchins' reply of 10 July 1880, which made it clear that the *Post* still wanted Harris and was willing to accept him at his own future convenience.

IV

Harris tried to keep his depression at a distance by immersing himself in his newspaper writing and by keeping his domestic circle of Esther, his mother, and his children close around him. Earlier his surrogate fathers—Turner, Harrison, Thompson, and Howell—and friends such as Mrs. Starke guided him in his personal and professional development. These adaptive measures of maintaining effective contact with the world and stimulating others to reassure and to pay attention, which Harris utilized in his rather reclusive circle of relatives and friends, prevented his depression from becoming more severe. Freud suggested that when depression breaks out in later life, invariably it is connected to an infantile depression that has perhaps been expressed in a veiled and incipient form only.[19] Persons suffering in this way, he pointed out, are extremely plastic, changing the object of their longing for one more easily attainable to avoid increased frustrations.[20]

So, too, Harris had experienced a chain of crises which took the form of personal losses or the threat of personal losses, failure, and new responsibilities. The recognition of the loss of his father and the anxiety that accompanied it; the separation from five jobs, and from three surrogate fathers and several close friends, within a five-year period; the emotionally trying courtship of Essie and later the threat of a new job and new financial responsibilities in marriage and in family life; and the death of his son Evan were deprivations and anxieties any or all of which could have brought on and sustained Harris's depression. It may, therefore, be more than coincidence that, at the end of a long series of crises, Harris created Uncle Remus, a literary father-figure and "a human syndicate. . . . of three or four old darkies" he had known during his idyllic years at Turnwold.[21]

Uncle Remus began to bring Harris considerable recognition not only from *Constitution* readers after November 1879, when the sketches became a regular feature of the paper, but also from newspapers across the country that began to reprint Harris's work. His self-confidence considerably bolstered, Harris actively sought more attention and recognition than he had received when his series appeared in the newspapers, by working to gather these folklore pieces into a publishable volume.

The standard account of how the first Uncle Remus book came to be published in November 1880 under the title *Uncle Remus: His Songs and His Sayings* was recorded by J. C. Derby, a representative of D. Appleton and Company, and in printed accounts by Harris himself. In telling of his visit with Harris in Atlanta in 1880, Derby said that he had previously been in correspondence with Harris "concerning the publication of a volume to be made up of his plantation stories" and, as representative of the publishers, he assisted Harris in selecting from the files of the *Constitution* those tales, sketches, songs, and proverbs that would make up the volume.[22] In one newspaper article Harris recalled that "The Representative of a New York publisher came to see me and suggested an Uncle Remus book. I was astonished, but he seemed to be in earnest, and so we picked out of the files of the *Constitution* enough matter for a little volume, and it was printed. To my surprise it was successful."[23]

Although Harris claimed the book caught him completely by surprise, referring to the experience as an "accident" and to himself as a "cornfield journalist" or mere "recorder" and "compiler" of the stories that he heard and collected, he nevertheless had already taken definite steps to have his work appear in book form. As early as 5 December 1879, in fact, Harris had written to Alexander Hamilton Stephens, then a member of the U.S. House of Representatives from Georgia, asking him to write *Harper's Magazine* in support of Uncle Remus. Harris explained to Stephens that he had "begun a series of Negro legends—comprising the folklore of the old plantation—which seems to be very popular" and "conceived the idea that such a series" would "afford a proper basis for a volume." Harris went on to say that he had already written the editor of *Harper's*, Henry Alden, asking if the firm would "undertake to get out such a book."[24] The New York *Evening Post* printed five legends from January through March 1880, and Harris wrote the editors of the paper on 19 May 1880 to thank them, fully aware of Uncle Remus's popularity: "I do not know whether the circulation of the 'Evening Post' covers all creation, but I do know that since you were generous enough to take up Uncle Remus and introduce him to respectable literary society, so to speak, we have received more than a thousand inquiries" (LL, p. 147). Also, Harris's readers had been expressing admiration for his work and were regularly asking him if he would publish a book. By May 1880 he knew that Appleton would issue it, but on 30 October 1880 Harris wrote to Mary Middleton Michel Hayne, wife of the poet Paul Hamilton Hayne, telling her that G. W. Carleton & Co. had first offered to make a book out of his work and that the offer had been followed by Appleton's (SL, p. 67). So at one time or another, Harris had considered at least three publishers for a book of Uncle Remus tales, and while the success of the Uncle Remus legends may have been an "accident," the appearance of the first Uncle Remus volume was the result, in large measure, of Harris's deliberation and planning. For the first time in his life, Harris saw that he had created a truly marketable literary character; he was determined now literally to sell Uncle Remus to the public.

From the last week in November to 8 December 1880, a little less than two weeks after publication, Harris saw his first book sell 3,000 copies (two printings of 1,500 each) and quickly go into its third printing. After the publication of the book more of Harris's work began to appear in various periodicals, including the *Critic* and *Scribner's*. To continue his earlier success and ensure another volume, however, he had to request friends and readers to send him outlines of stories. For example, in gathering some material for *Nights with Uncle Remus*, he wrote to the Georgia historian Charles Colcock Jones on 22 March 1883, telling him of the "great store of negro myths on the ncc [North Carolina Coastal] plantations and the Sea Islands" and of the difficulty he had in procuring them. Harris mentioned to Jones that a Mrs. Helen S. Barclay of Darien, Georgia, had sent him "three or four" additional coastal stories but that he hoped Jones would help him locate people who might furnish more, Harris being perfectly willing to pay for them (SL, p. 101).

Harris was extremely confident over the prospects of his second volume. He wrote his publisher, James Ripley Osgood, on 9 April 1883, saying that *Nights* would be "one of the most remarkable collections of folk-lore ever printed" (SL, p. 103). When Osgood forwarded him a copy of the book, Harris wrote back on 12 November 1883 to ask if copies had been sent to the New York papers, since there was a "Remus cult in New

York," and to suggest to his publisher that he "would not go far amiss to work it up a little."[25] That gaining recognition for his new book was on his mind, even when he was still reading revised proofs for the book and planning the introduction, can be instanced in his earlier letter of 12 August 1883 to Benjamin Holt Ticknor. Harris had asked Ticknor for advice on how to proceed if it was his "good fortune to be about to achieve fame" as a result of his new book (SL, p. 123).

While the reviewers' enthusiasm for *Nights with Uncle Remus* pleased Harris, the initial sales of the book did not. In a letter to Ticknor in July 1884 Harris expressed doubts about achieving financial success as a creative writer. And on the basis of preliminary returns, he worried that his third book, *Mingo and Other Sketches in Black and White* (1884), would also fail as *Nights* seemed to be doing—in spite of the critics' favorable notices. Discouraged about the marketing of his books, Harris lamented to Charles Scribner on 6 May 1885: "There was a lively demand for the book [*Mingo*] to begin with, but he [Osgood] allowed it to rest there. 'Mingo' has never been put fairly before the public" (SL, p. 160). Harris hoped, in fact, that Scribner would purchase the plates of *Nights* and *Mingo* from Osgood and market the books more effectively than had Osgood.

Scribner declined this proposition but did publish Harris's next volume, *Free Joe and Other Georgian Sketches* (1887); even with the new press behind it, however, sales of the book were disappointing. Harris wrote to the publisher on 2 February 1888 asking for an accounting of the book's performance, and Scribner replied that *Free Joe* had sold nearly 2,500 copies but that Harris should wait for more sales so that the firm could send him a larger payment. On 3 March 1888 Scribner wrote Harris to apologize for the poor performance of the book and offered to print a paper edition of 3,000 copies with a 10 percent royalty for Harris. On 31 March the paper edition was published. However, as late as 9 August 1889, Scribner sent Harris his regrets that nothing was due him for the past six months and that the firm had even had to take back 125 copies of the book in cloth from their largest wholesaler.[26] As a result of these disappointing sales, Harris wrote the firm of Houghton, Mifflin & Co. on 30 April 1889, asking them to approach the Scribners for the purchase of the plates of *Free Joe*.[27] Diffident Joe Harris proved to be remarkably aggressive with the Northeastern publishers!

It was not until Harris was back to writing Uncle Remus sketches for his newspaper syndicate and planning *Uncle Remus and His Friends* (1892), his third Remus book, that he developed a more realistic perspective about the financial rewards of authorship. As he implied in a letter to his son Julian on 10 February 1891, the answer was to stick by the Uncle Remus pattern—and to be happy with modest returns:

> I was waiting to get the half yearly reports from my publishers, and to see how my syndicate venture with Uncle Remus

sketches would turn out. The sketches which you see in the Sunday Constitution I have been trying to get in a number of other papers simutaneously [sic] with their appearance here. . . . The price varies from \$4 to \$5 each, according to length, making the returns 4 times 9 or 5 times 9, as the case may be, which is a very comforable [sic] weekly addition to my income if I can keep it up.—Very well. The book publishers have been heard from, and the syndicate is in sailing trim, the breezes seeming to be fair.[28]

Harris's considerable success with the first Uncle Remus book, and his belief in the enduring appeal of that kind of writing, prompted him to write the following comment to Scribner's on 21 October 1894: "I probably did my best when I got North American literature in the family-way with the Tar-Baby."[29] Although it may not have been conscious, his statement is the marvelously suggestive boast of a "proud father": it reflects Harris's pride in creative authorship, and it may even hint at his pleasure in having created in Uncle Remus a father to complete the "family" Harris never had.

V

Continued study of Harris will reveal more about the psychological complexities of the author and will clarify the themes and values that he sought to embrace in his writing. There are important clues to his more private self in his letters and reflections of it in his early poetry, *On the Plantation* (1892), *Sister Jane* (1896), *Gabriel Tolliver* (1902), and several other works. In fact, Harris's sensitivity to his own psychological needs and insecurities may even express itself in the very design of the Uncle Remus tales, where a wise and affectionate old Negro tells stories to a young boy whose father seems too busy or too remote to share such moments with his son. Harris's sense of deprivation may also help to explain his empathy with the plight of the Negro and, more universally, with the misfortunes of anyone who—like so many characters in Harris's writing—has at some stage in life been denied the natural support or "bracing" that all mankind is due.

Notes

I would like to acknowledge my indebtedness to my friend, the late Remus A. Harris, the youngest grandson of the author, and to his wife, Nancy Virginia, for their kindness in helping me secure the Harris letters project. Also, I wish to thank Lucien Harris, Jr., of Atlanta, and the Joel Chandler Harris Estate for permission to use Harris letters in my work.

1. Jay B. Hubbell, "Two Letters of Uncle Remus," *Southwestern Review*, 23 (January 1938), 218.

2. Julia Collier Harris, *The Life and Letters of Joel Chandler Harris* (Boston: Houghton, Mifflin, 1918), p. 83. All further references to this work appear in the text abbreviated LL.

3. "To Evelyn Harris," 5 April 1900, "Selected Letters of Joel Chandler Harris, 1863–1885," ed. Joseph M. Griska, Jr., Diss. Texas A&M 1976, pp. xiii–xiv. All further references to this work are abbreviated SL in the text.

4. There have been four major studies of Harris which have printed letters or parts of letters. Julia Collier Harris's *The Life and Letters of Joel Chandler Harris* (1918), while a valuable study, since the author was Harris's daughter-in-law and since she had access to materials available only to members of the Harris family, records mostly excerpts from more than 171 letters and not the full texts. Her *Joel Chandler Harris: Editor and Essayist* (Chapel Hill: Univ. of North Carolina Press, 1931), deals mainly with the author's political editorials and journalistic writings, and quotes from fewer than ten letters, many of which are taken from the excerpts in her *Life and Letters*. Robert Lemuel Wiggins, in *The Life of Joel Chandler Harris: From Obscurity in Boyhood to Fame in Early Manhood* (Nashville: Publishing House Methodist Episcopal Church, South, 1918), relies upon only a few letters and concerns himself mainly with Harris's early writings. Paul M. Cousins, in *Joel Chandler Harris: A Biography* (Baton Rouge: Louisiana State Univ. Press, 1968), quotes from letters printed in both books by Julia Collier Harris and from a few unpublished letters and aims primarily at placing Harris in historical and social context rather than telling the author's life story through his written correspondence with others.

5. Wiggins, pp. 161–62; Joel Chandler Harris, *On the Plantation* (New York: D. Appleton and Company, 1892), pp. 57–69.

6. I make this statement in SL, p. xxx; more recently, R. Bruce Bickley, Jr., in *Joel Chandler Harris* (Boston: Tawyne, 1978), pp. 23–24, writes that "Uncle George Terrell and Old Harbert, who are represented in the composite folk character Uncle Remus, may, like Turner himself, have helped fill the place of the absent father in Harris's life."

7. *Mississippi Quarterly*, 29 (Winter 1975), [91]–103. Jay B. Hubbell, *The South in American Literature 1607–1900* (Durham: Duke Univ. Press, 1954), pp. 793–94, Jay Martin, *Harvests of Change: American Literature 1865–1914* (Englewood Cliffs: Prentice-Hall, 1967), pp. 97–99, and Louis D. Rubin, Jr., "Uncle Remus and the Ubiquitous Rabbit," *Southern Review*, NS 10 (October 1974), 787–804, also examine Harris's writings in terms of his own insecurity and dualistic identity as optimistic advocate of the New South, in public, and nostalgic longer for the Old-Plantation South, in private. My essay shows that their positions on Harris's personality are supported and affirmed in light of Post-Freudian psychoanalytic theory and suggests that there was a profoundly deeper and more personal reason for this journey into his past and for the behavior that surrounded his writing and the publication of his works. Ed. note: Flusche's essay is reprinted on pp. 000 in this collection, Martin's on pp. 000, and Rubin's on pp. 000.

8. Norman Cameron, *Personality Development and Psychopathology: A Dynamic Approach* (Boston: Houghton Mifflin, 1963), pp. 412–13.

9. Cameron, p. 226.

10. Sigmund Freud, *A General Introduction to Psychoanalysis*, trans. Joan Riviere (New York: Liveright, 1935), p. 316.

11. Cameron, p. 417.

12. "Joel Chandler Harris Talks of Himself," *Atlanta Daily News*, 10 Oct. 1900, no page number, col. 2.

13. For a discussion of conversion and phobic reactions, see Cameron, pp. 276–337; for a different view of Harris's stuttering, see Jay Martin, p. 98. Martin sees Harris's avoidance of novel situations, such as his refusal to change his style of clothes as he grew older, as part of the "psychic complex" that underlies stuttering.

14. Samuel L. Clemens, *Life on the Mississippi*, Author's National ed. (New York: Harper & Brothers Publishers, 1911), IX, 351. Ed. note: Twain's account of this episode is reprinted on pp. 000 in this volume.

15. Cameron, pp. 417–18.

16. "Joel Chandler Harris Talks of Himself," no page number, col. 3.

17. "Joel Chandler Harris Talks of Himself and Uncle Remus" *Boston Globe*, 3 November 1907, p. 5, cols. 1–2.

18. Harris records his salaries on the two newspapers in "Joel Chandler Harris Talks of Himself and Uncle Remus," p. 5, col. 2.

19. Freud, p. 318.

20. Freud, p. 302.

21. "Joel Chandler Harris Talks of Himself and Uncle Remus," p. 5, col. 2.

22. James Cephas Derby, *Fifty Years Among Authors, Books and Publishers* (New York: G. W. Carleton & Co., 1884), p. 434.

23. "Joel Chandler Harris Talks of Himself and Uncle Remus," p. 5, cols. 2–3.

24. Letter to Alexander Hamilton Stephens, 5 December [1879], Alexander Hamilton Stephens Papers, Library of Congress, Washington, D.C.

25. David Bonnell Green, "A New Joel Chandler Harris Letter," *Georgia Historical Quarterly*, 42 (March 1958), 108.

26. The following letters, used with the permission of Charles Scribner, are in the Charles Scribner's Sons Archive, Princeton University Library, Princeton, N.J.: Joel Chandler Harris, Letter to Charles Scribner's Sons, 2 February 1888; Charles Scribner, Letter to Joel Chandler Harris, 21 February 1888; Charles Scribner, Letter to Joel Chandler Harris, 3 March 1888; Charles Scribner, Letter to Joel Chandler Harris, 9 August 1889.

27. Letter to Houghton, Mifflin & Co., 30 April 1889, The Houghton Library, Harvard University, Cambridge, Mass.

28. Letter to Julian Harris, 10 February 1891, Joel Chandler Harris Collection, Emory University Library, Atlanta, Ga.

29. Letter to Charles Scribner's Sons, 21 October 1894, Charles Scribner's Sons Archive, Princeton University Library, Princeton, N.J.

INDEX